DCU LIBRARY

190084146

D1766864

Teaching Primary Art & Design

WITHDRAWN

Sara Miller McCune founded SAGE Publishing in 1965 to support the dissemination of usable knowledge and educate a global community. SAGE publishes more than 1000 journals and over 800 new books each year, spanning a wide range of subject areas. Our growing selection of library products includes archives, data, case studies and video. SAGE remains majority owned by our founder and after her lifetime will become owned by a charitable trust that secures the company's continued independence.

Los Angeles | London | New Delhi | Singapore | Washington DC | Melbourne

Teaching Primary Art & Design

Susan Ogier

Learning Matters
An imprint of SAGE Publications Ltd
1 Oliver's Yard
55 City Road
London EC1Y 1SP

SAGE Publications Inc.
2455 Teller Road
Thousand Oaks, California 91320

SAGE Publications India Pvt Ltd
B 1/I 1 Mohan Cooperative Industrial Area
Mathura Road
New Delhi 110 044

SAGE Publications Asia-Pacific Pte Ltd
3 Church Street
#10-04 Samsung Hub
Singapore 049483

Editor: Amy Thornton
Development editor: Lauren Simpson
Production controller: Chris Marke
Project management: Swales and Willis Ltd, Exeter, Devon
Marketing manager: Dilhara Attygalle
Cover design: Wendy Scott
Typeset by: C&M Digitals (P) Ltd, Chennai, India
Printed by CPI Group (UK) Ltd, Croydon, CR0 4YY

© 2017 Susan Ogier

Apart from any fair dealing for the purposes of research or private study, or criticism or review, as permitted under the Copyright, Design and Patents Act 1988, this publication may be produced, stored or transmitted in any form, by any means, only with the prior permission in writing of the publishers, or in the case of reprographic reproduction, in accordance with the terms of licences issued by the Copyright Licensing Agency. Enquiries concerning reproduction outside these terms should be sent to the publishers.

Library of Congress Control Number: 2017936977

British Library Cataloguing in Publication Data

A catalogue record for this book is available from the British Library

ISBN 978-1-4739-9813-1
ISBN 978-1-4739-9814-8 (pbk)

190084146

At SAGE we take sustainability seriously. Most of our products are printed in the UK using FSC papers and boards. When we print overseas we ensure sustainable papers are used as measured by the PREPS grading system. We undertake an annual audit to monitor our sustainability.

Contents

About the author

Susan Ogier

Susan Ogier worked for many years as a nursery teacher and subject lead for art and design in a Surrey primary school, before becoming Senior Lecturer in Primary Art and Design Education at Kingston University and, since 2009, University of Roehampton, London. She holds a Master of Arts (Fine Art: Drawing) from Wimbledon School of Art, London, and maintains her own art practice whenever possible. Susan has worked with hundreds of student teachers, postgraduate teachers in training, as well as experienced teachers and teaching assistants to develop their subject knowledge and understanding of this subject. She is committed to the belief that having confidence in one's own creativity can make a hugely positive difference to an individual's life in so many ways.

Susan is the author of a series of art books for children and their teachers. She has written several peer reviewed journal articles and book chapters, and has contributed to many professional journals and magazines over the years. She has been involved in several EU-funded art education projects in collaboration with universities and schools across Europe: these include 'Images and Identity' (2008–10), and follow-up project, 'Creative Connections' (2012–14), both of which centred on teaching citizenship principles through art and design, and ICT. Her research interests relate to the contribution of visual arts practice to social and emotional well-being through a deepening understanding of personal identity, and how this can be an influencing and motivating factor for children to learn across the curriculum. Susan lives in a small village in Surrey with her two daughters and their dog!

About the Contributors

Anthony Barlow worked in primary schools for 11 years in London and Bolton before joining the University of Roehampton in 2011 to become Senior Lecturer in Geography Education. He is Vice-Chair of the Early Years and Primary Committee of The Geographical Association and has led many teacher development sessions for teachers as a primary 'Geography Champion'. Anthony has been involved in funded projects such as Making Geography Happen (DfES) and Young Geographers (TDA). He has written a chapter in Scoffham (ed.) (2016, 2nd edition) *Teaching Geography Creatively* published by Routledge, and curates a website for support with teaching primary geography. He is a fellow of the Royal Geographical Society and is currently writing *Mastering Primary Geography* with Sarah Whitehouse for Bloomsbury.

Edward Dickenson began his teaching career in Japan, returning to the UK to complete a PGCE at the University of Roehampton. He has worked as a classroom teacher and art and design coordinator in inner London primary schools for many years. He was inspired by the National Gallery's Take One Picture programme for primary schools whilst on his PGCE, and now includes gallery and museum education in his portfolio. Ed has worked for, amongst others, the Horniman Museum, Historic Royal Palaces and is currently at London's Ben Uri Gallery & Museum.

Dr Jonathan Doherty has worked in teacher education for 20 years. Until last year he was Head of Primary Education at Leeds Trinity University and before that held senior positions at Leeds Beckett University, where he taught PE specialism courses to primary students, and at Manchester Metropolitan University. He has led many INSET days for teachers in the north of England, and was Regional Adviser for the National Strategies for 3 years. He has authored *Supporting Physical Development in the Early Years*; *PE 3-11*; *PE 5-11* and contributed various chapters in books on curriculum PE. His doctorate investigated the role of critical thinking in PE and the teaching approaches that promote it. Jonathan is passionate about the role of PE in schools and in the lives of young people.

Karin Doull is a Principal Lecturer in Primary History and Holocaust Education at the University of Roehampton. She has taught in a number of London schools across the primary range. She is a member of the Primary Committee and trustee of the Historical Association. She is interested in Holocaust education and has written a wide range of papers and resources for teachers on this subject. Her most recent publication is a chapter in the book *Untold Stories of the East India Company*, published by Brick Lane Circle (2017). She is passionate about helping student teachers discover the excitement of teaching history.

Padraig Egan is a Senior Lecturer in Primary Science/Professional Studies in the School of Education at the University of Roehampton. Prior to this he was a Lecturer in Primary Science in the University of East Anglia. He is a qualified primary school teacher and a specialist in Early Years and KS1 phases. He is an active contributor to the *Association of Primary Science Journal* where he has several articles published. He also writes regularly for the *Irish Science Teachers Association Journal*.

Kerenza Ghosh is a Senior Lecturer in Primary English Education at the University of Roehampton. Kerenza is currently studying for her PhD and her research is centred around the development of children's visual literacy through comics. She has presented research papers at conferences both internationally and in the UK, and has written two published chapters: 'Walking with Wolves: Children's Responses to the Wolf Tradition in Stories' (in *Beyond the Book: Transforming Children's Literature*, Cambridge Scholars Publishing, 2014) and 'Who's Afraid of the Big Bad Wolf? Responses to the Portrayal of Wolves in Picturebooks' (in *Challenging and Controversial Picturebooks: Creative and Critical Responses to Visual Texts*, Routledge, 2015, edited by Janet Evans).

Alastair Greig is a Composer and Lecturer in Music Education in ITE at the University of Roehampton. He first studied composition with Oliver Knussen, then at the Royal Academy of Music, the University of Sussex and the University of Birmingham where his PhD was supervised by Vic Hoyland. He has worked with a number of composers including Hans Werner Henze, Dame Judith Weir, Sir Harrison Birtwistle, Giacomo Manzoni, Klaus Huber, Fernando Maglia, Dominique LeMaitre and Michael Finnissy. His music has been performed throughout Europe, the USA, South America and Australia and is published by Composers Edition (http://composersedition.com), Edizioni Suvini Zerboni Milano (http://www.esz.it/it/) and Taukay Edizioni Musicali (http://www.taukay.it/data3/index.php?lang=en). His music has been recorded on a number of occasions including Peter O'Hagan's 2010 CD, Chasing Boundaries (http://www.uhrecordings.co.uk/_shop/albums/UHR/Chasing-Boundaries.aspx).

Al Johnson is a politically engaged sculptor, and her work considers recent history, and the interplay between politics, power and the collective memory. She believes in the development of creativity as a founding principle of education, and in the empowerment that results from democratic participation in the arts. Al's work has been widely exhibited, and is held in both public and private collections. Exhibitions include *Reactions* at the Imperial War Museum North, *Flight and the Artistic Imagination* at Compton Verney and *Caught in the Crossfire* at the Herbert Gallery, Coventry. Sculpture commissions include the Royal British Legion, the Laing Gallery, Newcastle and the London Screen Archives. Al lectures and leads demonstrations and workshops in museums and galleries, including the National Gallery, Tate Gallery, Victoria and Albert Museum, the British Museum, the Wallace Collection and the Royal Collection.

Alistair Lambert is a visual artist based in North West London who enjoys the challenge of collaborative projects. He believes that groups of people develop their own power within creativity, and that people of all ages are capable of amazing and unexpected outcomes, usually far exceeding their individual expectations. He has 25 years of experience in running sculpture workshops with community and school groups, creating works for private and public spaces and institutions. He works with a wide range of materials and processes in new and ambitious ways that develop skills and confidence in workshop participants. http://www.alistairlambert.co.uk

Dr Robert Watts trained, worked and exhibited as a painter before becoming a primary teacher, and taught in inner-city schools in London for 10 years. Since his appointment as a Senior Lecturer in Art and Design Education at Roehampton University in 2000, he has been Programme Convener for the MA Art, Craft and Design Education, and is currently Course Leader for PGCE Secondary Art and Design. He continues to teach and supervise students on BA and PGCE Primary Education programmes. In 2016 Robert completed a PhD entitled *Children's Perceptions of Beauty: Exploring Aesthetic Experience through Photography*. The research investigated how children reflect upon and articulate their perceptions of beauty, and examined how these perceptions relate to philosophical thinking about aesthetic experience. Since 2002 he has co-edited two books on primary art education, written several articles for international journals and published over 200 creative projects and articles on education in various publications, a selection of which are available at: www.artandeducation.co.uk

Acknowledgements

I'm so glad to be able to officially thank my family, friends and colleagues who have been wonderfully enthusiastic in their support for the writing of this book. The contributors who gave their time and expertise so freely to add their voices to the rallying cry for creativity and expressive arts in primary schools, which make the messages in Chapters 6 and 7 so powerful: Ed, Robert, Alastair, Jonathan, Karin, Anthony, Padraig and Kerenza – thank you so much! To Al Johnson and Alistair Lambert, who generously gave me a unique insight into the life and thoughts of what it is to be an artist working with children and in schools – thank you! Thanks, also, go to Paula Briggs of Access Arts, whose conversation helped me more than she might know! To the children of Year 5 at Sacred Heart School and their lovely teacher, Jade, who let me photograph their work – thank you! A special thanks to my dear long-suffering friend and colleague, Robert Watts, who contributed the printmaking and the new media and technology sections of Chapter 4, and the piece on mathematics in Chapter 7, as well as supplying some of the better photographs in the book. I would also like to extend my appreciation to Peter Gregory and Lesley Butterworth for reading through and validating the work as it progressed, to Amy at Learning Matters for commissioning me in the first place, and to Lauren for keeping me on track during the process.

Lastly, I would like to thank all the student teachers I have taught for the journey of learning we have been on together over the years, and to those who have permitted me to photograph them for this publication. This book is for you, and for the children you will teach.

Love, Susan

Foreword

I am confident that this book could make a substantial difference to the lives and experiences of many thousands of primary aged children. I know that this sounds a big claim but I would like to set out my reasons for saying this and hopefully you'll not only follow my thinking, but be equally convinced yourself.

The last OFSTED subject survey inspection for art and design clearly indicated that the quality of both teaching and children's attainment was less than good in the majority of primary schools visited by inspectors. This is hardly surprising as the amount of time allocated to art in many teacher training pathways has now shrunk to an embarrassing low. Sadly, the story is now even worse, as the 2016 survey from the National Society in Education in Art and Design showed: very few qualified teachers are able to undertake further training in the subject, post-qualification. This means they must rely heavily on the precious time provided in their teacher training (and in some cases simply, or) their own childhood experiences. The book sets out to provide insights into the development of thinking and experiences which can be explored by any teacher, teaching assistant or arts volunteer who wants to expand their own capabilities in art to enrich their classroom learning. It is not a mini art school textbook however, but a repository of ideas, prompts, case studies and explanations, as well as clear links to the expectations of the current Teachers' Standards documentation.

Across the pages, you will find explorations into many, many different forms of art, craft and design education. You will not be limited to repeating old traditions from past centuries; neither will you be confined to the present – as exciting as today's technology may appear. Instead you will find inspiration, excitement and supportive encouragement to think about the principles and values that art embodies. These are applied across all time frames, as the fundamental principles are constructed in the form of the expectation of the National Curriculum as well as exploratory art classrooms. What results is an invitation to a spectacular learning adventure for each individual willing to embark on the journey towards the future.

The associations made with many school subjects provide scope for demonstrating demanding intellectual exploration through art. Rather than implying art is non-academic and only of value in illustrating ideas sourced from other quarters, the central message of this book is that art is a key and crucial aspect of human experience and learning. I think it is impossible to miss this message as you turn its pages.

Too often, resources for teachers reduce activities to step-by-step instructions and ultimately only develop the adult's confidence in following them. I am so pleased that Susan Ogier and her colleagues have resisted this approach. Instead they have sought the more challenging path which develops a greater depth of understanding and the creative freedom to mix ideas and experiment with media, which often results in surprising outcomes. Across the chapters you will be encouraged to consider the frameworks of knowledge, skills and understanding from which quality art can be produced.

Finally, let me return to the statement I made at the start – thousands of primary aged children could be enriched by this book. As the reader, you may influence a number of children each year. If you were to fully engage with the contents of this book, find extra confidence and the ability to articulate ideas to those children, as well as constructing, the net impact over a short period of time would quickly reach the level of hundreds. Then through word of mouth or other recommendations to colleagues, and by the sharing of the processes you have experienced, the impact could quickly be increased ten-fold and the figure of thousands across the country easily achieved.

I sincerely hope you enjoy this book and all the richness that it offers.

Dr Peter Gregory
President of the National Society for Education in Art and Design

Preface

They always say time changes things, but you actually have to change them yourself.

(Andy Warhol)

What is the place of art, craft and design within the Primary National Curriculum in England in the twenty-first century? During my 20-year career in primary education the arguments have always been the same: we know it is important and that children should be creative and have a rounded, well-balanced curriculum … but English and mathematics come first, and then we'll shoehorn in a bit of art if we have time. Increasingly this is the picture globally: at the time of writing, pressures are placed upon teachers to force children's learning in core subjects only, often at an unnatural and unsustainable pace, due to comparisons across international league tables. The relentless testing of children on finite knowledge as a measure of how schools perform has undermined the value that should be placed upon nurturing children's creative dispositions, and this is to the detriment of both the individuals themselves and future society. The impoverished diet that this type of narrow curriculum offers to children leaves us with far reaching consequences for children who are not given chances to reach their full potential, creating issues for child mental health and well-being, as well as preventing them from developing a questioning and critical outlook.

This book aims to begin the process of that change, to arm you with an accessible rationale, along with sound subject knowledge, skills and ideas so that you can become an excellent teacher in art, craft and design. (For writing purposes, the word 'craft' is omitted, but on the understanding that it is integral to the phrase, art and design, or art, where stated.) Whether you, the reader, are an art and design graduate or a complete novice in this subject, the aim of this book is give you the tools, the confidence and the justification to enjoy teaching art and design with your children, and to open their worlds to the joys of learning creatively through visual means.

Introduction

Creativity is allowing yourself to make mistakes. Art is knowing which ones to keep.

(Scott Adams)

Art and design in schools: the current context

Subject knowledge is at the forefront of debate and discussion in Initial Teacher Education in response to the government White Paper, *Educational Excellence Everywhere* (2016), and as the 2014 Primary Curriculum for England has become embedded in non-academy primary schools. OFSTED also has a renewed focus for observing and commenting on the teaching of foundation subjects during its primary inspections, and as a new teacher it can be difficult to know exactly what excellent practice looks like in subjects that you might be unfamiliar or unconfident with in relation to your own personal experiences, or from having only very short courses during your training.

Reports such as *Understanding the Value of Arts & Culture* (Crossick and Kaszynska, 2016) highlight the place and pertinence of the arts as a vehicle to facilitate deeper learning experiences. Specifically, this is through providing enabling avenues by which to develop enhanced cognitive abilities, motivation, communication skills, problem-finding and solving, as well as building self-esteem and confidence: in simple terms, it is about making children's learning experiences meaningful, accessible and palatable. It is therefore essential for you as a trainee, or as someone new to teaching art and design in primary schools, to have a thorough understanding of the discrete subject knowledge that is associated with art, craft and design education. It is imperative that you do this, for you to be able to offer appropriate provision and positive learning opportunities in art for the children in your class.

The 2009 OFSTED report, *Improving Primary Teachers' Subject Knowledge across the Curriculum*, stresses the importance of teachers having a wide knowledge base in *all* areas of the curriculum. It states that developing this kind of wider understanding is essential for raising standards in the quality of teaching and learning in primary schools generally. The report shows that findings from OFSTED inspections during 2007 to 2008 revealed that arts subject knowledge was undermined by teachers' lack of confidence, often stemming from misconceptions about how children might develop creative abilities: evidence showed that teachers often opted for sticking rigidly to closed and directed tasks, or published plans and schemes of work with fixed outcomes, therefore limiting children's creativity by placing a cap on what they could produce. A more recent OFSTED report (2012) shows that although there are indeed examples of very good practice to be found around the country, concerns remain whilst only one third of primary schools inspected during the period 2009–12 were seen to offer at least good art education to their children. The activities and case studies in the following chapters will specifically address concerns outlined by these reports. This should encourage you to experiment with teaching strategies that will develop your confidence to plan imaginative projects, as well as give you a sense of what is good practice in art and design teaching.

You might have already found that, when on placements, you are often under pressure to limit your teaching to 'core' subjects, such as English and mathematics. Sometimes, art, craft and design is taught by specialist teachers, who take the class whilst you are otherwise engaged in activities such as marking or planning. The result of this type of school organisation can be beneficial where the specialist teacher has good pedagogical knowledge, as well as artistic skills to share. There is a downside, however, which is that you might be excluded from ever seeing an art lesson in progress. Further impact of this situation is that you will not be able to gain the skills and confidence to teach the subject yourself, nor will you have the knowledge and understanding of how to plan and teach good quality art and design lessons should the school organisation change, or should you move to a new school where you are expected to teach the subject. Alternatively, if you are passionate and confident about teaching art, and are not given the opportunity to include the subject in your practice, then there is a chance you will feel disincentivised to teach art and design, and ultimately this could lead to you feeling or becoming deskilled. The intention of this book is to support you to teach art and design with enthusiasm and vigour, regardless of your own experience in art education – or lack of it. The following chapters will address your training needs no matter how long you have been teaching, or which route you are taking into primary education: for example, undergraduate or postgraduate university courses, or perhaps school-based routes. This book will be invaluable to you if you have only received superficial training in this subject area. It will provide you with support when you are a newly qualified teacher, and equally it will offer good practice models to experienced teachers who would like to refresh their skills.

Getting to know the National Curriculum

The 2014 English Primary National Curriculum for Art and Design seems noticeably scant in terms of statutory requirements, and only gives very little guidance on a few selected aspects of areas that are deemed important enough to be covered or achieved. Whilst this might at first appear less prescriptive, which is a good thing, problems can soon arise as to how this can be interpreted in relation to excellent practice in art and design education, without the deep knowledge and understanding that lies behind this basic guidance. For the novice trainee or teacher who is not art trained, the lack of detail is extremely unhelpful and could eventually lead to a lowering of standards. For example, where the curriculum states that 'mastery' in drawing should be achieved, a non-specialist teacher might read this as children having to practise and practise formal drawing skills, until they have learnt to draw like Leonardo da Vinci, which of course is nonsense. Teachers and trainees might find the lack of guidance off-putting if they do not have the pedagogical understanding or sound subject knowledge that is required to teach well in art and design. In Chapter 1, the National Curriculum will be analysed and re-interpreted, along with a more detailed explanation of current requirements, so that it is made wholly accessible for the generalist class teacher. It is also important to say here that the National Curriculum is not a compulsory document for all primary settings, therefore the interpretation in this book will essentially be about what constitutes high standards in art and design education, as basic good practice is rarely subject to change – unlike the National Curriculum.

Why is art, craft and design on the primary curriculum?

It could be argued that it is easier to question what would be missing if art and design education were not part of a broad and balanced curriculum. Try to imagine a world without art and design: no images to get us thinking or questioning; no visual link to history or culture; no way of communicating thoughts and ideas without using words; no graphic novels or comics; no film;

no photography; no visually exciting TV graphics; no creative advertising; no illustrations in children's (or adults') books; no exciting new fashions to wear; no video games; no new architecture or attractive interiors; no flower arrangements or garden design; no birthday cards; no new transport designs or furniture design. Only functionality would exist.

Reflection point

- What would that world look like? Colourless? Uniform? Uninteresting? Rather unpleasant? I'm afraid so!
- Have you created a visual image of that world in your mind? Because if you have, you are certainly using art-related skills to do that, namely *imagination* and *visualisation*.
- Take a moment to consider where an artist, craftsperson or designer has made a difference to your life.

A world without art certainly does not sound like a very pleasant or exciting place to live, and the Reflection point helps us to remember that. In fact, aspects of art, craft and design infiltrate every area of our lives, whether we are conscious of this fact of not. Everything that is manmade around us started life as a figment of someone's imagination, which was likely to be sketched on a page, before being transformed into an object in the world that we know and love: from the clothes that you are wearing to the mobile phone in your pocket; from the chair that you are sitting on, to the mug from which you are drinking your tea. We use our aesthetic senses all the time, and we engage in an increasingly visually orientated world. For example, perhaps you are momentarily distracted from reading this book and look away to appreciate a beautiful view in nature; or maybe you have felt disgust and dismay at seeing a litter-strewn street: in observing these views you are making informed, critically aesthetic judgements which affect your sense of self-worth and your emotions. Without the ability to view our world with an appreciative or a critical eye we would surely just have to accept whatever we see before us without question, or without having any sense of value. Chapter 1 will discuss this further, and enable you to base your teaching on firm values and principles, which in turn will keep children at the heart of your art and design teaching.

Tackling barriers to good practice

The value and practicalities of offering an inclusive subject base that places art and design securely within a primary school curriculum have been slowly but surely eroded over the past few years, in some cases almost to extinction. This is largely due to the increased importance placed upon the performative culture to which we now belong, in both English and international societies. This has forced arts education and activity to be viewed as less important than gaining knowledge in literacy and numeracy. Of course, literacy and numeracy are very important, *but so are all the other subjects*. The relentless pressure to stack subjects in a hierarchy, with literacy and numeracy at the pinnacle, has now become a huge problem for all of us. If knowledge of this type is deemed to be the end game in an educational race to the top, then what happens to other aspects of learning, such as enquiry and experimentation? Are these not important for future generations to be able to live their lives in a progressive way? These key skills for life and living in the twenty-first century, and beyond, are realised through working creatively with children, and what better way to nurture that creativity than by using art and design to underpin their learning. Creative thinking, and the implementation of creative ideas, is now crucial for the success of a future economy, as well as for developing cultural understanding through celebrating diversity, and for promoting and implementing social justice. Creative solutions will be a prerequisite to deal with the huge challenges and changes that the world faces now and in the future, and it will be the next generation who pick up the tab for that. Chapter 2 will explore these concepts further.

Reflection point

In his TED Talk of 2006, the creativity and education guru, Sir Ken Robinson, stated: *Creativity now is as important in education as literacy, and we should treat it with the same status.*

- Do you agree with this statement?
- Do you think it is possible to 'teach' creativity?
- Where have you seen 'creativity' happening in your classroom experiences?
- Do you consider yourself to be a creative person? In what way are you able to express your creativity?

Watch the whole talk here: **www.ted.com/talks/ken_robinson_says_schools_kill_creativity? language=en**

Unlike Robinson's vision, creativity in primary schools is currently relegated to a low priority in the teaching day. External pressures that create an environment where class time is mainly spent on core areas means that subjects such as art and design are often overlooked as an unnecessary luxury. The chance that the arts might help children in the real world by relieving stress, boosting self-esteem and confidence, and expressing themselves creatively is lost in favour of short-term goals, which might (or might not) push children successfully through tough testing regimes. But successfully for whom? Not necessarily for individual children. This success is more likely to be for the schools themselves, as they show their achievements in widely published league tables. Sadly, the measurements are very narrow and restrictive, unlike the personalities, talents and potential of the child population, whose futures are potentially at the mercy of these tests. The National Test results in 2016 showed that almost half of the country's population of 11-year-olds are already deemed as failures of this system, and faced re-testing as soon as they started their secondary education, just at the time they should have been encouraged to feel happy and welcome in their new school environments. If these children are offered a well-rounded curriculum, which helps them become resilient and resistant to personal challenge, they will survive these experiences and continue to progress. Right now, there is a renewed urgency for arts to be focused upon in schools to ensure that we provide the broad and balanced curriculum that we know is essential. It is imperative to prevent a future generation of people who are unable to fulfil their potential as creative individuals due to the lack of that broad education, and it is our responsibility, as their teachers, to ensure that they are offered a curriculum in which they can grow to discover and develop their individual talents and skills.

Subject-specific knowledge

I am enough of an artist to draw freely upon my imagination. Imagination is more important than knowledge. Knowledge is limited. Imagination encircles the world.

(Albert Einstein)

Another potential barrier to good teaching and learning in the subject of art and design is that many teachers have misconceptions of what the subject involves. Many primary school teachers and trainees might not have picked up a pencil or paintbrush since the age of 14 themselves, and even then their memories of engaging in art activities at secondary school are often not positive. They tend to remember just not being good enough for the GCSE class, or perhaps were counselled out of doing the subject they enjoyed because they would 'never get a job doing it'. There is sometimes a feeling that art cannot be taught or assessed, and that children can either do it or they can't, but no one would dare to say that about maths or English, nor about many of the other foundation subjects, so why should that apply to something as inclusive and enjoyable as art and design? Ironically, it is also unlikely that children will grow up to have a job 'doing' maths or English! But they will employ the skills they have learnt in all subjects, no matter what they end up doing in the workplace. Throughout this book, essential subject knowledge will be explained, along with examples and activities for you to try and case studies that will exemplify how this is put into practice in the classroom. Einstein stated that knowledge is limited, and that it is *imagination* that is needed to extend knowledge further, by pushing boundaries that are set by what we already know. It is, however, important for us to have the starting point of a secure understanding from which knowledge can grow, develop and change, and we need to bring this right back to the children we are teaching: no two groups of children are the same, therefore the knowledge they will gather during their work in art and design should also be different. As their teachers, it is important for us to keep a flexible view of where they are headed in their learning, and be open to their ideas, thoughts and new possibilities.

━━━ Case study ━━━━━━━━━━━━━━━━━━━━

A five-year-old child was sitting on the floor of the classroom playing with some randomly torn shapes of paper. As she pushed the tiny pieces around they were formed into patterns, which she suddenly recognised as such. She changed the formations, and the patterns developed into more complex arrangements, and eventually these transformed into images representative of familiar objects and creatures with recognisable features. 'I've made a 'picture-mover'!' was her excited response when the class teacher, Abbie, went to see what she was doing. The other children were inspired by this free flow 'play' activity and wanted to make their own 'picture-mover' so Abbie set up an area in the classroom where the children could create their own images and patterns using a variety of ephemeral materials that could be easily moved around, such as cardboard shapes, buttons, stones, shells, coloured paper scraps, flowers, leaves, and even pieces of construction kit.

┌───┐

▬ Reflection point ▬

- What learning do you think was taking place during this activity?
- What do you think that Abbie had learnt about this child from her observations?
- What subject knowledge in art and design would Abbie need to be able to progress this child's learning a step further?

└───┘

Analysis

Abbie had observed this child and engaged her in a dialogue about her activity. The child was using her imagination and sense of play to change and edit the shapes to create new compositions: she was learning to think flexibly and to visualise; to make decisions and to know that sometimes decisions can be reversed; she was observing shapes, lines, sizes and lengths, finding out how shapes fit together, and how to create balance through symmetry – all with just scraps of paper! This free flow activity was successful in promoting the child's open-ended, creative and flexible thinking.

How to use this book

The case study gives you a flavour of the pedagogical basis of this book: that it is not about how good you are (or not!) at art but about how you can promote a creative environment where children can thrive and express themselves visually. Your support can make or break it for some children.

Each chapter has theoretical and research foci so that you will have strong justification for teaching the subject, especially if you find you are in a school where art and design is not fully valued. You will find practical help in the form of advice, useful tables and diagrams that clearly explain different aspects to you. There are suggestions for planning formats linked to theory, and illustrations of key points, in the form of case studies.

Chapter 1 (Principles and values) will set the scene and lay down key features of good practice that are built upon throughout the rest of this book. This chapter will help you to situate your own position and to form your own philosophy for teaching art and design.

Chapter 2 (Creative learning: imagination and expression) and **Chapter 3** (Curriculum and concepts) will give you powerful arguments and tools for ensuring that you have very sound theory for your work with children in learning art and design.

Chapter 4 (Processes and practice) is the practical section. It contains all you need to know about individual processes, made easy to read and easy to find, so that you can identify how to do the processes quickly. You will find references to websites with information and demonstrations, which are most helpful – especially if you are not sure how a process might work.

Chapter 5 (Planning, assessment and progression) will support you in planning and assessing children in this subject. We shall look at the debates and difficulties surrounding this crucial aspect and seek solutions to help you plan to the best possible standard, pinning this to the theory explored in earlier chapters. It will help you to put theory into practice.

In **Chapter 6** we look 'Beyond the classroom and into the future', to help you to plan inspiring experiences involving art and artists, with contributions from Ed Dickenson, educator at the Ben Uri Gallery, as well as artist, Alistair Lambert, and our own artist-in-residence, Al Johnson, whose 'Artist's Stories' you will find throughout this book. For those with an art background, or a love and enthusiasm for art and design, this chapter also provides advice on how to progress the subject further and prepare for subject leadership.

Chapter 7 (The broad and balanced curriculum) is an array of contributions from experts in other curriculum areas, who advocate links with art and design in their individual subjects. This chapter will enable you to see the value of everything you have read in this book in terms of how it translates seamlessly to support and enhance learning across the whole curriculum. My deep thanks go to the contributors for their enthusiasm and commitment to promoting art and design in this way. Hopefully together we shall all start a quiet revolution to get art back on the menu for the joy and motivation it can bring to children in primary education.

1
Principles and values

The purpose of art is not a rarefied intellectual distillate: it IS life, intensified, brilliant life.

(Alain Arias-Misson)

Chapter objectives

This chapter will help you to:

- Situate your personal values in relation to teaching primary art and design.
- Formulate a principled approach to teaching in this subject.
- Consider art and design in the context of promoting social justice.
- Begin to answer the question, what is good practice in art and design?

The following standards apply within this chapter.

1. Set high expectations which inspire, motivate and challenge pupils.
5. Adapt teaching to respond to the strengths and needs of all pupils.

Introduction

At the beginning of any teacher training course, I ask the students about their personal values: what are the principles by which they lead their lives? How would you answer this question? How many of you would say that the main motivator for living a fulfilling life was being top of the class, gaining wonderful possessions, or becoming famous? Whilst we would all agree that these are nice-to-haves, some circumstances can enable us to reflect that these elements might not be as important as the code of principles by which we can lead a fulfilling life: principles that we can apply whether we have material assets or not. These principles might include things such as enjoying good physical and mental health; being caring and feeling the love of our family and friends; having emotional resilience in difficult situations; being a compassionate citizen, and other fundamental values for living a satisfying life. What has this got to do with art and design education, you might ask? The answer to that is *everything*. Engaging in artistic practice is essentially an engagement with holistic elements that make it possible to lead a well-rounded and well-balanced existence. The ability to communicate and express emotions and ideas, relate to others, accept feedback, give an opinion, make a comment, agree or disagree are all important, and we start developing those values as children.

What are values?

The Oxford Dictionary (2016) definition of the noun *value* in English originates from Middle English and from Old French (feminine past participle of *valoir* (be worth) from Latin *valere*). It states that it is:

1. The regard that something is held to deserve; the importance, worth, or usefulness of something: *your support is of great value.*

2. Principles or standards of behaviour; one's judgement of what is important in life: *they internalize their parents' rules and values.*

═══ Reflection point ═══

- Make a list or a mind-map of your top-ten determining personal values. Write them onto separate pieces of paper, or sticky notes, and try to place them in order of importance.
- Do you think these are in a fixed order, or do they move up, down or sideways as your priorities and circumstances change? Try to keep this exercise going over a few days or weeks and see whether your values change or shift in order of priority.
- What have you learnt from doing this exercise?

Analysis

Now there is an emphasis to engage schools with 'fundamental British values' as part of the Prevent Strategy, which became law in 2015. These values include democracy, the rule of law, individual liberty, mutual respect, and tolerance of different faiths and beliefs: possibly, you have listed some of these beliefs as values of your own in the Reflection point exercise. The ethical and moral codes that you apply to everything that you do might well have influenced your decision to become a primary school teacher in the first place (Benninga, 2003). It is, after all, simply about remembering your desire to contribute to society in some way, and becoming a participant in the human side of teaching. In this chapter, we shall explore ways that you can keep these values at the heart of your teaching strategies through the subject of art and design, which is, arguably, the most human of all subjects.

▬▬ Theory focus ▬▬▬▬▬▬▬▬▬▬▬▬▬▬▬▬▬▬▬▬▬▬▬▬

Becoming human

One of my favourite texts, that I go back to time and time again, is *Becoming Human Through Art* (1970) by the American, Edmund Burke Feldman. Humanist principles that underpin the work resonate throughout, and serve to remind us that we should endeavour to keep the child at the heart of the curriculum, and to frequently ask the question, what is education for? The book begins with a preface that states that it was written at a time of great uncertainty within the educational climate, when old assumptions were in the process of being challenged, and new forms of analysis and critique were commonplace. I wonder whether much has changed in all that time? Feldman argues that art in schools should not be about creating artists, which potentially limits its usefulness to the artistically talented alone. On the contrary, he proposes that it contributes to a much broader spectrum of life skills, knowledge and cultural understanding that no other subject can reach. Art and design education can instil in children and young people a sense that life is worth living, a sense that there is a deeper and more meaningful way of engaging in activities that go far beyond the narrow field of school testing regimes. Children, in Feldman's view, are given a feel for personal satisfaction that arises from creating something of their own, both physically and emotionally. Children are given 'permission' to justify their work by articulating the rationale for its existence, and to express their individuality. He makes the case that art is an essential way for us to respond to our world, and notes that every culture, every period in the history of humanity has produced artistic responses to social situations and cultural events. Evidence of this goes back as far as cave drawings, which have been found all around the world. Feldman suggests that children can learn to communicate effectively through unique visual vocabulary that can cross language barriers, enabling them to feel a sense of self-satisfaction in communicating their own individual visual responses. Importantly, by learning about culture and art, and by engaging in art activity, they have 'the values that permit civilised life to go on' instilled within them.

What is a principled approach?

So far we have gathered thoughts about your own personal values for living, and considered how teaching and learning in art and design are fundamentally about how we engage, reflect and comment upon aspects of life by using visual language. It is important to be able to ground yourself within a set of principles that are right for you, as much as they are right for the children you will teach. It is necessary, though, to underpin these with solid pedagogical foundations.

Dr John Reece, psychology professor at Melbourne Institute of Technology, puts forward a 'checklist' of doctrines, which can be applied to all teaching situations and to all age groups (Hurford, 2012).

He suggests key principles that might enable teachers to become reflective and to stand fast in what they know is right for children, no matter what stormy weather the educational landscape throws at them. The 12 principles he suggests are listed here.

1. Recognise, appreciate and foster knowledge and understanding of 'deep' learning.

2. Make learning enjoyable, without being trivial or flippant.

3. Remember that enthusiasm and passion on the part of the educator positively influences children's learning.

4. Educational approaches should be evidence-based and reflective.

5. Teach because you have a genuine love of helping children to learn.

6. Actively involve children in the learning process: empower their learning.

7. Win the 'battle of hearts and minds' when teaching challenging material.

8. Foster an appreciation of the real-world relevance of learning.

9. Be reflective and self-critical of your own practice; always strive for improvement.

10. Have respect for children, regardless of how challenging they may be: listen and learn from them; seek and value their input.

11. Incorporate educational technologies that will effectively enhance learning.

12. Self-knowledge: know what you're teaching and why you're teaching it.

This list seems like a sensible approach, with intentions that should apply no matter what subject you are teaching. In other subjects we are currently faced with a difficult problem when trying to apply these principles: we are in a time when the curriculum is narrow, and learning within that curriculum is prescriptive. We are, however, rather more fortunate with the subject of art and design in this respect, as we are not bound by prescription. We therefore do have permission to teach with the high degree of interactivity and child-focused methods that Reece suggests. So, how can you apply these principles to the area of art and design? That is the easy part once you fully understand the underlining pedagogical aspect.

Pedagogical perspectives

The Italian 'Reggio Emilia' preschool education system is one approach that fits extremely well with education in art and design at all levels – from nursery right through to degree level and beyond. Whilst the pedagogy is essentially an Early Years model, it is easily transferable to older age phases, although the possibilities that this presents is untapped in many schools; possibly for reasons already mentioned in these pages. The approach is established within a pedagogy of both scientific and artistic enquiry, which values children's personal responses to self-initiated lines of investigation. This mirrors the way that contemporary artists work in their own art practice. It is, therefore, worth investigating this further to develop principles to underpin our work for teaching and learning in art and design.

In 1991, Italy's Emilia-Romagna region was named by the American magazine, *Newsweek*, as having one of the best school systems in the world, and the preschools were hailed as examples of excellence (Wingert, 1991). Having been brought to the attention of the world, this educational system has since become an international role model for good practice in learning through creative and expressive mediums, and not just in preschool years. The history of how the methodology for the Reggio schools was formed is also very interesting, especially in relation to the potential for the subject area of art and design to be a platform for social justice and citizenship education principles. We shall return to this a little later in the chapter.

The history of Reggio schools

A young psychologist and pedagogist, Loris Malaguzzi, helped the local community to found the Reggio preschools soon after the Second World War. They were based upon the idea that both the children and their parents made a commitment to active citizenship principles, the intention being that this would help rebuild their society after the war. With Malaguzzi's drive, the people of the town of Reggio Emilia built the preschools with their own hands, after campaigning hard for funds to be allowed for investing in a good future for their children. The pedagogical model was centred on solid principles in which a specific 'image' of the child is key: it is a child who is competent, curious, imaginative and full of potential. The child is perceived as already having much knowledge, and the teacher's role is as a facilitator, or co-constructor, in developing this knowledge in ways that naturally expand and challenge children's preconceptions and views. The child's learning is made visible through the many creative ways that they express themselves, which Malaguzzi named the 'hundred languages of children'.

Reflective exercise

Have a look at Malaguzzi's poem, and think about your own learning experiences as a child.

The hundred languages of children

The child is made of one hundred.

The child has a hundred languages, a hundred hands, a hundred thoughts, a hundred ways of thinking, of playing, of speaking.

A hundred, always a hundred, ways of listening, of marvelling, of loving:

A hundred joys for singing and understanding;

A hundred worlds to discover;

A hundred worlds to invent; a hundred worlds to dream.

The child has a hundred languages, and a hundred, hundred more, but they steal ninety-nine.

The schools and the culture separate the head from the body.

(Continued)

(Continued)

They tell the child to think without hands, to do without head, to listen and not to speak, to understand without joy, to love and to marvel only at Easter and Christmas.

They tell the child to discover the world already there, and of the hundred they steal ninety-nine.

They tell the child that work and play, reality and fantasy, science and imagination, sky and earth, reason and dream are things that do not belong together.

And thus they tell the child that the hundred is not there.

The child says: No way! The hundred is there!

(Loris Malaguzzi, 1994)

Reflection point

- What thoughts did this poem invoke in you?
- How does this relate to experiences from your own childhood?
- What is your image of the child?

The Reggio philosophy is firmly based upon social constructivist positions, for example by theorists such as Jerome Bruner, Howard Gardner, John Dewey, Jean Piaget and Lev Vygotsky. It therefore lends itself perfectly to teaching and learning in art and design, with the notion that project work is collaborative: the best way to develop new ideas is from within a community of learners, and this is at the forefront of the Reggio philosophy. Reggio education is ever-evolving, and is a pedagogy that changes and adapts as society also changes and progresses. Peter Moss (2001, pp125–126) states that:

While we seek the answer which will enable us to foreclose, in Reggio they understand that even after 40 years or more, their work remains provisional, continually open to new conditions, perspectives, understandings and possibilities.

Since its discovery by *Newsweek*, this Early Years philosophy has been adapted to suit different settings right across the world, and when you look at the key principles upon which the Reggio school movement is founded, try to imagine that you are reading this from the standpoint of an art and design perspective.

- **Education is for finding out about who you are, and for discovering your place in the world:** Children do this through communicating and collaborating with others, therefore participating in group work and a dialogic approach are essential. Children are viewed as active citizens.

- **Children are capable of constructing their own learning:** they are not empty vessels to be filled with knowledge by the adult, but curious and motivated beings. The adult, therefore, has the role of facilitator, or lead learner.

- **The environment is the third teacher:** The learning environment is a conducive space for investigation and enquiry. It should be light, orderly and clutter free, with a range of interesting materials to inspire experimentation and creativity.

- **A multi-sensory and inclusive approach is required:** Learning and play are not separated. The child uses all their senses to learn, and there is not a hierarchy of ability or accessibility to learning experiences. Children with particular personal challenges have 'special rights'.

- **Project-based learning is key:** Learning opportunities are seen as part of a process, and children progress through a cycle of finding enquiry questions, researching, investigating through practical activities, experimenting with techniques and materials, and forming an outcome, which in itself has scope for development.

- **Parents as partners:** Parents are expected to be partners in decision-making and to reinforce school learning at home, and beyond that, the community also have responsibility to nurture and encourage youngsters: building upon the idea that children are active and valued citizens, the whole community is seen as having an investment in their education.

- **Documentation of learning:** Making learning visible by recording observations of the child at work, and a deep analysis and reflection of those observations together with practical outcomes is integral. This is how adults research how children learn. Again, the teaching pedagogy is a dynamic, ever-evolving research project, rather than a passive 'craft' approach favoured by some politicians.

- **The Hundred Languages of Children:** The languages, or ways of expression, are recognition that each child is an individual and will have their own idiosyncratic ways of learning, and responding to that learning.

Reflective exercise

Read the *Newsweek* article here.

www.europe.newsweek.com/school-must-rest-idea-all-children-are-different-200976?rm=eu

Case study

Recycling

A Year 4 class were studying the topic of recycling. Jane, a recently qualified teacher (RQT), asked the children to collect all sorts of recycled items and bring them from home. One morning they entered their classroom to find that all the chairs and tables had been moved to form a large circle around the room. In the centre was a huge pile of various recycled materials: plastic bottles; cardboard tubes; bottle lids; plastic bags; foam; sheeting; buttons etc. The children were excited, as well as slightly confused. The children had experience and knowledge about recycling materials, both from their homes as well as previous geography and science lessons in school, but Jane did not give them any further information at this point, as she wanted them to enjoy the surprise. The children were then invited to simply explore and experiment with these everyday materials, and to find out what they could do with

(Continued)

(Continued)

them. For example, they were asked to feel the textures, to discover whether they could cut or tear, twist or crush, stretch or change the shapes of the items. Jane posed questions to help the children progress in their investigations, such as: had they noticed whether a material was opaque or transparent, or were there holes or gaps they could use to thread through to join materials? The children soon began to come up with their own questions about the materials. They were challenged to try to find out brand new ways of manipulating materials, which they then shared with the rest of the class. This gave them more ideas of how to explore the objects in imaginative ways. They were asked to respond to their discoveries through visual means: by either drawing or using a camera.

Figures 1.1 and 1.2 Visual responses begin to emerge after exploring materials.

Reflection point

- Which of the principles of the Reggio philosophy can you apply to this case study?
- What is different about the approach taken towards teaching here?
- What is the role of the teacher?
- Can you think what the 'next steps' might be after this activity?

In teaching art and design we teach the whole person, not just one or two narrow aspects that some politicians think is best (often these people have few or no qualifications in educational studies themselves). Children are enthused to learn with a practical enquiry-based pedagogy, as it is one that excites and engages them, and encourages them to want to come to school. When taught well, art and design teaches children to consider important issues that can, or will, affect their lives. It is a valid method of communication, and can be a vehicle for change in relation to both children's personal lives and the wider community. It can help them to understand and contemplate world events and social injustices in a safe and non-threatening way. If we can view the children in our classes as active citizens, with a voice of their own, then we empower those children to change things for the better: art can allow children to discover their identity and find their voice.

Art and design, citizenship and personal values

The psychologist Jerome Bruner (1996) taught us that education is part of a broader cultural and social process. He states that:

> It is surely the case that schooling is only one small part of how a culture inducts the young into its canonical ways. Indeed, schooling may even be at odds with a culture's other ways of inducting the young into the requirements of communal living … What has become increasingly clear … is that education is not just about conventional school matters like curriculum or standards or testing. What we resolve to do in school only makes sense when considered in the broader context of what the society intends to accomplish through its educational investment in the young. How one conceives of education, we have finally come to recognize, is a function of how one conceives of culture and its aims, professed and otherwise.

(pix–x)

It is therefore essential that you see children's education within the social context in which it exists, and that they receive a well-rounded and mindful experience whilst they are in your care. By using a questioning approach with children, it is perfectly possible to explore their social attitudes and to help them develop and understand their own emerging personal values. Raising controversial issues that affect society will present a good opportunity for children to develop empathy and an awareness of others that can influence their developing mind-sets in a positive way. Teaching citizenship principles through art and design can help children to express their thoughts and concerns visually, and acts as a safety net by creating an outlet for their misconceptions and fears. Oxfam have produced some helpful guidance and they describe controversial issues as *those that have a political, social or personal impact and arouse feeling and/or deal with questions of value or belief* (Oxfam, 2006).

Contentious issues can be either local or global, and the children in your class will already have been influenced to some degree by images and materials they have absorbed through their environment, family, friends and the media. Often, concerning issues are complex to understand, even for adults, and children can be easily influenced by the strong views of others which they might overhear.

Practical activity

- Again, here it would be well worth revisiting your own attitudes towards your 'image of the child'. How much do you believe in their capabilities, and what is your knowledge of their existing understanding of the world?

- Which of the following controversial issues would you feel comfortable discussing with your class? Rate them on a scale of one to ten (one being that you would feel comfortable; and ten that you would not).

War

Pollution

Stereotyping

(Continued)

(Continued)

Death

Poverty

Global warming/climate change

Bullying

Racism

Terrorism

Gender

- Add your own items to the list.
- Do you think that primary aged children are too young to be introduced to contentious or controversial issues?

Reflective exercise

Exploring values through art

Have a good look at this image by the Singh Twins.

Figure 1.3 From Zero to Hero (2002), copyright The Singh Twins: *www.singhtwins.co.uk*

Use the questions to explore your personal values.

- What does this image remind you of, culturally?

- The Beckhams are quite a large size in the image – what do you think this signifies? What do you think of the elevated status they are given?

- At first you might think they are floating, but why do you think they have been presented on their throne balancing on pillars of magazines?

- What items are they portrayed with, and what might this tell you?

- What do you notice about the people at the base of the image, and about the offerings that are being made?

- At the top of the image you can see a cat and a dog in the form of angels: what are the qualities of cats and dogs in different cultures, and why do you think these two animals are portrayed showering the Beckhams with stars, eggs and clothed in £10 notes?

- How has this helped you to think about your own values and attitudes towards celebrity culture, traditions, multicultural Britain, and wealth and greed?

The introduction of contemporary art, as a basis for initiating discussion around tricky issues, can be a useful strategy for developing open-ended dialogue with and amongst children. This kind of questioning is appropriate for all age groups in the primary phase and allows you, as the teacher, to observe children's responses and to understand the values that already exist within them. See Chapter 6 for more examples of using artwork to inspire talk and enquiry.

▬▬ Theory focus ▬▬

Bruner's spiral curriculum

Bruner's notion of the 'spiral curriculum' advocates that concepts should be revisited at extended levels of depth as children grow, so that learning is embedded and understood completely. This concept is transferable to other areas of experience and learning, and means that we can teach anything, at any time, with increasing profundity and complexity. This theory applies well to art and design. For example, the same materials and techniques can be exploited by three-year-olds as well as 43- or 93-year-olds, and the results will all be different but no less original, valid or exciting. Returning to the concept of the Reggio schools, it will be advantageous to look in the direction of the Foundation Stage for inspiration: it is here that we can find a model for content of the art and design curriculum for primary aged children. Until the age of five, children are encouraged to experiment, explore the world around them and relate this to other areas of their lives: they look, think, respond, begin to articulate their ideas and solve complex problems; they have no inhibitions or doubts regarding their abilities to paint, draw, sculpt and make to express their ideas; they are encouraged to develop and learn through following their individual interests. When this happens, they are confident with materials, inventive, motivated and independent: these are positive traits in children that all teachers would find invaluable, no matter what subject is being taught. We should consider ourselves lucky in primary education that any outcomes for the subject of art and design

(Continued)

(Continued)

are not restricted by end-of-key-stage results from testing, and that we have every opportunity to develop thoughtful, imaginative and individual responses from our children. We must ensure that we use that opportunity.

Applying principles

The Independent Review of the Primary Curriculum (Rose, 2009) which came about through the Rose Review, and which was instantly disregarded by the Coalition Government in 2010, embraced three broad aims, shared across key stages including Key Stage 3, that all young people should become successful learners, confident individuals and responsible citizens. These aims, however, remain valid as a starting point for curriculum design, especially if one is to ask the question, what is education for?

In 2010, The Cambridge Primary Review published a report which was the culmination of 40 years of research into primary education (Alexander, 2010). The report identified a range of significant issues of great importance to this phase of education. Any curriculum, of course, should set out the key attributes that are valued by society, and which are reflective of what we hope our children and young people will become, because of the education we offer. These values relate to our relationships, our society, our environment and ourselves: education can influence the current values of society, and help to shape future society in a positive way.

Practical activity

- What would your aims be for an ideal curriculum?
- How would you educate children to be successful learners, confident individuals and responsible citizens?
- How would you develop an understanding of the principles needed for valuing ourselves as individuals, our relationships with each other, our engagement with the multicultural society in which we live, and the environment around us?
- How much would aspects such as creativity and imagination feature in your ideal curriculum, or do you think these are unnecessary luxuries?
- Make a list or spider diagram to record your thinking.

The outcomes of this activity will help you to focus on aims and values for an education that covers what *you* think should be of importance, while at the same time developing an understanding of art and design in the curriculum. Features such as equality, inclusion, progression, confidence and self-esteem, collaborative practice, well-being and a sense of achievement may have featured in your thinking about the broader issues to do with learning, and the needs of the next generation once they are in the workforce. An excellent curriculum should strongly emphasise children's personal, emotional and social development, alongside intellectual development, questioning and thinking skills, and this should be achieved through playfulness and active learning.

Practical activity

- Draw up a list of reasons to show how art and design can contribute to the education of the whole child: think about how these reasons are connected to children's personal, social and emotional development.

- Where do you place the value of personal, social and emotional skills in relation to children's learning?

Analysis

It might not be too difficult to think of reasons why the arts are important in children's education. With a holistic view in mind, we can set out some of these reasons and justifications for teaching art and design in relation to important life skills. I am sure that you will have listed some of the following justifications: the arts provide opportunities for children to express their thoughts, emotions and ideas, and to use their imaginations; children are able to experiment and to develop their ideas creatively; through group work and through working alongside each other on creative projects, the arts provide a key link with children's growth as confident individuals; art activity provides opportunities for children to work in creative ways with people of all ages, both inside and outside of the school, for example in community projects, and therefore to contribute to the wider cultural life of the school and community: through art and design projects, children are able to create performances or displays for a variety of audiences; they learn to work through a broad range of media including digital photography, use of computer graphics and video, etc.

Providing space for children to reflect upon and evaluate their work together allows them to develop critical thinking skills and an appreciation of creative products and processes. Through exploring a range of media and materials in an open-ended way, children will be able to empathise with different viewpoints, traditions and cultures, and begin to develop an understanding of the diversity of cultures in which they exist. We shall develop these ideas in the next chapter.

Eisner's ten reasons for teaching art

An important theorist within the art education fraternity is the late Elliot Eisner (1934–2014), who devised a top-ten list of reasons why art education is essential for children. In 1990s America, schools displayed the poster which explained this in no uncertain terms, and it remains very relevant today.

1. The arts teach children to make good judgments about qualitative relationships. Unlike much of the curriculum in which correct answers and rules prevail, in the arts, it is judgment rather than rules that prevail.

2. The arts teach children that problems can have more than one solution and that questions can have more than one answer.

3. The arts celebrate multiple perspectives. One of their large lessons is that there are many ways to see and interpret the world.

4. The arts teach children that in complex forms of problem solving, purposes are seldom fixed, but they change with circumstance and opportunity. Learning in the arts requires the ability and a willingness to surrender to the unanticipated possibilities of the work as it unfolds.

5. The arts make vivid the fact that neither words in their literal form nor numbers exhaust what we can know. The limits of our language do not define the limits of our cognition.

6. The arts teach students that small differences can have large effects. The arts traffic in subtleties.

7. The arts teach students to think through and within a material. All art forms employ some means through which images become real.

8. The arts help children learn to say what cannot be said. When children are invited to disclose what a work of art helps them feel, they must reach into their poetic capacities to find the words that will do the job.

9. The arts enable us to have experience we can have from no other source and through such experience to discover the range and variety of what we are capable of feeling.

10. The arts' position in the school curriculum symbolizes to the young what adults believe is important.

(www.arteducators.org/advocacy)

Eisner championed a philosophy in which educators can value the arts by realising that every small action can have ripple effects that are boundless; that arts celebrate multiple perspectives; and that arts teach children that problem-finding is as valid as problem-solving. He advocated that purposes are seldom fixed, but they change with circumstance and opportunity, and for the future we need children to be able to think with flexibility and open minds about the problems that we face, because it is their future, not ours.

Eisner (2002) states that:

> To neglect the contribution of the arts in education, either through inadequate time, resources or poorly trained teachers, is to deny children access to one of the most stunning aspects of their culture and one of the most potent means for developing their minds.

(p40)

Reflection point

- What do you think of Eisner's statement?
- Why do you think art and design education has become such a battleground for time and space on the curriculum?

What does good practice in art and design look like in the classroom?

I hope that, by now, you are starting to realise that teaching art and design is part of teaching about life in general. Good practice in art and design is firmly underpinned by sound principles that keep children and their worlds at the centre of what we do with them, and for them. An expectation of high standards based on clear personal values is paramount to good practice in all subjects, including this one, but with art and design we have the freedom to exploit a pedagogy of experimentation and enquiry without the pressure of having to perform to measurable targets, or having to fit in with any governmental plan. We shall be returning to this key point throughout the book, and building up a picture of what good practice looks like as we go.

Professional development

Hold a staff meeting to introduce the concepts you have learnt from this chapter to your colleagues.

Go to the Reggio Children website:

www.reggiochildren.it/identita/reggio-emilia-approach/?lang=en

Here you can view backdated newsletters of *Rechild*. These are full of wonderful examples of projects and images that can present ideas for art projects in your school.

Read the poem by Loris Malaguzzi, *The Hundred Languages of Children*, to your colleagues, and talk to them about the Reggio philosophy before asking them, what is their 'image of the child'?

Lead a discussion based upon their own principles and values, and ask them to work in pairs or groups of three to write down their thoughts and ideas, either on sticky notes or on large pieces of paper.

Use the Reflective exercises in this chapter to both initiate and develop the discussion.

Draw everyone back together and agree upon a final list together: you should now have a collective decision on what values and principles will underpin art and design teaching in your school, and you can use this to create or update a policy document for art and design.

Chapter summary

In this chapter, we have discussed the need to keep focused on the human aspect of education, as opposed to the preferred performative route taken by successive governments. We have reflected upon the reasons why you have come into the profession of primary teaching in the first place. We have questioned your own 'image of the child' and what this might mean for developing your philosophy for teaching art and design with your class. We have considered Bruner's 'spiral curriculum', as well as the Reggio Emilia Early Years pedagogy, and have explored how these relate to

(Continued)

(Continued)

developing an understanding of education in artistic practice, as well as offering children skills for life. In the next chapter, we shall look in more detail at attitudes towards teaching art and design, and the centrality of giving children permission to be creative and imaginative. We shall explore the fear that this sometimes invokes in unconfident teachers of art and design, as well as the sheer pleasure that is fully achievable for all.

Reflective exercise

- What have you discovered about your own attitudes, values and principles?
- What do you understand about why it is important to develop a rationale for teaching art and design in primary education?
- Revisit the list of the values that you made, and match these to the principles you have learnt about in this chapter.
- Make a list of the top-ten principles for teaching art and design with primary aged children. Which principles would you now apply to teaching art and design with your class?

Further reading

Butterworth, L (2016) 'The importance and value of art, craft and design'. Education Business (online). Available at: **www.educationbusinessuk.net/features/importance-and-value-art-craft-and-design**

Eaude, T (2015) *New Perspectives on Young Children's Moral Education: Developing Character through a Virtue Ethics Approach.* London: Bloomsbury.

Edwards, C P, Gandini, L and Forman, G (1998) *The Hundred Languages of Children: The Reggio Emilia Approach – Advanced Reflections.* London: Ablex.

Winner, E, Goldstein, T R and Vincent-Lancrin, S (2013) 'Art for art's sake? The impact of arts education'. Centre for Educational Research and Innovation, OECD Publishing (online). Available at: **www.oecd.org/edu/ceri/arts.htm**

National Society of Education in Art and Design website: **www.nsead.org/home/index.aspx**

2

Creative learning: imagination and expression

I would like to propose that we let the imagination take its place at the heart of learning, and that we create a climate in which it can flourish.

We need discovery; making; doing; exploring; creating; critical thinking; seeing; hearing; experiencing. Children have to be introduced to the arts in every form.

(Michael Morpurgo, *ImagineNation*, 2011, p1)

Chapter objectives

This chapter will help you to:

- Develop your understanding of the importance of being able to express ideas visually.
- Explore the role of imagination in children's lives.
- Understand the nature of creativity within art and design education.
- Begin to examine your own attitudes towards teaching art and design.
- Extend your understanding of how to teach the subject through optimising the learning environment for practical work.

The following standards apply within this chapter.

2. Promote good progress and outcomes by pupils.
3. Demonstrate good subject and curriculum knowledge.

Concepts and creativity

There has been so much written about creativity in education over the past couple of decades; at times it feels as if there is an overwhelming amount. The subject of art and design in primary schools is often seen as synonymous with 'doing' creativity, but how can we ensure that children are exercising their creative muscle during art lessons, and not just using processes and materials to fulfil a predetermined outcome set by the teacher? We should perhaps ask ourselves a few hard questions about our own understanding of what it means to be creative, expressive and imaginative. There are many good reasons, both simple and complex, why art is important, but none of those reasons is that it ticks a box called 'creativity'. In this chapter, we shall explore key concepts that concentrate on how creativity can be applied within art and design education, so that both you and your class will maximise creative opportunities to produce satisfying and thoughtful outcomes for the children. First we shall remind ourselves of some of the major research and readings that are relevant in discussing this important aspect of education.

Expression

Over many years of teaching primary art and design I have asked students and trainees who are just beginning their journey to become teachers, why they think art might be an important subject for children to experience and learn within. The most common answer is that they believe it is an expressive language, and we have already seen this exemplified by Malaguzzi's Hundred Languages in Chapter 1. Research by Watts (2005) bears this out: his enquiry with Key Stage 2 children into

Table 2.1 Table showing children's perceptions of how art is important

	Age					
	7	8	9	10	11	Total%
Communication	15	13	26	31	33	23
Personal development	26	43	15	25	16	25
Aesthetics/product	21	17	30	16	21	21
Fun	12	3	8	6	0	6
Money	5	6	9	5	8	7
Therapy	5	0	1	5	8	4
Physicality	0	0	1	0	0	0
There's no right or wrong	0	0	2	3	3	2
Don't know	17	17	8	9	10	12

Taken from: Watts, R (2005) Attitudes to Making Art in the Primary School, *The International Journal of Art & Design Education*, Vol. 24, No 3, p249.

why they make art was answered in a similar way by 16 per cent of the 11-year-olds in his study, whilst 57 per cent of the research group suggested that they made art because it was fun. This suggests that they did not have a very good awareness of what they were learning when engaged in an art activity. Table 2.1 shows the results from this research when children were asked the question, How is art important? As we can see, one of the key reasons from the children's responses is also *expression*, or ways of *communication*.

Reflection point

- How does this table of child responses match up with your own ideas of why art and design is an important subject?
- Can you think of occasions when it is easier or more efficient for you to communicate by creating a visual image?
- How often do you read images that communicate information or ideas in your everyday life (for example: road signs; advertising; apps such as Instagram; posters; etc.)? Make a list or keep a diary of these, and consider whether these communications would be better or more direct if the message was written as text.

Communication and self-expression are the most basic of all human needs (Alexander, 2009). Young children's independent artwork often derives from a desire to externalise their personal responses to everyday experiences and emotions, and it is a wholly natural exercise for them to use art activities, such as drawing or making, as a way of reacting to actual or imagined scenarios. Likewise, in school, we can use this natural motivation to encourage children to express their ideas visually, but we need to remember that we must hook them in first, and ignite their interest by providing stimulating – even irresistible – starting points. Very often, planned art and design activities are linked to topic or curriculum themes, but by including a personally invested approach you can allow children to express themselves as individuals more easily. For example, by using your children's home and school experiences, their interests, personal histories, friends, families, etc. as topics for artwork, you will allow them to use visual communication to 'speak' about their own lives, and at the same time give yourself an insight into them as unique individuals. Providing sensory activities of all kinds will give you scope to encourage children to produce original visual responses. These can be recorded or documented to ascertain children's understanding of their experiences, ultimately providing you with assessment material that shows you how they are processing information. Equally, children will learn how to interpret and respond emotionally, demonstrating that they are internalising the positive learning opportunities you have offered, and giving them confidence to express themselves through their art. As children progress through the primary years, they will become increasingly adept at using materials and techniques associated with this subject area. So alongside the acquisition of technical skills must ride increased confidence and enjoyment, brought about by exploring the world through engagement with sensory activity, thoughtful reflection and imagination.

Figures 2.1 and 2.2 Year 5 sketchbook pages with reflective comments.

Imagination

A small proportion of children in the aforementioned study by Watts (2005) stated that art was an imaginative response to the world they are learning about. An example is nine-year-old Georgie, who stated that, *I think children make art because they have more imagination than adults do. Then they draw it* (p291). What do you think of this child's statement? At what point in our lives do you think we grow out of imagination, creativity and our ability to 'draw it'? Why might this happen? Craft (2008) surmises that we are all capable of creative and imaginative acts, and says that, *Little c creativity involves the use of imagination, intelligence, self-creation and self-expression* (p45). She uses the terms 'Little c' and 'Big C' creativity, to help us understand the possibilities that are presented through small acts of everyday creativity: acts that each one of us uses to serve our daily lives (Little c), as opposed to the larger or more dramatic acts that are the result of high level creativity by creative experts (Big C). It is possible that not many of us would feel that we fall into the latter category, but we are all very capable of Little c creativity – maybe we just need to learn to recognise it a bit more. Little c creativity is the result of everyday imaginative acts that we need to do to live our lives well, yet I have met a lot of trainees, students and practising teachers who tell me, 'I am not at all creative', or 'I am not imaginative'. I have even met teachers who tell me their whole class lacks imagination.

So, how do we define imagination? The dictionary tells us that it is to do with conjuring things that are not real; to hold a picture, or solve a problem using one's mind; the ability to think of new things; to create something that is idealised or fanciful (Merriam-Webster, 2017). What a difficult job we have as teachers, to pin down the importance and the role that imagination plays in ours and in children's lives – especially as this, along with the concept of creativity, is something intangible and therefore immeasurable. Hickman (2005) goes much further in his analysis of the term, and gives us permission to recognise the educational purpose of utilising the imagination by linking it securely to developing thought processes and emotional awareness. He argues that:

Imagination involves thought, thought which is not simply fantasy or the conjuring up of mental images of things not experienced but the actual construction of new realities. Art making can be seen as an effective conduit through which imagination can flow. There appears to be a link between one's capacity for empathy and the ability to think creatively; empathy is made possible by imagination.

(p105)

Hickman also states that imagination is customarily associated with art and design, along with creativity, expression and understanding of personal identity. He describes creativity as 'elusive' (p112), and compares the pursuit of its meaning to catching butterflies or trying to grab a bar of soap, because it is notoriously hard to define, as Craft (2007) also acknowledges. He suggests that the trouble in defining creativity lies within its nature as a brain-based function: the concept is ethereal and so cannot be physically seen, captured and monitored, which takes us back to the possibility that imagination is something not real enough, or too difficult to justify, to be concerned with in education, where accountability is king. Let us, however, take a quick look again at where we would be without the very human ability to imagine. For a start, we shall have to use our imagination to do exactly this. Albert Einstein famously said that imagination is more important than knowledge, because it reaches beyond current thinking and into unchartered areas of human achievement. Interestingly, the 2013 National Curriculum for England does mention the word 'imagination' in the guidance for art and design, but only once, and that is at Key Stage 1, where it states that pupils should be taught:

- *to use a range of materials creatively to design and make products.*
- *to use drawing, painting and sculpture to develop and share their ideas, experiences and imagination.*

(DfE, 2013)

We shall look in more detail at the 2013 National Curriculum for England in the next chapter, but suffice it to say here that imagination shouldn't really stop at Key Stage 1. Contrary to what Georgie, aged nine, from Watts's research suggests, imagination is not just for children.

Research into the human brain and how we learn is constantly making progress, with the advent of MRI scanning and new discoveries being made about how the brain works (Caine et al., 2008; Blakemore and Frith, 2005), but the workings of the mind and how, or whether, we utilise our imaginative inner lives to their full effect remains an enigma to this day. The American philosopher Professor Nigel J T Thomas wrote:

Imagination is what makes our sensory experience meaningful, enabling us to interpret and make sense of it, whether from a conventional perspective or from a fresh, original, individual one. It is what makes perception more than mere physical stimulation of the sense organs. It also produces mental imagery, visual and otherwise which is what makes it possible for us to think outside the confines of our present perceptual reality, to consider memories of the past and possibilities for the future and weigh alternatives against one another. Thus, imagination makes possible all our thinking about what is, what has been and, perhaps most importantly, what might be.

(www.co-bw.com/BrainConciousness%20Update%20index.htm)

The role of imagination cannot be underestimated, even if it remains somewhat misunderstood and unknown. Primary teachers, however, deal with the unknown every day, as we can only guess at what a child is fully capable of, and we may never know whether they achieve their potential at some point in the future or not. We must use our imaginations to try to visualise that potential, and use our creativity to not leave stones unturned in their education by leaving out essential subjects such as art and design, so that children have every chance of personal fulfilment. Imagination alone is not enough, however, and should be supported by strategic progression of other aspects of art and design learning, so that children are satisfied by their efforts in expressing imaginative ideas. Technical skills, as well as lots of encouragement to make and record detailed observations, will avoid a situation where children are embarrassed by the efforts they make to express their ideas visually, as we shall see in the case study that follows.

━━ Case study ━━━━━━━━━━━━━━━━━━━━━━━━━

Creative Connections research project (2012-14)

Thomas, a ten-year-old Year 5 boy, attended a two-form entry primary school situated in the outer suburbs of London.

He was a quiet boy who, according to his class teacher, was a middle achiever. He showed enthusiasm towards project work and was good at sport, but not very enthusiastic or competent at literacy. He preferred maths but was not a particularly high achiever in this area. The school offered art and design on the curriculum, but the teacher, who was newly qualified and unconfident in the subject himself, avoided teaching it as much as possible. Some children opted to attend the after school art club, but Thomas was not one of them.

An artist was brought in to work with the class through an EU funded Art and Citizenship research project, 'Creative Connections' (2012-14), which aimed to explore children's concepts of personal, national and European identity though art. In this project, pupils connected with children of similar ages in other European countries by responding to existing art images and creating their own artwork. They then posted these onto a secure blog, where they were able to comment on and question each other's work through immediate online translation. The class chose to explore their sense of European identity through studying the built environment.

Thomas was the very first UK child in the project to try the blog, and he did this in his own time, during the half-term holiday. He uploaded an image of his own and asked, 'Hi Spanish! Are you there?' When later questioned about how he had learnt to do this, he said that he had watched an online tutorial to find out how to use the blog: 'It was just an app. I watched the video to see how to get the Wordpress app on my iPad.'

Thomas then began to find other images of buildings that he liked and posted those onto the shared site. One was of London's Shard, which he titled, 'My favourite building' and he immediately followed this up with a question to encourage responses: 'This is mine. The Shard. What's yours?'

This drew no fewer than 40 responses from partner European schools, as well as others from his own classmates, and the project had begun.

Thomas remained a key participant in the project and was clearly inspired by the topic, his imagination having been sparked. His family responded by taking him to see The Shard one weekend, and he used photographs from this trip to develop his own imaginative drawings. Subsequent group work in school saw Thomas as a central instigator for the creative outcomes that resulted from the project.

Figures 2.3 and 2.4 In the Shard they have these stilts that's why I did that there. Then it's like a steel pole where the lift is and it goes up into this big orange glass like in churches – like stained glass. Thomas, aged ten.

When interviewed, the class teacher stated that he was amazed at the quality of Thomas's initiative, as well as his sustained involvement and his leadership in the group work. He acknowledged that he had not seen evidence of Thomas's creative potential during general class work. Thomas's self-awareness of his own potential as an artist/designer was also not apparent at this stage. When interviewed, this was the conversation:

Thomas: *Yes, but I'm really terrible at art.*

Researcher: *Why do you say that?*

Thomas: *It's just not my thing.*

Researcher: *What about all these ideas – your photos and the drawings you've done here?*

Thomas: *Yes I like those – but it didn't really seem like work.*

┌───┐

━━ Reflective exercise ━━━━━━━━━━━━━━━━━━━━━━━━━━━━

Have a look at the Creative Connections research project.

creativeconnexions.eu/

└───┘

Analysis

This case study is an example of how easy it could be to miss spotting a child's creative potential. Thomas was unremarkable in the class of 30, and had reached Year 5 before a teacher was given an unexpected insight into his personal interests and his imaginative responses, through this project. Thomas's own thoughts on his ability in art and design reveal a child whose confidence and understanding of the subject had been negatively affected by his experiences so far (Holt, 1997). It highlights the necessity for us, as primary teachers, to create windows through which children can believe in their own capabilities, foster their imaginations and unlock their creative possibilities. If this is not justification enough to allow time and space for creativity through art and design in our daily practice, in the next section we shall look at research that will help us to further value arts education in our classrooms.

━━ Theory focus ━━━━━━━━━━━━━━━━━━━━━━━━━━━━━━━━━━

All Our Futures (1999)

No student leaves my lectures without knowing about the important report, *All Our Futures: Creativity, Culture and Education* (NACCCE, 1999), even though this was written a long time ago. The National Advisory Committee on Creative and Cultural Education (NACCCE) was established in 1998 by the then Secretary of State for Education and Employment, and the Secretary of State for Culture, Media and Sport. The committee was tasked with making recommendations on the creative and cultural development of young people through both formal and informal education. The committee was asked to take stock of provision at that time, and to make proposals for principles, policies and practice, to move forward with the goal that education would be fit for purpose in the twenty-first century. The results and recommendations of this report were far reaching in relation to the impact it had upon creative approaches in primary schools during the following decade, and in fact are still resonant and relevant right up to today.

The report usefully determines a variety of definitions of the term 'creativity', noting that there are incumbent attitudes that colour how each of us personally view the term. The three views of the creative process, according to NACCCE, are:

1. Sectoral: that creativity is firmly encased within the arts. To some degree, this attitude is borne out by the schools who use subjects such as art and design to justify that they are offering a creative curriculum.

2. Elite: there is an elitist view, which purports that true creativity is rare and confined to special people with special talents (as in Craft's notion of 'Big C' creativity). There is, within this view, a sliding scale denoting degrees of mastery and genius.

3. Democratic: the democratic view advocates that everyone is capable of being creative, and that it should be the aspiration of a democratic society to ensure that every child has the opportunity to fulfil their creative potential.

NACCCE, which was made up from people with a range of different expertise and interests, including scientists and mathematicians as well as those from arts backgrounds, offered their own definition, that creativity is: *Imaginative activity fashioned so as to produce outcomes that are both original and of value*. This, when coupled with the democratic view as described in point 3, lends itself well to a practical and accountable *raison d'être* for creativity being placed firmly on the agenda of any school curriculum. The report unpicks the three key components for us, and helps us to understand the co-dependency of the terms: *Imaginative activity* is not enough on its own without an outlet for experimenting with those ideas and bringing them to fruition; *Originality* both creates and solves problems, and both of these aspects are essential to the progression of societies, as the world becomes a more and more uncertain place; *Value* can be seen as both on a very small, personal scale as well as a larger, or even global, scale. As teachers of art and design with primary aged children, it is very important for us to remember that we might not see all that value play out whilst children are in our schools or in our care, but we shall know that by offering our children the strategies and confidence to be creative individuals, in whichever way suits them, that we have done our job well.

Reflective exercise

Read chapters 2 and 5 of the *All Our Futures* report which can be found here:

www.sirkenrobinson.com/pdf/allourfutures.pdf

- What is your own view of creativity?
- The idea of flexibility and open-mindedness comes across strongly in the report as important across all subject areas. How does this fit in with your personal philosophy for teaching? How does this match with the school experience you have encountered so far?
- Which areas highlighted by the report do you recognise as continuing to be problematic for art and design education, nearly 20 years after this report was presented?

Analysis

All Our Futures (1999), chapter 5, section 147 states that:

We welcome the Government's commitment to reduce the content of the National Curriculum and to allow schools more flexibility and freedom. But many schools are also worried about the impact on the breadth and balance of the curriculum, and particularly on the status of the foundation subjects. The problem as we see it is that in practice the relaxation has been in the interest of concentrating on the core subjects, rather than promoting increased flexibility across the whole curriculum. Our argument for greater flexibility is not to reduce provision in arts and humanities, but to allow more freedom for them to flourish on an equal footing with the existing core subjects.

Greater flexibility is important to allow schools more freedom to innovate within the requirements of the National Curriculum, but it will be counter-productive if it is seen as an encouragement to drop or neglect vital areas of children's education.

(p94)

Do you recognise this scenario? It is the same one that we have right now in 2017, but this is directly discussing the then forthcoming National Curriculum of 2000. The hierarchy of subject areas continues to pervade our education system, despite the fact that there is so much research to say that a wide range of skills, talents and creative capacities are needed and wanted by society, today and in the future (Wahl, 2016; CBI, 2015; Batey, 2011).

In 2011 Ken Robinson, who headed the committee on *All Our Futures*, was asked whether he still stood by the report. Whilst he accepts that some things have changed, and some of the bodies that they made recommendations for at the time no longer exist, he believes the report continues to be of enormous relevance. You can watch the interview on YouTube here: **www.youtube.com/watch?v=wqjQ6iMGYKk**

Reflection point

- Why do you think arts subjects are continually sidelined in favour of core subjects?
- Go back to your vision of the child. How will you begin to place your priorities in order, so that children in your class or in your school are offered a chance to be truly creative?

Creativity or culture?

Craft and Hall (2014) suggest that over the past few years, creativity has lost some of its sense of value in its own right and has become subsumed within the cultural debate: that creativity is perhaps most useful as an 'aspect of culture' (p17). The Henley report (2012, commissioned by the Coalition Government at that time) validates this position by investigating and researching 'The Case for Cultural Education' (p12). The arts were acknowledged as being key to unlocking cultural understanding, but the truly creative aspect that had been so well articulated by the *All Our Futures* report, and certainly the 'Little c' element, was rather buried underneath an effort to promote the arts as something rather special, giving what could be interpreted as an elitist viewpoint, even if that was not the intention. The National Society for Education in Art and Design (NSEAD, 2013) acknowledges the relationship between cultural understanding, creativity and practical engagement in the arts to promote and encourage a sense of identity and belonging within a community or culture. They state that this point is integral within the National Curriculum for England:

The current National Curriculum (DfE, 2013) advises that Art and Design should be viewed as a valuable subject, which contributes to the holistic education of the individual child. Additionally, the National Curriculum's (DfE, 2013) statutory guidelines explicate that there are more abstract reasons as to why the teaching of Art and Design is important, such as the notion of 'how Art and Design both reflect and shape our history, and contribute to the culture, creativity and wealth of our nation'.

(NSEAD, 2013, p1)

Two more recent reports would back up the assessment of the situation as described by Craft and Hall: 'The Warwick Report' (2015) led by Jonothan Neelands, and 'Understanding the value of arts and culture' (2016) by Geoffrey Crossick and Patrycja Kaszynska. Both reports place creativity under the banner of 'culture', perhaps as a means to invigorate a tired old term, or maybe in an effort to underpin its importance in a new way that governments would understand better. Crossick and Kaszynska have picked up where Robinson left off, by presenting us with clear guidance that underpins the value of arts in education, and this has come just at the right time now that we are entrenched in an age of austerity – a time when it would be very easy to cut art and design education back even further, due to the high costs of resources, and the little return for schools in the performance league tables. The case is clear, however, for arts education to provide future citizens who will be able to work within the creative industries, now understood to be worth around £84.1bn per annum. See **www.gov.uk/government/news/creative-industries-worth-almost-10-million-an-hour-to-economy**

Crossick and Kaszynska's 2016 report is the result of a thorough research-based investigation, called 'The Cultural Value Project' (2013–15). One of its findings questions the concept that has become ingrained, in which we ask how the arts contribute to other domains of learning – and especially what they can do to boost results in the core areas. An example given in the report relates to another art form, but the principle is the same: it asks whether studying the subject of music can improve upon mathematical learning and acknowledges that it rarely, if ever, occurs to us to ask the opposite: does mathematical knowledge improve music learning? It is a fresh and interesting way to look at the arts in education, as well as the contributions they offer as very important ends in themselves. This raises questions about the hierarchy of disciplines and learning outcomes. A turning of priorities could lead us to look again at the hierarchy in which we place subjects, and bring the debate to the fore. In relation to this, it might be apposite to consider the many benefits that arts education does bring to every other subject. The report highlights key skills and habits of mind, or dispositions for learning (Gardner, 2006; Katz, 1993), that the arts instil so naturally within those engaged in artistic practice: the 'soft skills' that we so often hear are desperately needed by the workforce now, and will be in the future. As Crossick and Kaszynska explain:

Extensive systematic research indicates that there are more significant gains in cognitive and behavioural areas than in formal attainment – what might be seen as building the crucial platform for all learning and development, through positive effects on the processes involved in learning, remembering and problem-solving, and the formation of communication skills and social competency skills.

(2016, p118)

Reflective exercise

Read Chapter 8, 'Arts in education' (pp113–118) of the report 'Understanding the value of arts and culture', available at:

www.ahrc.ac.uk/research/fundedthemesandprogrammes/culturalvalueproject

---

Reflection point

- How does this resonate with your own experiences of engagement with arts activity as a child or a young adult?
- What do you think you gained from having time and space to work through and try out your ideas in creative and expressive ways?
- Were you ever dissuaded from following an arts education because you 'wouldn't get a job doing that'? I know I was.

Practical activity

Fostering creative behaviours in the art classroom

Check your responses to these practical do's and don'ts for creative activity in art and design teaching. Look at the lists in Table 2.2 and score yourself on a scale of 1–5 for fostering creative behaviours in the art classroom (1 = strongly agree).

Table 2.2 *Fostering creative behaviours in the art classroom*

Do you allow for these good things to happen?		Are you guilty of these bad things? Do you ...	
❑ Playfulness		❑ Introduce a competitive element – celebrate only the 'best work'	
❑ Curiosity		❑ Allow for fear of being judged	
❑ Sensitivity		❑ Apply pressure for work to look a certain way	
❑ Self-awareness			
❑ Independence		❑ Feel stress – because of not enough time or space	
❑ Risk taking		❑ Give negative reinforcements	
❑ Tolerance for ambiguity		❑ Impose restrictive guidelines	
❑ Problem-finding		❑ Operate an over-controlled atmosphere	
❑ Looking at problems in different ways		❑ Show your fear of mess	
❑ Making links between unusual concepts and circumstances		❑ Show anxiety	
❑ Calmness and a relaxed atmosphere		❑ Allow children to copy other artists' work	

Adapted from: Bartel, M (2001) available at: **www.goshen.edu/art/ed/creativitykillers.html**

┌───┐

━━━ Practical activity ━━━

What does 'creative' look like?

- Collect a range of drawing materials together. What do you think a creative person looks like? Draw an image of what you imagine that to be.

- Do you think you are a creative person?

- Try to take a broad view of this question: How do you express your creativity?

└───┘

Creativity and control

In a constructivist frame, learning and creativity are close, if not identical.

(Craft, 2005, p61)

If, as Craft states in the quote above, creativity is at the heart of all teaching and learning, it is essential for us to understand the theoretical perspectives on fostering this. We have already established that art and design is often seen as synonymous with creativity, so it is not difficult to utilise this so that the children you teach will feel enabled and empowered to express their imaginative ideas visually, in a safe environment where they feel their efforts are valued. They should feel as though they can 'have a go' without recourse, that they can learn by making mistakes and without fear of failure. It is important here to look inside yourself, and acknowledge your own feelings towards teaching art and design. I hope you are excited and enthused to teach this wonderful subject, but it is *very* common for trainee or student teachers to feel anxious about teaching art and design, and research shows that this has been the case for many years (Green et al., 1998; Pavlou, 2004). Reasons for this are convoluted and multitudinous and would include, as we have already discussed, the performative culture and the focus on core subjects, which is the same in many westernised countries all over the world right now, with profound effects for arts education (Irwin, 2016). To make matters even more challenging, since the implementation of the English Baccalaureate (EBacc) in English schools in 2014 (DfE, 2014), where art and design as a subject has not been included, it is less likely for pupils to choose to study this at GSCE or A level (NSEAD, 2016). This is because young people are forced to concentrate on a set of core and humanities subject areas, so that they pass the EBacc. The chain reaction of this is that those who continue onwards to become a teacher in primary education (for instance, after A level as an undergraduate, or in postgraduate routes) are not confident in the value of the subject, nor in the skills and processes that they need to be able to teach it.

Even if we take these external pressures out of the equation we are still faced with difficulties that place barriers in front of teaching art and design to a good or high standard. For example, you might think that you cannot draw, and therefore cannot 'do' art, which implies that you have the perception that you are not going to be able to teach it very well either. Again, this is a very common reaction when I ask students how they feel about teaching art and design. If this is your perception, I hope you will take comfort that you are not alone in your feelings. It is a challenge for young people who are brought up in an environment where failure is the worst thing that can happen, to have a go at something they do not think they are any good at. Ironically, in this subject some of the best creative work will happen as a result of a 'mistake' (or 'happy accident', as we like to call it).

For you to facilitate an atmosphere for children in your class where mistakes and failures are supported, even celebrated, you must let go of *control* to some extent, however hard that seems right now. Removing your own emotional barriers will allow true creativity to manifest within your teaching and the children's learning. The possibility of giving children degrees of ownership is key to this, so that you develop a sense of trust and freedom, and, although this can sometimes be easier said than done, it is essential to examine your personal attitudes towards the subject.

Art and design is sometimes rather narrowly viewed in relation to its ability to develop only practical skills, and as the children in Watts's research (see Chapter 1) suggested, is perceived to be just 'a bit of fun'. Even our case study of Thomas shows that he has already learnt a distinct prejudice about the value of art, and states that what he had done did not seem like work at all – implying that it was not of value. To re-establish the value of learning in art and design, let us go back to Craft's suggestion that creativity and learning are one and the same, and look at what OFSTED says about this. The 2010 OFSTED report, 'Learning: creative approaches that raise standards', found that:

> Teachers were seen to promote creative learning most purposefully and effectively when encouraging pupils to question and challenge, make connections and see relationships, speculate, keep options open while pursuing a line of enquiry, and reflect critically on ideas, actions and results.

> (p5)

We see here that the same principles of good practice in teaching generically apply once again in art and design. Bearing this in mind, it further demonstrates that art and design is every inch an intellectual activity, as it is a practical one. Challenges can occur, however, when tight or predetermined lesson plans can seemingly prevent you from 'keeping options open'. How can you allow for flexibility and open-endedness when you have a very good lesson plan, that you have worked extremely hard to produce, and now want to see through to completion? Do you notice that the emphasis in this question is upon you, rather than the children? Can you put the children at the centre of that planning and build in space and time for experimentation and 'happy accidents'? What would happen if you allowed a more flexible approach to that planning? What would that look like, and how would you feel about releasing some control? We shall look at planning in more detail in a later chapter, but it will be useful for you to now consider your current method of planning for art and design.

Creative environments

Setting up your classroom to be conducive to fostering children's creativity will go a long way in helping you to feel comfortable allowing children to freely investigate and explore through materials and media, without causing you stress and anxiety. A 'workshop', or 'studio', approach can help you think about the learning environment in a new way (Claxton et al., 2012). If we remember Malaguzzi's principle that the environment is the third teacher, we can design the classroom to include physical, social and emotional aspects that are essential for good learning (which is also creative learning), and these aspects are certainly within your own control.

- **Emotional.** Halpin (2003) states that pupils should be able to feel confident enough to take risks and learn from failure instead of being branded by it. They should react positively to self-help questions like, 'Am I safe here?, Do I belong?, Can I count on others to support me?' (p111). Grainger and Barnes (2006) suggest that we need to provide an environment for children to flourish and grow which *also depends upon a climate of trust, respect and support, an environment in which individual agency and self-determination are fostered, and ideas and interests are valued, discussed and celebrated* (p3).

- **Social.** The classroom arrangement can foster cognitive development by providing opportunities for children to classify and find relationships (Dodge, 2004). Where they are taught in a context that is social and enabling they are likely to be motivated and absorbed in learning. Albert Bandura's social learning theory (1977) specifies that learning occurs in the individual by incorporating behaviour that has been observed in others. It is linked to Vygotsky's social development (1978), and Lave and Wenger's situated learning (1990) theories, which also emphasise the importance of social learning.

- **Physical.** The environment should support children to be active participants in their learning. They should be able to make independent choices and investigations, which will require a well thought through physical space, with materials and resources that can be easily accessed. Children can and should be encouraged to be respectful of the physical environment and learn that they share the responsibility for maintaining a calm and attractive atmosphere.

These three aspects of the environment are symbiotic in nature, as one is not good enough without the others: Burnard et al. (2008) agree that all children are capable of creative achievement, provided the conditions are right, and they are taught the relevant knowledge and skills. This can be achieved by developing an environment that resembles a workshop approach when teaching art and design in your classroom.

Reflective exercise

Crack open creativity in your classroom, by providing a creative climate.

- Have a good look at your classroom from the point of view of facilitating teaching and learning in art and design.
- Use the checklist in Table 2.3 to see whether you are optimising the potential for artistic creativity to flourish in the space you have.
- Use an online design program, such as **www.teacher.scholastic.com/tools/class_setup**. Play around with ideas for manageable changes to your classroom that will facilitate practical activity and give children the social, emotional and physical environment that they need for art and design activities. Remember that you need to be able to foster an atmosphere that is supportive of children's creative and imaginative visual expressions.

Use the following checklist to create a studio approach within your classroom which will provide a balance to cater for children's emotional, social and physical needs.

Table 2.3 Creative environment checklist

Key point	Aspect	Rationale	✓	Your to-do list
Are the desks/ tables organised for collaborative and group work?	Social	Essential for dialogue between peers, developing communication skills, as well as learning to share, negotiate and appreciate each other's unique contributions. Moving tables around to create new arrangements and spaces for different activities can help you mix the children into new working groups. This can also be a strategy for ensuring good behaviour during art and design activities.		
Are display boards reflective of children's current work in terms of topic or theme?	Emotional/ Social	Create a supportive atmosphere which values children's efforts by displaying their work. All children should have something on display at some point each term. Displays should be updated regularly so that they reflect current learning.		
Do you have too many published posters, slogans and texts on the walls? How can you determine whether children are engaging with these displays?	Physical/ Emotional	Avoid having too much environmental print, especially if these are made up of commercially produced charts, word banks and information posters that the children have no emotional connection with. Some children, and others with certain learning difficulties, will be overwhelmed by too much information. Some might simply be put off by having to work hard just to find the information they need.		
Is information placed at a good height for children?	Physical/ Emotional	Think about keeping key information or resource material in a low position on the walls.		
Are some display boards left clear to create a sense of space?	Emotional	This will help to provide a studio feel to your classroom.		
Are all surfaces, such as windowsills, bookcase tops, work surfaces, your desk, etc. clutter-free?	Physical/ Social	Keeping a physically clutter-free environment is essential for providing good space for fresh ideas, and for new work to emerge. A workshop approach means that the space belongs to the class community, rather than becoming a dumping ground for teaching resources and piles of books for marking.		

Are art materials well organised, readily available and easily accessible to children? Can you create an area where art materials are kept so that children can both help themselves and replace in a tidy fashion at the end of the activity?	Social/ Physical/ Emotional	Permitting children to access their own materials from a well organised, accessible place will cut down the time you spend setting up for art and design activities. Teach children to respect and care for art materials so that they learn to clean and tidy them away after use. This will help you to stay calm and in control of the organisation.		
Is there enough natural light, or do you rely on fluorescent lighting?	Physical/ Emotional	Natural light is ideal, but ambient lighting can also be achieved by bringing in spotlights or lamps. This relaxes the mood and creates a calm atmosphere in the classroom. You can use spotlights to focus on objects and artefacts for drawing, or for studying tone and colour. Using lighting in this way can be a good strategy for making art special, and different from other subjects. A calm environment keeps children's excitement for practical work under control.		

Reflective exercise

Watch this inspiring video from Australia, which shows how one primary school has developed the idea of using the school environment as the 'Third Teacher':

http://bit.ly/1S7nG3d

Professional development

During a staff meeting, use the information and activities in this chapter to open a debate around creativity and creative approaches, both within the subject area of art and design and, more broadly, through other subjects in your school.

Show staff the YouTube video of Ken Robinson's seminal TED Talk, 'Do schools kill creativity?' Follow this up with a discussion on how to develop creativity and imagination in your school curriculum.

www.ted.com/talks/ken_robinson_says_schools_kill_creativity?language=en

(Continued)

(Continued)

Build in discussion where colleagues can openly share their feelings about teaching art and design without fear of being judged. Introduce them to some of the ideas for making their classrooms 'workshop ready' by using the activity tables in this chapter. Collectively formulate a plan to ensure that every child has opportunities to explore and express their imagination and creativity every day.

Arty ideas could include the following.

- Devising five-minute creative starter activities at the beginning of morning or afternoon sessions.
- Allow children to access their own personal sketchbooks during quiet periods, when they have completed set tasks, between lessons, during break time and after school.
- Create an area of free choice materials in your classroom for children to access, explore, invent and make. Change the resources available at frequent intervals.
- Develop a 'sparkle-box' of ideas for children to lucky-dip into, filled with ideas to spark their imaginations.
- Value children's ideas and efforts by using a class display board to showcase the work they have done independently, at home or outside of teaching hours.

Chapter summary

In this chapter, we have developed the notion of our fundamental obligation to ensure that children are free and confident to express themselves through visual means. We have looked at both historical and recent research reports that underpin the rationale for teaching creatively, and for nurturing creativity in the children we teach, through valuing the role that imagination plays in our lives. We have started to consider our own attitudes towards teaching the subject of art and design, and have examined some of the barriers that can prevent us from feeling confident to teach this subject well. To round off, we have considered the learning environment within Malaguzzi's paradigm of the Third Teacher, and I hope you have started to think about how you can change the space in your classroom, which will begin your journey towards a studio approach when teaching art and design with your class.

Reflection point

- What have you understood about creative processes and the relevance of this for education, and the futures of the children we teach?
- Do you provide opportunities for children to communicate things that are important to them and make them unique individuals, and to express these visually?
- How much do you believe in the power of imagination? Can you think of ways to develop and value children's imaginative responses during your everyday teaching?
- Do you provide a safe space for children to share their ideas and thoughts, either visually or through dialogue? Can you ensure that your classroom is emotionally, socially and physically supportive for them to be an independent community of learners when you are teaching art and design?

Further reading

Cameron, J (1995) *The Artist's Way: A Course in Discovering and Recovering Your Creative Self.* London: Souvenir Press.

Davies, D et al. (2013) Creative learning environments in education: a systematic literature review. Centre for Research in Early Scientific Learning, *Thinking Skills and Creativity*, 8: 80–91. Available at: **www.sciencedirect.com/science/article/pii/S187118711200051X**

Dissanayake, E (1988) *What is Art For?* Seattle: University of Washington Press.

Fleming, M (2008) *Arts in Education and Creativity: A Review of the Literature.* London: Arts Council England.

Wilson, A (ed) (2015) *Creativity in Primary Education.* London: Sage/Learning Matters.

Find out about brain-based learning at: **www.edutopia.org/article/brain-based-learning-resources**

3
Curriculum and concepts

It is better to have enough ideas for some of them to be wrong, than to be always right by having no ideas at all.

(Edward de Bono, 1990, p88)

Chapter objectives

This chapter will help you to:

- Understand key skills and concepts that are required in art and design teaching and learning in relation to UK National Curriculum models.
- Learn about the formal elements of visual language and how to put these into practice in the classroom.
- Develop your own philosophy for outcomes in art and design that value the idea of 'process not product'. You will learn how to embrace the unexpected, and celebrate originality and diversity of outcome.

The following standards apply within this chapter.

3. Demonstrate good subject and curriculum knowledge.
4. Plan and teach well structured lessons.

Introduction

From what you have read so far, I hope you are becoming more intrigued as to the many ways in which teaching art and design can benefit both you and the children in your class. You should understand by now that many of the concepts lying behind good teaching in art and design are exactly the same principles that exist for teaching any subject. You might also have discovered how art can enliven your classroom practice by introducing pedagogies that unite the physical, intellectual, social and emotional aspects of the developing child. This means that you are teaching holistically, for the 'whole child', and not just from the neck upwards.

In this chapter we shall focus upon the practical skills and knowledge that you need, to teach the subject to a high standard. We shall continue to build upon the theoretical bedrock, so that you will feel confident and secure as a class teacher in art and design, and feel able to teach the subject to the best of your ability. We shall see how this can be managed in relation to planning for art and design, and look at how it is possible to 'keep options open' (OFSTED, 2012) to enable children to be imaginative, expressive and creative in your lessons.

═══ Theory focus ═══

Cambridge Primary Review (2010)

The Cambridge Primary Review (2010), led by Professor Robin Alexander, is a significant document for anyone planning to teach primary aged children. It is a comprehensive piece of research that is important because it does not solely focus on the formal school curriculum, but embraces many wider aspects of contemporary life that might affect a child's potential to learn. These aspects, therefore, should intrinsically impact upon features of any potential primary curriculum. The research took place over a six-year period, between 2004 and 2010, and was the culmination of 40 years of research into primary education. The data was collected from over 4,000 published sources, and the report also includes extensive evidence from written submissions, face-to-face interviews and searches of official and historical data (Alexander, 2010). The Review investigated what primary aged children's lives are really like, the impact of imposed measurements and accountability on schools and children's attitudes to learning, and the outcomes and suitability of successive governments' educational policies over the past 40 years. It explored values that would be necessary to underpin a curriculum that would enable children to function as socially active participants in the future.

In relation to the subject of art and design, there are many key points that make the Cambridge Primary Review a very attractive document, as the principles, values and creative approaches that we have already discussed in previous chapters are validated by this research. One of the recommendations for the organisation of the curriculum is that it should be mapped across eight domains of knowledge, skill, enquiry and disposition, and these are seen to be of equal status. The first of these is *Arts and Creativity*, as the Review states that:

> *The renaissance of this domain, which takes in all the arts, creativity and imagination, is long overdue. A vigorous campaign should be established to advance public understanding of the arts in education, human development, culture and national life. There should also be a much more rigorous approach to arts teaching in schools. However, creativity is not confined to the arts. Creativity and imaginative activity must inform teaching and learning across the curriculum.*

> (Alexander, 2009, p44)

━━ Reflection point ━━

Use this link to read a synopsis of the Cambridge Primary Review:

http://esmeefairbairn.org.uk/uploads/documents/Publications/CPR-booklet_low-res.pdf

The 12 aims that the Cambridge Primary Review recommends should underpin a primary curriculum are:

- Well-being
- Engagement
- Empowerment
- Autonomy
- Encouraging respect and reciprocity
- Promoting interdependence and sustainability
- Empowering local, national and global citizenship
- Celebrating culture and community
- Exploring, knowing, understanding and making sense
- Fostering skill
- Exciting the imagination
- Enacting dialogue

Have you noticed that personal, cultural, social and emotional aspects are embedded throughout these 12 aims?

Consider your understanding of how the arts influence learning in all these areas, and relate this to the aims.

Understanding the curriculum for art and design

Access to art and design education is a statutory right for children in the UK, as stated in the National Curriculum guidance framework (DfE, 2013). The programmes of study for art and design in the National Curriculum for England is a slimmed down version of practical guidance. In fact, at only two pages long, it is a very basic document in terms of requirements for the subject. It could be argued that its predecessor, the National Curriculum (2000), was far too prescriptive in content and resulted in many schools, up and down the country, trotting out the same old interpretations-on-a-theme year after year. This became stale and uninspiring for teachers, let alone the children, who knew exactly what was coming up next because they had seen the same projects done many times before in their schools. Ironically, the units of work in this version of the National Curriculum for England (which are still used in some places) were never statutory, but they were often interpreted as such in some primary schools, where they were relied upon for planning in art and design. We are now in a position, however, where not all primary schools are under compulsion to use the National Curriculum (2013); for example, free schools and academy affiliates, as well as independent schools, do not have to comply. It is therefore important for us to look at the National Curriculum with a slightly different eye, and not to think about what those minimal requirements tell us to do, but to understand more fully exactly what good practice means in the context of this subject. In some cases, it should be said, minimal guidance is freeing for teachers who have a good grasp of what to teach and how to teach it, but equally it is rather unhelpful for anyone coming into teaching without a good understanding of our subject, and it can be a challenge to know exactly where, and with what, to start.

Before we take an in-depth look at the 2013 requirements for England, we could remind ourselves of the principles and values that we have already established as fundamental to good practice. We can also look at other models of curriculum guidance for art and design that exist in the UK, as there are certainly good examples that we can go to for information and ideas for art and design within alternative versions of the National Curriculum. The Scottish Curriculum for Excellence (2010), the National Curriculum for Wales (2008) as well as the Northern Ireland Curriculum (2007) can all be very helpful when looking for advice and inspiration. The message is that good or excellent practice is always the same, whichever way it is dressed up.

Reflective exercise

Take a look at these examples of curriculum guidance for art and design from different UK countries, and compare them for differences and similarities:

Scotland

https://www.education.gov.scot/Documents/expressive-arts-eo.pdf

Northern Ireland

www.nicurriculum.org.uk/curriculum_microsite/the_arts/art/

Wales

http://learning.gov.wales/resources/browse-all/creative-development/?lang=en

http://learning.gov.wales/resources/browse-all/art-and-design-in-the-national-curriculum-for-wales/?lang=en

England

www.gov.uk/government/publications/national-curriculum-in-england-art-and-design-programmes-of-study

Reflection point

- What do you notice about the visual impact of these curriculums? What messages does the mode of delivery of these documents send out to readers?
- Which of them are you more likely to be drawn to and use, as a visual learner yourself? Compare the Northern Ireland version to the one presented by DfE England. Which one do you favour, or find more accessible? Why?
- Have you noticed any major discrepancies between the different models of curriculum guidance for art and design?
- What do they all have in common?

Analysis

Whilst each of these guidelines has its own distinct characteristics, the key skills and concepts are fundamentally the same, although much less specific in the DfE (2013) version. The questions in the Reflection point should help you to think about how important the impact of the visual presentation of these documents is upon you as a reader, as subliminal messages are given in this way: you are using *visual literacy* skills to do this (read more about visual literacy in Chapter 6).

The Welsh curriculum differs from other UK curriculum models in terms of organisation, in that the Foundation Stage is inclusive of children aged three to seven years. This is consistent with many other European countries with child-centred educational systems, such as Finland, where a play-based education for young children is extended beyond the age of five. The Welsh curriculum was revised in 2015, and is designed to encourage children to be creative, imaginative, and to make learning more enjoyable and more effective (Welsh Government, 2016). At the time of writing, the whole curriculum is under reform and the intention is to extend the Foundation Stage pedagogy across older age ranges. This is congruent with the values and principles introduced in Chapter 1, where we looked at how the philosophy of the Reggio schools, essentially an Early Years pedagogy, can underpin good practice in art and design right through the primary years.

The Scottish Curriculum for Excellence (2010) is a very interesting model for those of us who do need a more explicit rationale and more guidance on key skills and concepts in art and design teaching. The Curriculum for Excellence was introduced after an extensive consultation and with the intention of creating a flexible curriculum fit for the twenty-first century. Fundamental principles underpin children's work in all subjects and across all age bands, from three through to 18 years of age, which resonate well with the scrapped Rose Review (2009) and the Cambridge Primary Review (2010), both of which were cast aside by politicians very soon after publication. The four capacities that pervade the entire Scottish Curriculum for Excellence are explained here, with a specific focus on the expressive arts:

1. ***Successful learners***, *who can express themselves, think innovatively, meet challenges positively and find imaginative solutions to problems and who have developed knowledge and skills related to the different arts and broader skills such as the use of technologies.*

2. ***Confident individuals***, *who have developed self-awareness, self-discipline, determination, commitment and confidence through drawing on their own ideas, experiences and feelings, and through successful participation.*

3. ***Responsible citizens,*** *who can explore ethical questions, respond to personal and social issues, and develop stances and views, who have deepened their insight and experiences of cultural identities and who have come to recognise the importance of the arts to the culture and identities of Scotland and other societies.*

4. ***Effective contributors,*** *who can develop and express their creativity, work cooperatively and communicate with others, and in so doing, show initiative, dependability, leadership and enterprise.*

(SNC Expressive arts: principles and practice, 2010, p1)

Reflective exercise

Read the following purpose of study for the 2013 National Curriculum for England. Can you match aspects of this statement to the four capacities that underpin the Scottish National Curriculum, above?

Art, craft and design embody some of the highest forms of human creativity. A high-quality art and design education should engage, inspire and challenge pupils, equipping them with the knowledge and skills to experiment, invent and create their own works of art, craft and design. As pupils progress, they should be able to think critically and develop a more rigorous understanding of art and design. They should also know how art and design both reflect and shape our history, and contribute to the culture, creativity and wealth of our nation.

The 2013 National Curriculum for England

Having looked at these curriculum models, you might begin to develop an understanding of exactly what learning should occur within the art and design curriculum. We can now look more closely at the National Curriculum for England (2013) and learn how to interpret this in a useful way.

The curriculum aims, which stretch across Key Stage 1 and Key Stage 2, state that the intention of this guidance is to ensure that all pupils:

- *Produce creative work, exploring their ideas and recording their experiences.*

What does this mean?

This means that children should be encouraged to visually record and use their own observations and experiences to create original work, which springs from their own ideas. They should be encouraged to use enquiry-based learning through imagination, exploration and experimentation, to develop their ideas into individual and original visual responses.

- *Become proficient in drawing, painting, sculpture and other art, craft and design techniques.*

What does this mean?

This means that children should consistently be given opportunities to experiment with a wide range of materials and media, so that they develop confidence in applying these in a variety of contexts, and make decisions by understanding which material would be best for different purposes. They should develop the ability to observe the world around them in detail, and to express this visually. They should develop both gross and fine motor skills and hand–eye co-ordination to produce personally satisfying outcomes.

- *Evaluate and analyse creative works using the language of art, craft and design.*

What does this mean?

This means that children should be articulate and confident to review and evaluate their own work and the work of their peers. They should become resilient when receiving feedback, and be able to make decisions about their work in the light of review. They should be taught subject-specific vocabulary, and the unique language that applies to visual literacy and expression.

- *Know about great artists, craft makers and designers, and understand the historical and cultural development of their art forms.*

What does this mean?

This should be seen in the widest context, and means that children should be introduced to a range of artists, craftspeople and designers from different cultural and historical positions, including the present day. A range of artists' work should be chosen to ensure it is relevant to any topic or project work that is being undertaken, so that children learn to situate their own artwork within an extensive artistic tradition.

Reflective exercise

The National Society for Education in Art and Design has produced a complementary and detailed analysis of the National Curriculum guidance for art and design in England, including a breakdown of every aspect of the requirements (NSEAD, 2014).

Have a look at the guidance for subject content in both Key Stage 1 and Key Stage 2.

www.nsead.org/curriculum-resources/england.aspx

This analysis of basic requirements will give you a good understanding of key skills and concepts that you can use to develop more detailed planning for art and design. We shall look at this in more depth in Chapter 5.

Key learning in art and design

The building blocks that structure every single work of art, piece of design or craft artefact are known as the 'Seven Elements of Art'. Understanding each of these is essential subject knowledge for you, so it is worth spending some time getting to know them. These elements are so fundamental to the creation of artwork that no art, craft or design would exist if it was not for these visual ingredients. You do need to be aware that, whilst this is important knowledge for functional purposes, these elements do not act alone, and we need to take account of other key processes and decisions that artists make or use in creating unique artwork (for example, elements such as subject matter, social comment, symbolism and originality). It is, however, very useful for you to understand how to teach children to recognise the seven elements in their own work and when observing the work of others. The elements can be taught separately or given a specific focus for a lesson or project, but in practice you will soon discover that many of them overlap, or are present in varying degrees, whenever artists (and by that I include the children) are creating artwork of their own.

Practice

The elements are explained for you here, followed by activities that you can try out alone or during CPD (continuing professional development) training sessions. Alternatively, they can be adapted to use as lessons with the children in your class.

1. **Line.** A line is a mark or stroke, long in proportion to its breadth; an elongated dot is a line! Almost everything in our world can be interpreted in terms of Line: it is all around us. The artist, Paul Klee, once said that drawing was like taking a line for a walk.

Figure 3.1 Look for lines in the built environment.

Look: Look around your environment. Make a list of everywhere you see lines, for example, venetian blinds, radiator grills, furniture, stacked books, etc.

Draw: Take some drawing materials and paper and see how many ways you can draw lines. Ideas might include straight, vertical, horizontal, diagonal, wiggly, curved, sweeping, wavy, curled, thick, thin, swirled, jagged, dotted, dashed, etc.

Make: Tear up your piece of paper and arrange the pieces into a line on the table or floor. Move the pieces around to recreate some of the lines that you discovered by drawing.

2. **Shape.** A shape is a two-dimensional, flat space, which can only have height and width, enclosed by a line. Shapes can be either geometric, for example, circle, square, etc., or organic and irregular like the shapes we observe in nature.

Look: Look at the work of Henri Matisse, and particularly the 'cut outs' that he made in his later years: **www.henri-matisse.net/cut_outs.html**

Draw: Take some drawing materials and some coloured cellophane. Draw a variety of geometric and irregular shapes of different sizes onto the cellophane and cut these out.

Make: Place the cellophane shapes onto a piece of white paper, or a light-box, and play around with the shapes, overlapping some, or arranging them symmetrically or asymmetrically, until you are happy with your arrangement. Have you created new shapes or tones where these have overlapped? What aesthetic decisions did you make? How did you know when you had finally achieved a satisfactory outcome?

3. **Space.** Space deals with the area around or inside shapes. 'Positive space' is the area occupied by an object and 'negative space' is the area around an object. This element is used to give the illusion of depth in a two-dimensional image, such as making an object look as though it is either near or far away. Specific vocabulary that relates to this is 'foreground', 'middleground' and 'background'. Space can be explored in three-dimensional work, as well as in two-dimensional.

Look: Place one hand near your face and the other at arm's length. Compare the sizes of your two hands whilst in this position: your near hand appears larger, although you know in reality they are the same size.

Explore: Look at the work of Swiss contemporary artist, Sabine Jeanne Bieli: **www.sabinejbieli. com**/. Bieli uses the medium of thread to explore perceptions of space. How could you develop children's spatial awareness using similar materials?

Make: Download the SketchUp program, which is free, from **www.sketchup.com** and explore drawing and designing in virtual 3D. You will find that you are using a variety of maths skills at the same time.

4. **Tonal value.** Tonal value refers to the degree of lightness or darkness, or shade, of an object or colour. Artists use this element to create the illusion of depth in two-dimensional shapes, by shading and adding shadow. 'Tints' make colours lighter by adding white or, in some cases, yellow can help tones seem brighter; 'shades' make colours appear darker, which is achieved by adding black or darker colours, such as purple or blue. 2D shapes can have the illusion of being 3D by the clever use of tone.

Look: Look at an image of the painting *An Experiment on a Bird in the Air Pump* (1768) by Joseph Wright 'of Derby' (National Gallery, London).

www.nationalgallery.org.uk/paintings/joseph-wright-of-derby-an-experiment-on-a-bird-in-the-air-pump

- How has the use of tonal value enabled you to feel a sense of drama in this scene?
- How does the use of light force you to focus on different areas of the work?
- What emotional response do you have to the image, and how far is this due to the use of tone?

Observe: Shine a spotlight onto a plainly coloured (preferably white) object, such as an egg or a paper cup. Notice the variation in hue of white tones and where the shadows fall. A video about teaching tonal value to Key Stage 1 can be found here:

http://archive.teachfind.com/ttv/www.teachers.tv/videos/ks1-ks2-art-messy-art-at-ks1.html

Make: Create a tonal value drawing by collecting some charcoal, chalk and paper. Use the charcoal to lightly sketch the shape of the object that you have been looking at in the observation activity. Draw in the dark areas with the charcoal and use your fingertips to smudge the dark colour towards the lighter areas. Use the chalk to draw in the very light parts. Bring the dark and light areas together by blending the tones; first with the drawing materials and then with your fingertips. Softly apply the charcoal to denote where the shadow falls.

Figure 3.2 Encourage children to explore tone by using charcoal and chalk.

5. **Colour**. Colour is all around us: light is reflected from objects to the back of the eye, where colour is registered in our brains. Colour has three main properties: *hue*, which is the name we give different colours; *intensity*, which relates to the vividness of the colour; and *tonal value*, which relates to the shade or tint of a colour. Colour influences our lives profoundly every day: getting dressed in the morning will involve making colour decisions; it affects mood, emotions and even our appetite, for example, food that has a grey tinge might indicate that it is no longer edible.

Look: Observe the colours in your own environment at different times of the day. How does the light make subtle changes to the colours you can see as the day progresses and turns into night? How does the weather affect the colours around you? Do this exercise on a bright sunny day and contrast it with the same exercise on a dull rainy day. How has this affected your mood?

Claude Monet made several studies that documented the changing light and the effect this has on colour: **www.nga.gov/content/ngaweb/features/slideshows/claude-monet.html**

Explore: Know your *primary* (red, yellow and blue) and *secondary* (green, purple and orange) colours. The 'double primary' combination, consisting of 'cold' colours (lemon yellow, crimson and turquoise) as well as 'hot' colours (cadmium yellow, scarlet and ultramarine), as shown in the middle row of Figure 3.3, will give you the widest range of colours when mixed.

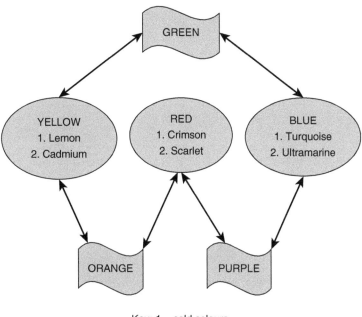

Key: 1 = cold colours
2 = hot colours

Figure 3.3 Use this chart, which shows 'double' primary colours in the centre, to experiment with combinations of these to create secondary colours of green, orange and purple.

Make: Practise mixing primary colours to make secondary and tertiary colours: squirt red, yellow and blue poster paint onto a sheet of thick paper and see how many hues of secondary colours you can achieve. Mix the secondary colours together and see if you can make browns and greys. Add white and black to achieve an even greater range of tints and shades.

6. **Texture.** This element relates to how the surface of something feels, or might feel if you could touch it. For artists, this could mean either real surface quality, such as in a sculpture, or the illusion of surface quality, as represented through, for example, painting or drawing. **Pattern** can also be explored by observing texture.

Look: Find examples of different textured materials, both natural and manmade, such as crumpled paper, fur, wood, etc. and look at the surface patterns. Make a list of vocabulary related to texture, to introduce to your class. View contemporary works of art online at London's Saatchi Gallery (**www.saatchigallery.com**) and see where you can use your vocabulary list to describe surface texture in both 2D and 3D work.

Draw: Collect a range of materials that you can make marks with: chalk, charcoal, shoe polish, candle wax, oil pastel, earth, etc. Experiment with these materials to recreate some of the textures you have observed. For instance, try to make marks that resemble a shiny surface, or give the illusion of feathers or fur.

Figure 3.4 Year 4 work on 'Landscapes'. Use a combination of paint and collage to explore texture.

Make: Do you remember making wax rubbings when you were young? This is a good way to explore surface texture in the local environment. Take a large sheet of paper and some coloured wax crayons or oil pastels. Use the crayons by holding them sideways on, and take imprints of surfaces and textures that you find indoors and outdoors. For example, computer keyboards, wicker baskets, manhole covers; even the bottom of your shoes will have a surface texture that you can capture visually by texture rubbing.

7. **Form.** All objects that have three dimensions are examples of this element. 3D forms will have height, width, depth and volume. The world we live in is full of forms, and artists have designed all the manmade ones somewhere along the line. Everything in the manmade world started life as a sketch on a page. Forms can be viewed from all sides, either by picking them up or by walking around them.

Look: Look for 'geometric' forms. These are usually manmade items and could be cone shaped, cuboid, spherical or cylindrical. Also look for 'organic' forms; these could be irregular shaped objects that are either natural or manmade. Learn how artists express a deep understanding of form, for example by looking at the work of sculptor Henry Moore (**www.henry-moore.org/pg**) or Antony Gormley (**www.antonygormley.com**).

Draw: Collect a range of recycled items of different shapes and sizes and arrange them together on a table. Use a spotlight to highlight one side of the composition and make a study of the dark and light areas only, by using charcoal and chalk on large paper, much like the exercise for tone. After a while you should see the forms emerging in your drawing.

Make: Use a grapefruit sized lump of clay to explore organic shapes. Manipulate the clay in as many ways as you can to change the shape. You might include pulling, pinching, twisting, flattening or rolling the clay. What other ways can you find to move the clay into new forms?

Subject content

Subject content of the art and design curriculum lies in the processes, materials and subject-specific language, as well as knowledge and understanding of the world of art, craft and design, historically and culturally. These four main components are interdependent in practice, as you can see in Figure 3.5.

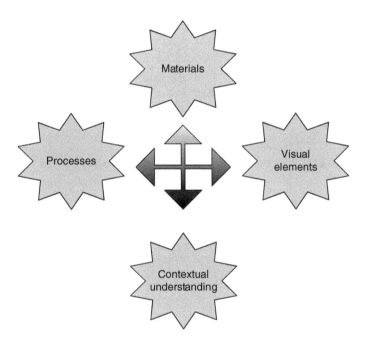

Figure 3.5 The four main components of the art and design curriculum.

When art and design is taught well, all these aspects are incorporated into class planning over the course of a project. Later in this book we shall look at how we can incorporate contextual knowledge and understanding, as well as explore in more detail how the elements of art, materials and vocabulary are individually related to each of the practical processes.

Pedagogical perspective

Subject-specific knowledge includes an understanding of pedagogical approaches. This is important to remember, as sometimes the term 'subject knowledge' can imply that you should know *what*, *where* and *when*, but not necessarily *how* and *why*. Learning in art and design can, and should, be seen as part of a process and can be likened to a journey. Many forms of meaningful art-making will follow a path of their own, no matter what level of art practice we are talking about: from very young children in nursery right through to adults who have been making their own art for many years. This can be a useful way of beginning to think about how to structure an art project over the duration of a few lessons; whether you do this in a span of days or weeks will depend upon the idiosyncrasies of your placement experience or school setting. Look at Figure 3.6, which explains how the learning journey might evolve throughout an art and design project. The case study that follows will demonstrate how this can be easily incorporated into your practice.

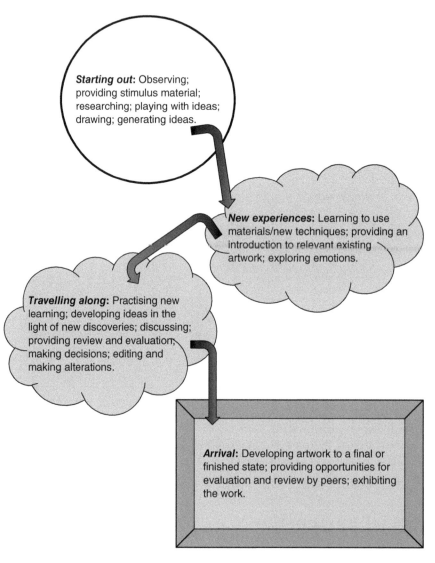

Figure 3.6 The learning journey through an art and design project.

—— Case study ————————————————————————————

Student story

Natasha, a third-year BA primary education student, was on her final teaching placement in a Year 5 class in an inner-city school. The curriculum was tightly focused on raising standards in the core subjects of English and maths because the school was required to make improvements, following a recent OFSTED inspection. The children found collaborative work very difficult and many children were unable to share or negotiate in group tasks. Natasha already had some experience of teaching art and design on previous placements, but these had been as one-off lessons, so she was keen to plan a project during her three-month placement that would facilitate collaboration amongst the children. The class teacher was nervous about using so much time for a foundation subject, but Natasha convinced her that the children would learn many new skills and gain practical and transferable knowledge, whilst allowing them to enjoy a collaborative, shared experience. Natasha suggested that they could link the work to the class topic of 'movement', which they could also utilise to extend learning in other subjects. She planned consecutive learning experiences over half a term that followed the journey of learning within the theme.

Starting out. To begin with they looked at body shapes in images of people participating in active sports; researched art images that represented movement; introduced a variety of new materials and media and used these to explore mark-making that could represent movement.

New experiences. Children were shown Rodin's *Cambodian Dancers* (1906) and were provided with a variety of different sized papers and a range of materials, such as graphite sticks and watercolour paints. Children worked in pairs to draw each other whilst moving to music, using the marks they had observed in Rodin's work.

Travelling along. Natasha introduced Matisse's 'cut outs' and looked at his painting, *Dance* (1909–10). Children cut out organic shapes resembling different parts of the body from sheets of coloured foam, card and paper; they then arranged these onto a long paper roll.

Arrival. Children edited and changed the shapes until there was a general consensus that they were happy with the arrangements. They secured the shapes to the background with glue and used coloured pastels to add detail and pattern. They reviewed the work as a whole group before the final collaborative work was exhibited in the school hall and enjoyed by everyone.

You can use the following websites to look at Rodin's *Cambodian Dancers* and Matisse's *Dance*.

www.musee-rodin.fr/en/collections/drawings

www.hermitagemuseum.org/wps/portal/hermitage/digital-collection/01.+Paintings/28411/?lng=

—— Theory focus ————————————————————————————

A curriculum that exists as a guide for desired outcomes, or one that describes the content of exactly what children should learn, is known as a 'product' model. This theory depends on the belief that there is a finite amount of knowledge, or subject content, that should be transmitted or

(Continued)

(Continued)

delivered to the learner, which can effectively be ticked off once they have gained that knowledge. This theory has its foundations in the American movement towards social efficiency in the early part of the twentieth century, when the establishment of the time accepted the ideas of the educationalist Franklin Bobbitt. Through his writing, and especially his two books, *The Curriculum* (1918) and *How to Make a Curriculum* (1924), he developed a theory for teaching and learning based on his belief that people should not be taught what they would not use. Another educationalist, Ralph W. Tyler (1949) further developed the ideology towards the outcome-based educational philosophy that we are familiar with today in many schools in the UK. In the classroom context, this model of learning is, to a large extent, dependent on behaviourist pedagogy (Skinner, 1972). By looking at the dates of these writings, you can see how pervasive that tradition continues to be in today's primary schools, despite all that we understand from more recent research, such as the Cambridge Primary Review and NACCCE, amongst others. The product model is usually the type of curriculum that many governments prefer, because the outcomes can be easily measured and teachers can be held to account by results.

The 'process' model

In Chapter 2, we talked about the necessity for you to relinquish some control when you are teaching art and design so that children retain ownership of their work. The theoretical position of this places the production of art within a wider arts-based curriculum, where learning *how to learn* is key (Bartel, 2014) and this is the part of the process that we have already looked at earlier in this chapter. It has probably become clear to you that the 'product' model is an unsuitable one for teaching and learning in art and design, where we celebrate diversity of outcome and personal individualism, so we need to find another paradigm for this subject within curriculum theory and practice. This can be found within the 'process' model. I expect that you are already very familiar with many of the theoretical positions that support a process driven curriculum model, as these are often the ones that are taught on ITE courses to promote pedagogy that is holistic and child-centred, such as those embedded in 'social constructivism'. Lev Vygotsky's theory of social constructivism (1978) requires a collaborative method, in which children learn from each other as well as from a more competent 'other' person. This means that a teacher who is involved through praxis, who is both an active participant and able to perform the role of guide, or more experienced 'other', can encourage children to progress in their own learning. Vygotsky stated that: *What the child is able to do in collaboration today he will be able to do independently tomorrow* (1987, p211); in application, this theory is known as the 'zone of proximal development' (ZPD). It is a useful theory for our subject area as it permits teachers to both learn alongside children, and to use questioning skills to push their personal or collective enquiries much further; often way beyond the limits imposed by more product driven paradigms. When we are looking for a theory to underpin our work in art and design, in which all the core values that we hold as our principles for good learning are set into motion, social constructivism ticks all the boxes.

Understanding the work of the British educationalist, Professor Lawrence Stenhouse (1926–82), might be another good theoretical position to examine. Stenhouse believed that education itself is a process of enquiry, as opposed to one that celebrates the achievement of prescribed goals. His theory is inclusive and democratic: that in order to create an equitable and emancipated society, every child or young person, no matter what social, cultural or economic background they originate from, is not only capable of defining their own learning, but of progressing to individual fulfilment through an enquiry-based methodology. In one of his many essays, Stenhouse wrote that: *although educa-tion is inevitably concerned with the transmission of skills and information, its heartland is in giving access to knowledge as a medium and discipline of thinking* (1980, p1). He championed the idea of teachers as researchers, active participants, observers and facilitators. He saw teaching as a vehicle for social justice and his ideals are still relevant in society today, where topics such as this are often in the news. Stenhouse's theories, which acclaim personal independence, thinking skills and understanding, rather than knowledge-gain, are much more attuned to the philosophies that we have already studied in this book, and are therefore more conducive to teaching and learning in art and design.

Reflection point

- Think about classroom practice that you have observed. Where or when have you seen examples of either process or product based pedagogy?
- Where do you situate your own practice within these two models? Which of these two paradigms are you more comfortable with and why?
- How do you feel about using the process model when teaching art and design? Can you use this in other subjects as well?

This reflection will help you to think about your own philosophy for teaching and confirm what sort of teacher you want to be.

Professional development

You can use or adapt activities in this chapter to teach the staff in your school about the 'formal elements' of art. The diagrams and information presented here will also be very helpful to explore teachers' understanding of art and design subject content, and to establish expecta-tions for pedagogical approaches when teaching in this area.

For a staff development session, print off examples of each of the National Curriculums for art and design from across the UK. Alternatively, you could ask staff to bring iPads and look at the curriculums online. Divide the staff into four separate groups (ideally groups should have members from different age phases or key stages, so that teachers are working alongside oth-ers who they might not normally be in contact with: this is to ensure that the conversation facilitates a whole-school cohesion). Give each group one curriculum model from a different part of the UK. Ask them to use sticky notes, or make mind-maps, to draw out what they inter-pret to be subject-specific content or key learning points. They should make a note of anything they are unsure of, or do not fully understand.

Give them around ten minutes for this activity and ask them to feed back their findings to the other groups. Facilitate a discussion to agree a good curriculum model for your own school to develop and use in the future. Explain to them that subject content is only part of the knowl-edge they will need for teaching to a high standard in art and design, and talk to them about

(Continued)

(Continued)

the process model of learning. The following short, interactive practical activity will take them through a journey of learning in art and design.

- Teachers stay within their four groups.
- Give each group an image that signifies a different part of the journey: 1. Starting out; 2. New experiences; 3. Travelling along; 4. Arrival.

Examples might include:

1. Starting out: Vlassis Caniaris, *Image* (1971).

   www.tate.org.uk/art/artworks/caniaris-image-t13269

2. New experiences: Richard Long, *A Line Made by Walking* (1967).

   www.tate.org.uk/art/artworks/long-a-line-made-by-walking-p07149

3. Travelling along: Ian Hamilton Finlay, *Sailing Dinghy* (1996).

   www.tate.org.uk/art/artworks/hamilton-finlay-sailing-dinghy-ar00021

4. Arrival: Mark Wallinger, *Threshold to the Kingdom* (2000).

   www.tate.org.uk/art/artworks/wallinger-threshold-to-the-kingdom-t12811

- Using easily accessible materials (such as paper, drawing materials, tape, scissors, string and even furniture), ask the groups to create a visual representation that signifies their part of the journey, in response to the image they have been given; give them just 15 minutes to do this. Ask them to think about which skills they are using to complete the activity.

Figure 3.7 Teachers developing creative ideas through the theme of 'journey'.

- Plenary: Ask each group in turn, starting at the beginning of the journey and ending with the 'Arrival' group, to explain what they have done and what they have learnt from the session.
- Photocopy Figure 3.6, which explains the learning journey, or scan and send copies to the teachers. Place a copy of this diagram with your art and design planning.

Working quickly will ensure that the groups do not have too much time to worry about the activity and they will feel a sense of urgency, which will force them to make decisions. It will enable the groups to experience a feeling of being creative and flexible, as well as having to negotiate and collaborate through dialogue and enjoyment. Make sure you draw out these points during the plenary.

Chapter summary

We have covered a lot of essential groundwork in this chapter. We have looked in depth at currently available models of the National Curriculum from across the UK, and have compared these in our search for essential subject understanding. We have examined key theoretical positions and considered the most appropriate paradigm for good learning in art and design. You should now have a good understanding that learning in this subject has both formal and informal elements at work. These can be applied by teaching specific subject knowledge, whilst bearing in mind that there are intangible elements, over which you do not have control, as these belong to the individual children who are making their own artwork. In Chapter 4 we shall explore the processes, techniques and materials that are fundamental to learning in art and design.

Further reading

Dweck, C (2008) *Mindset: How You Can Fulfil Your Potential*. New York: Ballantine.

Elliott, J and Norris, N (2011) *The Work of Lawrence Stenhouse: Curriculum, Pedagogy and Educational Research*. London: Routledge.

Hickman, R (2010) *Why We Make Art and Why it is Taught*. Bristol: Intellect.

Sefton Green, J and Sinker, R (2000) *Evaluating Creativity: Making and Learning by Young People*. London: Routledge.

Read more about the work of Lawrence Stenhouse: **www.uea.ac.uk/education/research/care/resources/archive/lawrence-stenhouse**

Find out more about how we learn: **www.funderstanding.com**

4

Processes and practice

Chapter 4 will provide you with subject knowledge relating to the physical processes and technical skills that are required for you to teach art and design with confidence. The format here is slightly different from other chapters; the sections are full of information and practical guidance so that you can dip in and out as you become more confident to try new and different techniques and materials, which you can then demonstrate to the children. You can therefore use this chapter to develop new learning in art and design, as well as extending your existing knowledge of the processes, materials and techniques that are most suitable to use with primary aged children.

Chapter objectives

The chapter is split into the following sub-sections:

- 4.1 Drawing
- 4.2 Painting
- 4.3 Printmaking
- 4.4 Three-dimensional work and the physical world
- 4.5 Craftwork and making
- 4.6 New media and technology

The following standards especially apply within this chapter.

1. Set high expectations which inspire, motivate and challenge pupils.
2. Promote good progress and outcomes by pupils.
3. Demonstrate good subject and curriculum knowledge.
5. Adapt teaching to respond to the strengths and needs of all pupils.

Theoretical context: learning through making and doing

Whilst there are many theories on how people learn, how many times during your training have you heard that you should employ a 'multisensory' approach within your teaching and learning strategies? There is a good theoretical rationale behind this, as well as a common sense one: think about how *you* like to learn. Sometimes it is very appealing to sit passively and listen to an interesting lecture by an inspirational speaker, and you might come away from that feeling excited and ready to put what you have heard into practice. On other occasions, however, you might learn best by participating in a hands-on experience, or even by being 'thrown in the deep end'. It is likely that you will remember the practical one more clearly because of the physicality of that experience, coupled with the emotional reactions that were brought about whilst 'having a go'. With more practice and experience, the knowledge you have gained by 'doing' becomes almost second nature, but it can also be rather hard to define, and harder still to describe *how* you know what you know. Activities such as making an omelette, driving a car or riding a bicycle are examples of this, and it is known as 'procedural knowledge' (Anderson, 1976). Much of what we know and understand so that we function in our everyday lives is due to this kind of knowledge, and it is deeply embedded within our psyche. In addition, we use our understanding of the visual world to make everyday decisions and judgements. For example, the act of getting dressed in the morning will require you to make decisions based on your knowledge of colour, shape, texture and pattern: your friends and colleagues might tell you how stylish you look, but in fact you may feel that you made little effort in putting the outfit together. This requires another form of knowledge that is to do with an intuitive, emotional response to the world, which is known as 'tacit knowledge' (Polanyi, 1967). This is a deep well of personal knowledge that we all hold within us, and it relates to individual experiences and personal insights. Procedural and tacit knowledge are key features of learning in art and design, and are amongst the intangible elements that make it more difficult to understand how we might assess or progress children in this subject area. We shall explore this in more depth in Chapter 5. For now, we might do well to remember that the children you are, or will be, teaching will each have their own bank of tacit knowledge, that you will add to through utilising the multisensory learning opportunities that they will experience in art and design.

Experiential learning

You might already be familiar with the work of David Kolb (1984) who proposed a four-stage cyclical learning process model. This theory involves different practical elements at determined stages of each cycle of learning, as well as points of reflective activity, where the experiences are internalised. This is an interesting theory for the subject of art and design, as when learning is internalised and understood on a deeper level, it can become part of our reservoir of tacit knowledge. Kolb believes that the learner can enter the cycle at any point, and can continue to develop

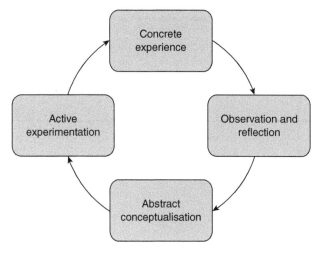

Figure 4.0.1 The experiential learning cycle (Kolb, 1984).

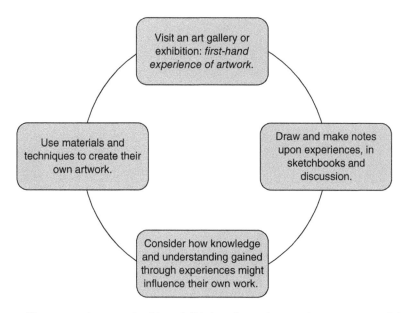

Figure 4.0.2 An example of how Kolb's learning cycle can relate to an art and design activity.

their understanding by going through the cycle any number of times. This is often referred to as 'experiential' learning (McGill and Beaty, 1995) because it is grounded in practical activity and real experiences. Figures 4.0.1 and 4.0.2 show Kolb's learning cycle, followed by an example using a gallery visit, to demonstrate how this works both theoretically and in practice.

—— Reflection point ——

As we have already looked at process paradigms for teaching and learning in art and design, Kolb's theory is one that sits well as a pedagogical basis.

As you read through this chapter, try to link the pedagogical aspects and the theoretical contexts to each of the processes.

The processes

The following sections in this chapter will guide you through the various technical processes associated with learning in art and design.

4.1
Drawing

For the artist drawing is discovery. And that is not just a slick phrase: it is quite literally true. It is the actual act of drawing that forces the artist to look at the object in front of him, to dissect it in his mind's eye and put it together again; or, if he is drawing from memory, that forces him to dredge his own mind, to discover the content of his own store of past observations.

(John Berger, 2005, p3)

Fear of drawing

What are your feelings about the most fundamental process of them all: drawing? For children, drawing or making marks on a surface is not only an extremely pleasurable and satisfying activity, it is quite simply the most natural and accessible form of visual communication and expression available. Our duty, as their teachers, is to ensure that they continue to feel empowered and confident in their efforts to draw as they progress through the primary years.

Many people, teachers included, have a real fear of failure with this process, and believe that their graphic efforts will be judged harshly by anyone who looks at their artwork. Do you feel this way, or do you know someone who does? Emotions that are brought about by anxieties such as these can have a very stifling effect not only upon you, but on the children who you will teach: that is, if you let your fear show. If a teacher is resistant to promoting drawing as an enjoyable, freeing and productive activity, then a negative bias can be transmitted to the children. A discouraging or dismissive attitude towards art and design – drawing in particular – can present serious implications for children who encounter this mindset. It can prevent them from discovering the usefulness that having confidence in drawing brings for success in a wide range of pursuits and future careers. In a worst-case scenario, it could even prevent some children from finding their talent. As a trainee teacher, or a teacher just starting out, this is the last thing you would want to happen, so this is a good point for you to reflect upon your personal feelings towards and experiences in drawing. If you discover that they have a negative slant we can address that right now.

Good drawing

Sometimes anxiety can arise from misconceptions that a 'good' drawing is an exact copy of an object or image, not unlike the picture one might find in a photograph. Of course, a great deal of

Figure 4.1.1 Build confidence by lending a helping hand to draw for a friend!

skill would be a prerequisite to produce such polished work, and as we are dealing with primary aged children, who are still developing physically, emotionally and intellectually, that is an unlikely scenario: therefore, to expect children to work at this level would have no purpose other than to set them up for failure. Observation work and learning pencil drawing techniques are very important, but there are fresh ways of approaching such activities without applying pressure, stress or by introducing a competitive element to be the 'best' at drawing. This is an appropriate time to also consider a very different view of *what drawing is* and *what it is for.* In the world of contemporary art and design, the act of drawing is seen to have a much broader base, and the role of drawing is understood to have a much deeper impact upon how we engage with the world in ways which might surprise you. The following case study exemplifies how drawing is essential in the world of science.

Case study

Fay Penrose trained as a fine artist before beginning a career as an anatomist. She is now lecturer in anatomy at the University of Liverpool Institute of Veterinary Science. Fay is emphatic that her art background has given her many of the skills, aptitudes and understanding that she has needed to develop her career, and she is frustrated by the perception, prevalent in the current education system, that there are stark divisions between sciences and the arts. She explains how she uses drawing with her first-year undergraduates, many of whom arrive on the course with underdeveloped fine motor skills and a narrow understanding of what it means to work in a practical field, such as veterinary medicine. The students are all high achievers, and would usually have been encouraged to study sciences and maths at school; they are therefore surprised to find that drawing is a compulsory module. Fay says: *Anatomy is essentially a visual and tactile science: when you are learning about anatomy you must be very tuned in to what the body looks like – it is all about form, function and spatial relationships. Pathology is about being able to see what is normal and what is not, so new veterinary students have to be trained to look, and to look in great detail.*

She emphasises that surgical operations rely upon the physician's skills in observation and recognising visual references, as well as their tactile and three-dimensional understanding and dexterity. All these can be developed through engaging with drawing and art processes.

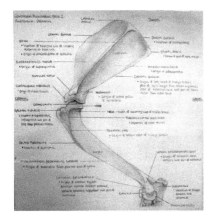 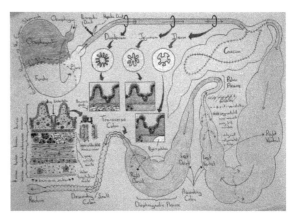

Figures 4.1.2 and 4.1.3 Veterinary students develop observation, fine motor and hand–eye co-ordination skills, as well as their ability to express their understanding of anatomy.

Fay describes how the students develop an insight into how drawing can be a means of both learning and working efficiently in their studies: by giving them an alternative method of communicating, which is much more direct than any writing. They are encouraged to use drawing for revision purposes, so that they learn to visualise. Fay states that the most able students are the ones who embrace this innovative practice, and she acknowledges that schools do not value the role that art and design plays enough to form well-rounded, physically and visually literate people for the future workplace.

Analysis

This case study is just one example of how drawing has a unique and pivotal role within many professions. Sometimes our perceptions of what one or other occupation entails is not quite the truth of the matter. Fay says her students tend to have expectations when they begin the course that they will be studying by traditional academic means, such as memorising facts, much as they did for their A levels. This shows that they have misconceptions of the wider skills and practical knowledge they will need in order to become vets. Having read this case study, how have your perceptions changed in view of the role and place of drawing with primary aged children? Can you think of other professions where the skills associated with drawing are regularly employed?

The power of drawing

If you have read the quote at the beginning of this chapter by the artist and art critic John Berger, you could already be thinking that there might be more to drawing than you had first realised; although as we have discussed, many peers on your training course, or teachers in your school, might still have a fairly narrow view of what constitutes a drawing, or what it is for. Drawing is the most direct and elemental method of creative activity and communication, and has been practised since the beginning of man's existence on our planet: handprints and creatures that were etched and scraped onto cave walls are evidence of this. Archaeologists suggest that there are many theories why prehistoric man might have decorated their caves, but we shall probably never know the real reason why. Theories are plentiful, however, and one of these suggests that cave dwellers did this for the same reason we decorate our own homes today: for aesthetic reasons. There is a possibility that animals were a chosen theme because these were so important to their very survival, and this theory purports that prehistoric man either documented hunting expeditions, or desired simply to record their observations of animals that lived alongside them. Yet another possible reason is that the drawings could have been considered a form of magic to help the hunters: the images would have been revered and respected, and seen as an important part of the hunter-gatherer process, as if by capturing animals through drawing, the hunters believed this gave them power over the creatures and a psychological advantage to prepare them for the terrifying job of feeding their communities. There is further evidence that some caves, such as the famous caves at Chauvet in France, were so remote and far from living areas, they were possibly used for ritualistic purposes. A special journey would have been necessary to visit and view these drawings, therefore the suggestion is that these caves were possibly the very first art galleries (Zorich, 2011). For whatever reason they exist, these images have been handed down to us through the centuries so that we have a glimpse into the lives of our forefathers; there is certainly no more powerful way for them to have communicated so directly with us.

Practical activity

Draw like an animal

Figure 4.1.4 Draw like an animal: tape pieces of charcoal to your fingers, put some music on and draw with your claw!

In the classroom

In our contemporary world, drawing remains a most powerful method to communicate across ages and cultures without the barriers that spoken or written language can present. Table 4.1.1 shows the most commonly available materials that you will find in schools for drawing activities, along with an explanation of how and when to use these. There are also some suggestions for artists' work you can show children when demonstrating the teaching points.

Table 4.1.1 Materials for drawing

Media	Best for...	Concepts and key vocabulary	Skills	Context
Soft drawing pencil: 2B; 6B ('B' stands for 'blackness') Hard drawing pencil: HB	2B – all-purpose pencil For creating initial shapes; outlines; fine detail; sketching. 6B – for depth and contrast; blending; shadow; tone. For light sketching. Technical drawings.	Line Tone Pressure Shade Dark Light Shadow Soft Curve Straight Wavy, etc.	Hand-eye co-ordination Fine motor control Observation Attention to detail Concentration	Adonna Khare www.youtube.com/watch?v=BLdlkgjTOYE Paul Noble www.tate.org.uk/art/artists/paul-noble-2767 Tom Kundig architizer.com/blog/how-architecture-is-born-olson-kundig-architects
Graphite sticks: 6B	Bold, sweeping marks on large scale work. Very soft 'blackness' can achieve depth of tone. Good media for texture rubbings; carbon copying.	Tone Line Shape Space Texture Pattern	Gross and fine motor control Expressive Exploring	Rembrandt www.rembrandtpainting.net/rembrandt_drawings_start.htm
Charcoal: made from slowly charred wood Available in thin and thick sticks	Thick willow charcoal: Exploring tone; sketching; blending; blurring; spreading; smudging; sweeping marks; quickly cover large areas; easy to erase with soft cloth or screwed up paper; achieving depth through building up layers. Thin willow charcoal: Adding detail; delicate marks.	Subtle Gradation Gesture Blend Shade Shadow Tonal values Density	Freeing and expressive Imagination and visualisation Gross and fine motor control Manipulation Working with mistakes Potential to work on large scale/ group work	Many contemporary artists use charcoal: www.saatchiart.com/drawings/charcoal Frank Auerbach www.tate.org.uk/art/artworks/auerbach-sketch-from-titians-bacchus-and-ariadne-t07629 Käthe Kollwitz www.moma.org/artists/3201

(Continued)

Table 4.1.1 (Continued)

Media	Best for...	Concepts and key vocabulary	Skills	Context
Compressed charcoal	Very black, dark lines; add detail; create very black areas to add depth and drama to a drawing. Sharpen the end to create a fine point for drawing detail; good for emphasising a shadow or very dark area; not easily erased.	Black Fine lines Smudge Sharp Darkness	Observation and imagination Quality of line Decisive mark making Problem solving	Albrecht Dürer **www.albrecht-durer.org** Eileen Cooper **www.royalacademy.org.uk/exhibition/ drawings-by-eileen-cooper**
Chalk White chalk	Bring drawing to life by adding highlights; add lighter areas to show a light source; emphasising a specific area of a drawing.	Dusty Reflection Highlight Light and tone	Understanding light sources Responding Observation	Angelica Kauffmann **www.metmuseum.org/blogs/now-at-the-met/2015/neoclassical-drapery-studies**
Coloured chalk pastels	To add colour to a drawing; use light colours instead of pencils or charcoal to sketch shapes; mix colours on the paper; blend with fingertips or soft cloth; use side of the pastels to cover the whole paper to create a background; use tips of the pastels in contrasting colours to draw over background.	Strokes Side strokes Feathery Blocks of colour Mixed colour Cross hatch Layers Background Foreground Hue	Exploring Experimenting Developing an understanding of the importance of colour in our lives.	Many famous painters from the Impressionist period used this medium: Edgar Degas, Mary Cassatt, Berthe Morisot, Auguste Renoir, Paul Gauguin and Edward Munch are just some that you might recognise. Paula Rego **www.tate.org.uk/whats-on/tate-britain/ exhibition/paula-rego/paula-rego-1994-2004-recent-pastel-works**

Media	Description	Vocabulary	Skills	Artists and resources
Oil pastels: made with wax and oil, so will feel a little greasy to the touch	Intense colour; use like paint; blend by adding a little sunflower oil; not so easy to control; create colourful patterns and wash over with watercolour to create a resist effect.	Texture Intensity Bright Contrast Pattern	Controlling medium Discovering Enjoyment	Sonia Boyce www.tate.org.uk/learn/online-resources/from-tarzan-to-rambo/about-sonia-boyce
Drawing ink	Use straight from the bottle with drawing pens, wooden barbeque sticks or Chinese brushes; make little splashes to create texture; dilute it down with water and use with small paintbrushes to create a wash; draw with candle wax and use an ink wash over the top to create a resist effect; usually permanent so use with care.	Line Splash Intense Fluidity Transparency Opaque Lively Wash Resist Subtlety	Experiment and exploration Understanding and respecting materials Hand-eye co-ordination Using mistakes Confidence building	Leonardo da Vinci www.howtodrawjourney.com/leonardo-da-vinci-drawings.html Stephen Wiltshire www.stephenwiltshire.co.uk/gallery.aspx Quentin Blake www.quentinblake.com David Remfry www.davidremfry.com
Pens: ballpoint; felt pen; marker pen; whiteboard marker; graphic pen; metallic marker; gel pen, etc.	Doodling; crisp lines; no rubbing out possible; thick markers can cover larger areas quickly; creating contrasting areas; adding detail; pattern; low-cost; no mess; portable, so good to take on trips and visits;	Doodle Pattern Detail Hatching Cross hatching Scumbling	Freedom and imagination Observation Decision making Making choices Independence Confidence	Alighiero Boetti www.archivioalighieroboetti.it/eng/alighiero-boetti/gallery-works/#/tra-se-e-se Karen Hull www.youtube.com/watch?v=Z7ZEoKFfISE

(Continued)

Table 4.1.1 (Continued)

Media	Best for...	Concepts and key vocabulary	Skills	Context
	add tone by drawing lines very close together (hatch), crossing these with more lines (cross hatch), or drawing round and round with lines overlapping one another until you have achieved a dark area (scumbling).			
Collage materials: various papers; glue; scissors.	Making collages	Colour Tone Texture Shape Image Juxtapose Matching Opposites Edit Compose Layer	Experiment Using tools safely (scissor/craft knife skills) Confidence Decision making	Wangechi Mutu **wangechimutu.com** Kara Walker **www.artsy.net/artist/kara-walker** Kurt Schwitters **www.tate.org.uk/art/artists/kurt-schwitters-1912**

Collage as a process for drawing

Many people who have a fear of drawing will feel much happier using collage to express their ideas visually. Pop into the Foundation Stage classes of your school or placement and you will find that *cutting and sticking* activities are readily available for children to access every single day. In this way, it is as fundamental a process as conventional drawing for recording and working through ideas, as children learn to compose an image by placing, layering, overlapping, juxtaposing and making visual decisions. Collage, as a process, is an important medium for many contemporary artists, designers and craftspeople. Invented by the Cubists (Picasso and Braque) at the beginning of the twentieth century, it broke with the usual tradition of drawing and painting by incorporating found items, such as newspaper, tickets, music manuscripts, etc., into artwork. This set the ball rolling for using found materials to make art in both 2D and 3D (think about installation work, such as Tracey Emin's *My Bed* (1998)). When using collage the same motor skills and thoughtful decision making is required, as with drawing, to express and communicate ideas. This can be used in conjunction with almost every process to create mixed media pieces as final outcomes.

Reflective exercise

Figures 4.1.5 and 4.1.6 Collect some magazines and different types of paper together, tear out images that interest you and then sort other torn or cut out pieces into colour families. Arrange your selected colours and images to create a self-portrait by arranging and sticking the pieces of paper onto a coloured or drawn background.

Look at artists who use collage and see how they have cut up or placed fragments to create surreal images.

Hannah Höch: **www.artsy.net/artist/hannah-hoch**

John Stezaker: **www.saatchigallery.com/artists/john_stezaker.htm**

Another collage artist who is good to look at with children is Joseph Cornell.

Practical activity

Getting dirty: exploring opposites

Potential mess can be a real reason for anxiety in the primary classroom, and even children can sometimes come to school at a young age with an aversion to getting their hands dirty. However, as the teacher in charge it is your job to ensure that children have plenty of sensory experiences that will help them to feel a connection to the real world. It is also up to you to keep the messy elements under a certain amount of control, so that you feel the learning situation is manageable. To get past the fear that making art, including drawing, can create too much mess, try out this activity with a group of your colleagues or with the children in your class.

Materials

- Large (A1 sized) white paper or cheap paper on a roll, such as lining paper (available from hardware shops or decorating retailers)
- Masking tape
- Glue
- Thick sticks of charcoal
- Chalk
- Pencils
- Wax sticks or candles
- Oil pastels: black and white only
- Soft pastels: black and white only
- Containers with earth, flour, sand and salt
- Graphite sticks
- Black drawing ink
- Cocktail sticks or barbeque skewers
- Black paint
- Paintbrushes
- Old toothbrushes
- Water in a large container for cleaning brushes
- Paper towels/rags/sponges
- Washing up bowl with warm, soapy water and dishcloths for cleaning at the end of the activity

Organisation

1. Make sure you offer aprons for this activity.
2. Place the materials on a surface that can be easily accessed by everyone participating in the activity.
3. Arrange tables so that they are ready for group work.
4. Protect the tables with easy-wipe covers.
5. Cover the tables with large sheets of paper: tape sheets together underneath so that there are no gaps.

6. Use masking tape to draw lines across the paper so that you end up with a grid of empty squares.

7. Encourage groups of four or more people or children to work together around one table.

Preparation

Make a list of adjectives/words that are 'opposites'. Examples might include:

spiky/wavy	neat/messy
matt/shiny	blurry/sharp
light/dark	velvety/whiskery
soft/hard	muddy/clear
smooth/rough	reflective/dull
fluffy/coarse	... add your own.

Draw

Use the drawing materials to explore ways to express the qualities of the words on the vocabulary list, by filling each square with a visual interpretation of each one. Try to use the materials in new ways that you haven't tried before, for example by crushing the charcoal and pressing the fragments onto the paper, or by dipping a piece of rag or sponge into black paint and smearing it across the surface. Use your hands and fingers to smudge and blend the materials. Try using the graphite stick to draw a solid, dark shape before rubbing the surface with a cloth or your fingertip to create a shiny appearance. Use barbeque skewers to dip into drawing ink and see what marks you can achieve to describe a 'spiky' mark. Combine materials together and see what happens.

When all the squares are filled, make sure you have clean hands and that the work is dry before carefully peeling the masking tape strips off the paper.

Ensure that everyone is involved in tidying up and that they leave the materials as they were found: tables cleaned, covers and aprons put away and the room restored to its normal layout.

Figure 4.1.7 Teaching students to explore drawing materials whilst working as a group.

━━ Reflection point ━━━━━━━━━━━━━━━━━━━━━━━━━━━━━━━━━

- Place the work onto a display area and look for the variety of marks and tones that have been achieved. See if you can match these to the correct vocabulary from the 'opposites' list.
- This exploratory, sensory work should look well-ordered and aesthetically pleasing because of the regularity of the grid, created by the masking tape boundaries.
- Think for a minute about which other subject areas you have touched upon in this activity.
- How has this activity helped you to think about fresh ways of introducing drawing activities to the children in your class?
- How do you feel about getting your hands dirty? Were you able to keep the mess under some control?
- To extend the learning in this activity you could encourage the application of some or all of these techniques to other drawing or painting activities that you set up in the future.

━━ Further reading ━━━━━━━━━━━━━━━━━━━━━━━━━━━━━━━━━━━

Briggs, P (2015) *Drawing Projects for Children*. London: Black Dog.

Cox, M (1992) *Children's Drawings*. London: Penguin.

Edwards, B (2008) *Drawing on the Right Side of the Brain*. London: HarperCollins.

Kolbe, U (2005) *The Drama of Drawing*. Byron Bay, NSW: Peppinot Press.

You can find resources and information on drawing and about annual Big Draw events at: **thebigdraw. org**

4.2
Painting

Introduction

Along with drawing, painting is probably one of the most widely used art processes in primary schools and is often concerned with elements such as colour and surface quality. For such a commonly used process, it is not always exploited to its full potential as a learning experience, so in this section we shall explore some of the possibilities that will help you to make the most of this highly adaptable medium. First, however, let us consider your own experience of using paint. What do you remember from your own school days, and what do you think you learnt by painting? Perhaps you have observed painting lessons, or seen displays showing children's paintings whilst on placement or in your school: what do you think the context was for making these works? What role do you think painting plays in children's education today? We shall look at some examples from research that demonstrate clearly what kind of learning can take place when children use paint, and begin to build a profile for this medium that will leave you in no doubt of the aims and objectives which you can put into your lesson planning.

Theory focus

John Matthews (2003) famously documented his own son as a small boy, engaged in the act of painting. His research, in which he studied his own and other nursery aged children's approaches to painting and drawing, was captured over a period of time by observing and interacting with them during naturalistic, self-directed tasks, rather than through staged or controlled tests. He described in detail how his two-year-old son, Ben, painted arching shapes with blue paint across paper in an energetic way, seeming to use his whole body whilst engaged in this activity. He then pushed and pulled the brush vigorously from the top to the bottom of the paper, creating a cross shape. The boy changed brushes and colour and, as he brought the loaded brush over the painting, he noticed drips that created contrasting spots onto the blue below. The child stopped in his tracks as the realisation took hold, and began to shake the brush so that more spots and splashes were created. The story of this little boy goes on to describe how he develops the painting into his own narrative and, with another colour change, he makes new shapes, mixes new colours and edits the newly formed areas and edges. Matthews acknowledges that this scenario is one that

(Continued)

(Continued)

any parent or Early Years educator might recognise when observing a young child using paint, but further analysis of the incident is helpful for us regarding understanding painting as a process, as a medium for learning about the self, and for teaching about materials and cause and effect. Matthews questions the opinion that the child's action could be *mindless scribbling, impulsive activity,* or *just the clumsy beginnings of a long apprenticeship towards 'correct' drawing and painting* (2003, p11) and that his physical actions are irrelevant to the process of painting. He argues that in this act of painting Ben was constructing knowledge that was closely linked to both his emotions and his previous experiences in everyday operations, such as talking, eating, drinking and bathing. Therefore, not only had the child understood the process in relation to his own experiences, he had used this to communicate his story and acquired a scientific knowledge base of the materials themselves along the way. In addition, it shows that he had learnt about spatial boundaries to keep the image contained within the surface of the paper, as Matthews states:

> *Arranging one's attention and actions towards a blank sheet of paper in readiness for the act of painting might be taken for granted by an adult. Yet even a blank sheet of paper is a product of a theory about space and representation developed over many years by a society. Before brush has been set to paper, Ben, in his attitude and stance, is doing something just as intelligent as using painting tools. This means that he has already acquired some insights into a particular mode of expression and representation.*

(2003, p16)

Figure 4.2.1 A young child explores the world through paint.

Analysis and the theory of 'flow'

Figure 4.2.1 shows this small child's absorption in the painting task. It demonstrates a holistic engagement of his own physical, emotional and intellectual realities, which becomes equitable to the situation of an adult artist engaged within the same process: an exploration of materials; new discoveries that are uncovered; the emotional and physical energy that is given to the task are all equivalent to those experienced by the child. The artist allows him/herself to enter a state of creative 'flow', which the psychologist Mihaly Csikszentmihalyi describes as: *a state in which people are so involved in an activity that nothing else seems to matter; the experience is so enjoyable that people will continue to do it even at great cost, for the sheer sake of doing it* (Csikszentmihalyi, 1990, p4). Csikszentmihalyi identifies specific elements that are present in achieving a state of 'flow', which when applied to painting with children give us important considerations to make in reflecting upon our own attitudes and ability to relinquish control over the outcomes, as we have discussed in previous chapters in this book. This can be a very useful way to think about setting up painting tasks for primary aged children. Csikszentmihalyi suggests that:

- clear goals are set at each step;
- feedback is provided to actions;
- there should be balance between skill development and challenge;
- action and awareness are brought together;
- distractions are eliminated;
- there is no worry of failure;
- self-consciousness disappears;
- sense of time is lost;
- the activity becomes an end in itself: process-, rather than product-led.

(Adapted from Harmat et al., 2016)

Figure 4.2.2 Student exploring paint techniques.

▬▬ Reflection point ▬▬▬▬▬▬▬▬▬▬▬▬▬▬▬▬▬▬▬▬▬▬▬▬▬▬▬▬▬

Have you heard children say that they 'love' painting activities? Have you ever experienced the time seeming to pass very quickly when you are absorbed in a creative task yourself? This state will occur for children when they have ownership over the work they are involved with, but cannot be achieved in the same way by completing competitive tasks, working to limited or predetermined outcomes, or by copying existing artworks, as these activities are likely to instil or increase feelings of anxiety. Matthews maintains that asking children to paint by copying shows a disconnection from their learning needs and that if, as adults, we only value 'correct copying' then we are guilty of misunderstanding the meaning and significance of children's art 'to the detriment of children's intellectual and emotional development'. He states that a great teacher *is an adult companion to the child on an intellectual adventure* (2003, p139).

Choosing media for painting

It is essential for you to become aware of the different types of media that can be used for painting, so that you can decide what experiences to plan for your class. Some of these will be readily available in school, such as bottles of poster paint, watercolours, powder paint, dyes and pastels, and other materials that can be obtained easily. The practical exercise from the previous section, Drawing, might already have given you some ideas about the wide variety of materials and techniques that can be used to achieve different effects and textures: now we just add colour into the mix and you have a vocabulary of marks and materials that can be used to enhance any painting.

There are many circumstances in school where painting will be the most appropriate medium to employ, but how do you know which is the most appropriate type of paint for the task? Table 4.2.1 gives you a checklist of resources that you will need for painting. It also shows you which materials to choose to best fit your learning objectives and suggests ways in which you can use them.

Organisation

Sometimes just the thought of trying to organise painting activities can lead to feelings of panic. This might be because it takes time and effort that you feel you can't always provide, so by involving children in the setting up and clearing up, you can build social and citizenship learning into your organisation and management of the lesson. To do this you will need to agree rules and procedures with the children and teach them to be independent and responsible, so this works best if it is part of school policy, which the children become well practised in over the years. You will find helpful ways to organise the class for paint activities in the second column of Table 4.2.1.

Table 4.2.1 Resources for painting, and key learning opportunities

Materials and tools for painting	Best for...	Skills and concepts	Key language
Paper	A1: Large painting, best for paired or group work. A2: Individual paintings that are quite large. A3: Small sized individual work. Postcard size: for working on a small scale.	Offering children different types of paper and surfaces to paint upon will allow them to discover how materials respond when a wet substance is applied.	Blank Clean Light Soft Textured Tissue Thin Thick Strong Fragile Wet Dry Flat Shaped Glossy Matt Transparent Opaque
Thick 'brushwork' or sugar paper	Everyday painting. White or buff is a good choice because the background colour will not interfere with the applied painted colours.	Working on a variety of sizes allows children to learn spatial awareness and to gain a sense of scale. For example, working on a very small painting feels very different from working on large-scale work with rollers or large brushes.	
Cartridge or lining paper roll	For large-scale and group work.		
Watercolour paper	Thick, textured paper that supports very wet work. Wet on wet (dampen paper first before applying wet paint).		
Other surfaces Cardboard	For 3D work, or for use with thick paint that needs a strong support.		
Perspex, polythene, ceramics or glass	Paint onto transparent surfaces by mixing a little PVA glue into the paint to help it stick to the surface.	Painting on a transparent surface means that the work can be seen from both sides, so large-scale hangings can be created. Children can learn how light affects colour.	
Natural material such as stones, wood, leaves, shells, etc.	Add PVA as above.		
Recycled materials	Use poster paint to create surface pattern.		

(Continued)

Table 4.2.1 (Continued)

Materials and tools for painting	Best for...	Skills and concepts	Key language
Brushes **Large**	Backgrounds, covering large areas or shapes.	With your guidance, children will learn to make their own decisions about what tools to use for which purpose. Ask them to think what would be the best tool in relation to scale and medium; even the theme or topic might dictate which implement to use.	Fine Thick Soft Flat Bristle Broad Stipple Stroke Handle
Medium	Painting inside shapes, and covering areas that need more careful control.		
Small/thin	Adding detail, line work.		
Decorators' brushes or rollers	Covering large areas quickly, large-scale work.	Decision making is an important part of the process of making art at all stages, and giving children the independence to do this will benefit them in other subject areas too.	Tip Round-ended Wide Synthetic Knife Load Flexible Wash Wipe Smear Blend Explore Experiment
Rags and sponges	Covering areas that require a bit of texture, applying paint through a stenciled shape.		
Painting knives, spatulas	Use with thick paint: apply paint over a pre-painted background.		
Watercolour brushes	Soft-haired, flexible brushes especially for carrying various quantities of water.	Children can make their own painting tools from recycled or natural materials, for example by bunching and tying sticks or straws together, or by securing a small scrap of fabric to the wrong end of a paintbrush. They will learn to invent, explore and test ideas.	
Hands and fingers	Even older children love to use their hands for creating paintings.		

Aprons/old shirts	One for each painter.	Children will learn to be responsible for keeping clean.
Table covers/newspaper	Tables should be arranged for group work and covered, for easy cleaning after the activity.	Try to involve the children in both setting up for painting and tidying away. This helps them to take an attitude that is about collective responsibility and enables them to become independent.
Mixing palettes	Each child will need their own palette. Paper plates or plastic trays will do, or ask children to cut some A3 sized heavy paper, such as sugar paper, into a shape resembling an artist's palette and use this to mix colours. These will make a beautiful display to show their learning in colour mixing, whilst also saving on washing up.	This gives children ownership of their work, and helps them to be cognitive of the changes that happen during colour mixing. They learn to become thoughtful and intuitive in their use of colour.
Buckets for water	For washing brushes between colours: place these near to where the children are working so that there is minimal moving around to the sinks. Ask one child from each group to be in charge of changing dirty water.	Children learn that they need to keep colours and painting tools clean so that a maximum colour intensity is maintained.
Rags or paper towels	For cleaning and wiping excess water from brushes.	Children learn to sequence their actions.

(Continued)

Table 4.2.1 (Continued)

Materials and tools for painting	Best for...	Skills and concepts	Key language
Paint receptacles **Large containers or buckets** **Paint trays or pots for poster paint**	For large-scale work. For table painting and sharing colours: children can scoop the colours they want with small spoons and place these on their individual mixing palette from the central resource. This saves waste.	Children learn to work together as a group to keep the colours clean. They learn to respect materials and resources and to understand that they need to use these efficiently.	
Poster paint	General purpose paint. Water it down or add textured materials, such as sand, flour, etc. Mix with PVA for a glossy finish, and for acrylic work.	Through paint, children will learn to enjoy using colour and become aware of how colours interact and react. They learn to visualise, imagine, transform and adapt. They learn to be flexible and work with 'mistakes'. Children learn about the properties of different types of paint. They should be encouraged to mix their own colours and use this knowledge in every painting activity, including those where paint is used in other curriculum subject areas, for example, when painting a model made in history, or to describe the course of a river in geography.	Colour Fluorescent Tint Shade Pattern Texture Hue Layers Splash Drip Spot Scumble Shape Complementary Harmonious Clashing Depth Flash Intense Pastel Dark

			Vocabulary
Powder paint	Mix up big tubs for large-scale work. Dry on wet: use dry paint by sprinkling onto wet paper – draw into this with fingertips or sticks to create linear marks, or let this air dry for a powdery texture. Mix with cellulose glue to make finger paint. Make thick paint by adding to cooked up cornflour: mix one tablespoon of cornflour with a little cold water, add one cup of boiling water, and paint.	When working on a large scale and with large quantities of paint, children will learn to work collaboratively and towards a common goal. For example, this could be in making backgrounds for large work or for creating paintings of scenery for school productions, etc. They learn how it feels to be motivated and trusted.	Primary Secondary Tertiary Cool Warm Pale Spectrum Greyscale Spread Stain Pour Composition Balance Rhythm Tone Deep
Watercolour paint	Translucent finish Useful for washes, layering. Resist techniques: wash over oil pastel or candle wax drawings. Easy to transport for field work.	Children will learn to control the materials, develop hand–eye co-ordination and fine motor control. They will learn to observe and interpret what they see. They develop confidence in expressing ideas and how to communicate through visual means.	Translucent Detail Wash Layers Resist Block Muted Bright Definition

━━━ Practical activity ━━━

Abstract art

Revisit the section in Chapter 3 (page 54) on *colour* as one of the visual elements, which describes the double primary system for colour mixing. Use these colours to explore a range of painting techniques to further develop your subject knowledge. Try the following activities with your colleagues in a staff meeting, or with your class.

1. Set up for painting, using the checklist in Table 4.2.1.

2. Look at some images of abstract art to inspire ideas on how to use colour, shape, pattern and texture in painting, such as:

   Patrick Heron

   artuk.org/discover/artists/heron-patrick-19201999

   Gillian Ayres

   www.artsy.net/artist/gillian-ayres

   Molly Zuckerman-Hartung

   www.mollyzuckermanhartung.com/index.php?q=Slideshow&ID=56

3. Use decorators' brushes to cover a large piece of thick paper with colours of your choice, and put it aside to dry. (Use a long piece of wallpaper lining if you are working collaboratively.)

4. Experiment with ways of using paint on smaller pieces of paper.

- Roll marbles, stones or conkers across wet paint to create a textured pattern.
- Squirt poster paint colours onto some card or paper before running a comb through it, to create patterns.
- Place blobs of primary coloured paint into the centre of a piece of paper, fold the paper and smooth the central fold to spread the paint inside, then open this out and see what the shapes remind you of.
- Use feathers, leaves or sticks dipped into paint to draw across the surface of your paper.
- Cover paper with oil pastel or wax crayon. Paint over this with a black or dark blue poster paint. Draw through, or scrape the paint away with a barbeque skewer or cocktail stick, so that the colours from the layer underneath show through.
- Make coloured patterns on paper with oil pastel and paint over this with watercolour. The oil will resist the watery paint to produce a good effect. Try the same thing, but by drawing first with household candles.
- Add poster paint and washing up liquid to a small amount of water in a container; blow into the mixture with a straw and take a print from the resulting bubbles.
- Take an old toothbrush, dip it into paint and use your thumb to spray the paint onto a surface, or lay some objects onto paper and spray paint over these to achieve negative images of the objects.
- Take some wax rubbings from the environment using coloured crayons; paint a wash over these patterns and textures using block watercolour.

- Use decorators' foam rollers to roll paint onto paper shapes for a smooth effect. When dry, use fruit bag nets or small gauge chicken wire to roll paint through in a contrasting colour, or use everyday objects, such as bubble wrap, sponges, washing up brushes, etc. to print texture and pattern.
- Wet thick paper with water before sprinkling powder paint onto the surface. Use your fingers to draw into the paint to create an image or design.

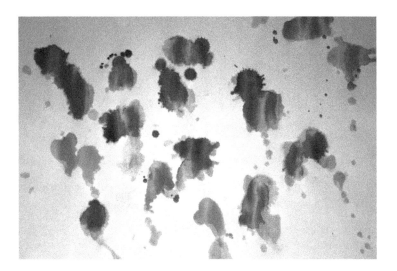

Figure 4.2.3 Rain painting.

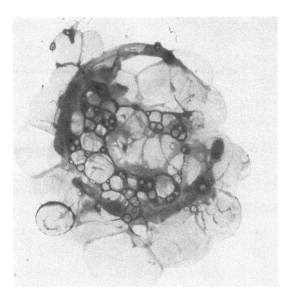

Figure 4.2.4 Bubble painting.

(Continued)

(Continued)

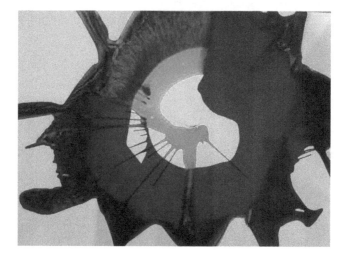

Figure 4.2.5 Spin painting.

Once these experiments are dry, tear or cut them into shapes. Organise these shapes onto the large painted background that you left to dry. Play with the shapes until you have achieved a balanced, aesthetically pleasing composition. Stick them down with glue and continue to use paint to accentuate or disguise areas, eventually bringing the whole piece together. Place the work onto a display board, stand back and admire!

——— Further reading ———

St Clair, K (2016) *The Secret Lives of Colour.* London: John Murray.

Watson Garcia, C (2009) *Painting for the Absolute and Utter Beginner.* New York: Watson-Guptill.

Take a journey through colour at London's National Gallery: **www.nationalgallery.org.uk/ journey-through-colour**

Read about the science between colour and emotion: **www.designshack.net/articles/graphics/ the-science-behind-color-and-emotion**

Mihaly Csikszentmihalyi talks about the theory of flow on TED: **www.ted.com/talks/mihaly_ csikszentmihalyi_on_flow**

4.3

Printmaking

Introduction

Printmaking is both the simplest and most complex of art processes. Sometimes it can be so easy – think of those muddy footprints on a kitchen floor – while at other times it can be so complex: look at the amazing layers of colour and tone in something like Picasso's linocuts. Printmaking lessons might require some thoughtful planning but, whichever age group you teach, you'll find that the process offers unique opportunities for children to explore, experiment and try something new.

What is printmaking?

So, what exactly is printmaking? Today, most children might assume it's simply something that happens when they point the cursor on their computer screen to 'File' and 'Print', but printmaking has a tradition that stretches back many thousands of years, to when cave-dwellers pressed their pigment-covered hands to the walls of their caves. Essentially, printmaking encompasses a range of methods for transferring an image, design or pattern from a surface to a piece of paper. A printmaker will create an initial design on a tile, plate or other surface, then apply ink and transfer the design to paper or fabric.

At the centre of the printmaking process is *repetition* and printmakers will often make repeat patterns, or a set of identical images. Vincent van Gogh was one of many well-known artists drawn to printmaking, and he thought the process was nothing short of miraculous. In a letter to his brother, Theo, he explained his love of the process in poetic terms, describing how: *one's drawing is sown on the stone or etching plate, and a harvest is reaped from it.* Today's artists can use printmaking to provide an income, as they can produce editions of 50 or 100 prints that collectors can buy. Children can also use printmaking to make multiple copies of their creations to use as Christmas cards for their friends and families, for instance.

There are three basic printmaking processes that we use in primary schools, and we'll explore each of them in this section. We'll begin by thinking about why we make prints; we'll then reflect on an example of how printmaking can inspire even the youngest of children to create their own works of art, before outlining some practical ideas for printmaking in Key Stages 1 and 2.

Why do we make prints?

There are many reasons why we make prints. Younger children will be drawn to the immediacy, the physicality and the simplicity of printmaking: picture a five-year-old squashing her hand into a palette of ink and squidging it onto paper. At the other end of the scale, older children will be intrigued by the complexities of printmaking and the opportunities it offers for making decisions about their work: they'll enjoy exploring different options for their prints and creating a range of effects through experimenting with line, tone and texture.

Above all, and whatever their age, children love the colours of printmaking. As they progress, children can experiment with applying several layers of colour to the same image or pattern, and try alternative colour combinations. 'Real' printmakers use printmaking ink (rather than paint) to create their work and, as soon as you squeeze the first drops from the tube, you'll see why. Printmaking ink is intensely coloured, thick and sticky, and adheres well to various surfaces, whilst mixing different colours and tones in a palette is a particularly pleasurable part of the printmaking process.

Printmaking has several other special qualities. First, there's an element of unpredictability. This might sound like a problem, but unpredictability can be great. When children make prints, they have only limited control over the way they transfer ink to paper and the resulting marks can be unexpected. While there may be times when they are a little disappointed with their print, more often than not children are pleasantly surprised by what they see: the moment at which they peel their paper away from the tile to reveal their print can be almost magical. As children become more experienced printmakers they can even learn to embrace mistakes. Encourage them to always look for the unexpected: a successful print is often a combination of the intentional and the unintentional.

Second, there are certain aesthetic qualities to be found in prints that are seldom seen in drawings or paintings. For example, when we apply a second layer of ink over a previous layer, often some of the first layer will show through, creating unexpectedly rich textures. Sometimes the accidental and unexpected marks turn out to be the most effective; patterns that would take hours to paint can be created in a matter of seconds in a print.

This brings us to the third special quality of printmaking: it encourages children to focus firmly on the artistic decisions they make. Decision making is one of the most important aspects of the creative process, and we'll explore this principle in more depth through looking at some examples of children's work.

=== Case study ===

Key Stage 1 teacher, Megan, provided children with a range of natural and manmade objects as starting points from which to explore printmaking. By pressing objects into ink, and printing these onto paper, children started to notice the patterns and textures that emerged.

Making prints using found objects can be surprising and rewarding: the unique patterns and textures of objects such as leaves, vegetables or household items can be overlooked until they are inked and pressed onto paper. Printmaking offers children opportunities to experiment with colour, tone, texture and shape, and they'll enjoy the range of results that can be achieved with even the simplest of everyday resources.

Megan's sequence of lessons began with the simplest of images: her own handprint. She prompted the children to look carefully at the print and to think about how it was made. Their observations highlighted several key characteristics of printmaking: some noticed that the lines indicated the texture of skin; others saw that some areas of the image were lighter than others; whilst one or two recognised that the printed image was a reverse of the original object. Megan built on each observation through discussion, to help children understand the principles of printmaking, before illustrating some of the points raised by demonstrating a simple print process.

Taking a leaf, the teacher pressed it into a palette of ink and then onto paper. She emphasised how to apply enough ink to the leaf to ensure that its texture was visible on the page: too much or too little and the texture was lost. She showed how the harder she pressed the leaf to paper, the darker the tone was on the page and, finally, she pointed out how the image of the leaf was the reverse of the original. Children collected natural objects from outside the classroom and explored their shapes and textures by rolling ink onto them and printing them onto paper. The lesson not only provided children with an introduction to the techniques of printmaking but also drew their attention to details of the natural world that are often easily overlooked.

=== Theory focus ===

As they progress through Key Stage 2, children should be encouraged to return to printmaking with the aim of creating more complex images and diverse outcomes. This is a theme that American art educator, Elliot Eisner, wrote about in several of his books. Eisner helped to identify many of the principles that currently underpin teaching and learning in art and design and to celebrate the characteristics of the subject that distinguish it from the rest of the curriculum. In *The Arts and the Creation of Mind* (2002) he wrote:

> The teacher of spelling ... seeks **unity** of response from students. The same is true for most teachers of arithmetic ... What schools seem to teach best is rule following. The arts, however, march to a different drummer. In most of the arts we seek **diversity** of outcome.

> (Eisner, 2002, p44)

If you've ever seen a classroom display of identical paintings or drawings, you'll know that the teacher responsible will have provided children with too many instructions and too few opportunities to make *decisions* about their work. In an ideal world (or classroom) children would never have to write their names on the backs of their artwork because each one would be so distinctive that they could recognise it immediately. Eisner's notion of 'diversity of outcome' is one that teachers should bear in mind before, during and after each art lesson, whether planning activities, providing feedback or reflecting on outcomes.

Diversity of outcome

Printmaking, perhaps more than any other art process, offers opportunities to encourage children to think about what we mean when we talk about diversity of outcome. As children progress through Key Stage 2, ask them to make four of five copies of their prints, as they will then have opportunities to experiment with each print in a different way. Encourage children to look carefully at their work in progress and to visualise how they might develop it further. This may sound a little complicated, but the support that teachers need to provide can be summarised in a few words: What next? What if …? These two simple questions can be enough to prompt children to reflect on what they have learnt so far from the process, to think about how they could change their print and to experiment with further techniques.

Once children have made their first print they should consider what they might do differently a second time. Again, some simple questions can focus their minds on this task: Will your second print sit alongside your first, or will they overlap? What if you tried different coloured inks? What if you tried pressing harder or softer? Encouraging children to consider these questions carefully will lead to greater diversity in their outcomes.

Finally, a printmaking session requires a few more resources than a drawing or painting lesson, and some techniques can be tricky to manage. There are a few simple rules that children will need to follow if they are to achieve the best results. We'll explore these challenges by reflecting on a selection of examples of printmaking in primary school.

Preparing your ink

Printmaking inks are a little more expensive to buy than ready mixed paints, but use them if possible: the ink is thicker than the paint and the results are better. You'll only need the primary colours, plus black and white.

Squeeze small amounts of ink from two tubes onto a palette (a teaspoonful is enough) and mix them together with a plastic palette knife (two colours combined are almost always more interesting than one straight from the tube). White can be added to create lighter tones.

Take a roller, roll it through the ink and apply to the surface of your block. Take care with the amount of ink that is applied: too little will mean the print will be only partly visible; too much and the detail that will make the print interesting will be lost.

Resources for printmaking

- Printmaking inks
- Sheets of thin, white newsprint paper (A3, A4)
- Small sheets of cardboard for string prints
- String
- PVA glue
- Sheets of polyboard
- Perspex sheets or similar for monoprints
- Rollers and palettes
- Plastic palette knives
- Sharp pencils or biros
- A drying rack or washing line

━━ Practical activity ━━━━━━━━━━━━━━━━━

Press-prints

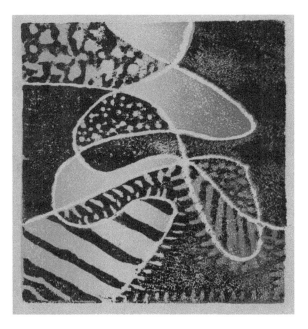

Figure 4.3.1 A press-print.

The best way to begin making press-prints is to encourage children to create abstract designs rather than make representational images. As they become confident with the process they can experiment with more figurative imagery, but this can involve making some tricky decisions about sequencing colours in a manageable way, so initially it's easier to concentrate on exploring patterns.

Press-printing involves removing parts of a flat surface and printing what remains. Using polyboard offers children greater control over the outcomes.

- Practise drawing your design on paper before carving it into a sheet of polyboard.
- Squeeze a small amount of ink into a palette. Ideally, mix two colours together.
- Roll your roller into the ink, ensuring it picks up an even layer, then transfer the ink to your tile, applying a thin, consistent layer. Work right to the edges, then place a sheet of paper over the tile and press down firmly, smoothing out to the edges.
- Carefully peel away the paper to reveal the print. Repeat four times. You will find it's much quicker to ink up a second time and you can experiment with each print to create something different every time.
- Now give your tile a quick wash to remove ink from the first layer, then remove some sections of the tile with a craft knife.
- Ink up your tile with a different colour and carefully place it over one of your prints.

(Continued)

(Continued)

- Flip the tile and paper over and press carefully on the back of the paper to make sure the ink has transferred.
- Peel away the paper to reveal the print.
- What next? What if ...?

Older children could experiment with making continuous designs across several tiles. They could draw a line that starts at a point on one side of a tile, then curves around and leaves the tile at precisely the same point on the opposite side, meaning that it will synchronise with the line on the next person's tile, and so on.

Practical activity

String prints

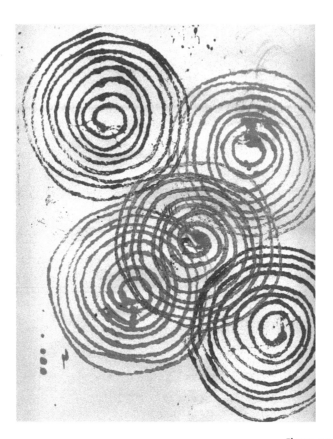

Figure 4.3.2 A string print.

- Begin by demonstrating how to spread a very thin layer of PVA glue over a piece of thick card: the glue should be so thin that it's transparent after a few minutes.
- Cut a length of string and arrange it onto the card. When you are happy with the way the string is placed, press it firmly onto the card and set aside to dry; this won't take long, assuming your glue isn't too thick.
- Squeeze ink into a palette (experiment by mixing a new colour or tone) then roll your roller through the ink.
- Roll the roller across the string, taking care to avoid getting too much ink on the card.
- Print by placing the paper on top of the card.

Having made the first print, encourage children to consider how they might change the image they have made. Do they want to make a second impression, similar to the first? Will their second impression sit alongside the first, or overlap it? Do they want to use different coloured ink? (Sharing palettes is a good idea.) These are simple questions, but encouraging children to consider them carefully can make the difference between a set of prints that are almost identical and a collection that features a range of distinct approaches.

Practical activity

Monoprints

Figure 4.3.3 A monoprint.

(Continued)

(Continued)

- We'll start this monoprinting activity by creating a colourful background layer. Choose two primary colours and squeeze a small blob of each into the top corners of your palette.
- Roll your roller through the ink and down the palette towards you and aim to create a *blend* of the two colours, then transfer the ink to your paper. (If you have too much ink on the roller, roll off the excess onto some newspaper.)
- You now have a colourful background layer for your monoprint. Ideally, allow time for this layer to dry, though if you want to complete your prints in one lesson then use a second piece of paper to blot off the excess from the first (you can then use this second piece for another print).
- Roll a very thin layer of black ink onto a perspex sheet, or any smooth surface that can be wiped down later. The ink needs to be so thin that it looks matt and not at all shiny: you should be able to just see light reflecting on the surface. Place a sheet of paper very lightly onto the inked surface, then draw your design in pencil on the back of the paper. The pressure at the point of contact will transfer the ink to the paper.
- Now trace over the image, and transfer it to the background layer. Experiment with mark making. You'll find that using harder or softer drawing pencils, or applying different amounts of pressure to the drawing, will create different marks.

▬ Further reading ▬

Garner, L (2014) *The Little Book of Printmaking*. London: Bloomsbury.

Printmaking in the Primary National Curriculum with Access Art: **www.accessart.org.uk/curriculum-planning-printmaking**

Ideas for projects: **www.teachkidsart.net/category/process/printmaking-lessons-by-process**

4·4

Three-dimensional work and the physical world

Introduction

Sculpture and working with three-dimensional materials in primary schools has been problematic for many years, and this has been well documented by OFSTED inspection reports, such as 'Drawing together' (2009) and 'Making a mark' (2012). There are, however, important reasons for including 3D experiences in the art and design curriculum for primary aged children. Using physical materials in the art classroom will involve children being up and out of their seats, moving around and being physically active, so it is perhaps no wonder that it is a popular choice as a way of working for boys, in particular; in fact, for all children who like to move to help them think (Robinson, 2006). Children moving around, picking things up, feeling texture, weight and size of objects through handling them, provides important tactile and sensory understanding, and is another key feature of working within this process. There is an indication that children's lives are becoming more sedentary, as they opt to watch TV and use mobile devices and other technologies rather than being engaged in physical activities or going outside to play, and there are serious health and well-being concerns regarding this trend (Biddle and Asare, 2011) which has strong implications for us all. Cancer Research UK has released figures that on starting primary school, one in five children are already overweight or obese, but that figure rises to one in every three children by the time they leave Year 6 (2016). These children are at risk of both mental illness and other life threatening diseases, and these shocking statistics should help us to reflect about the part we can play in encouraging participation in active, playful learning (Cardon et al., 2014).

Up and about in the classroom

There is a perception in many primary schools that working with 3D techniques is rather challenging, and this could be due to several reasons: a lack of teachers' confidence in exactly what to teach and how to manage it is possibly exacerbated by the shortage of CPD available in this area (NSEAD, 2016). Other prohibitive factors can often be related to everyday practical difficulties, simply in terms of collecting appropriate materials and resources together. Not knowing how to organise space and time for this type of learning can be a further challenge, as can wondering where to store and display work once it is done. As with painting, sometimes just the physical aspect of classroom organisation for 30 children in a carpeted room can appear to be complex and unmanageable. It is essential, though, that you put these fears aside to give children the opportunities to explore, experiment and to become physically involved with all sorts of 'stuff': this is key for developing children's understanding of the physical and material world, as well as their ability to solve problems, think flexibly and be resourceful. As defined by the aforementioned OFSTED report of 2009 only one-third of the 91 visits to primary schools showed that the art and design curriculum was operating at a 'Good' standard or above. It highlighted that boys were likely to enjoy and achieve well when working with three-dimensional materials, but they are less likely to be offered opportunities to learn about and through working with sculptural techniques. The report states: *Despite boys' preference for 3D work, they were often given little encouragement or guidance to explore or present ideas in this form* (2009, p32).

═══ Case study ═══

Gender differences and art

Figure 4.4.1 Boys become actively involved in using 3D materials.

Susan Coles, artist and educator, created a project aimed at encouraging boys' engagement with art and design through 3D processes, with a focus on the built environment. This was designed specifically as a reaction to the 2009 OFSTED report, which acknowledged that boys, especially, were being put off from making art. She said:

> It seems that boys of all achievement levels love the chance to make things in three-dimensions. The abstract nature of the sculpture task that we set meant that they did not have to try to make something that already existed, therefore they had more chance of success. They were learning by making and doing, without being afraid of the outcomes, so the outcomes looked after themselves. Our project gave them permission to play imaginatively with the question, what if ...?

Karen, the Year 6 teacher who worked with Susan on this project over a four-week period, was surprised by the children's engagement and motivation to do this work. She said: *I was concerned that the class did not really enjoy art before this, and it has made me realise that perhaps I did not talk to them enough about why they are making art. They were much more motivated when they knew there was a real purpose to the creative work.*

Analysis

This case study exemplifies that inclusivity in terms of gender is another consideration that we should be aware of in planning for art and design. Susan's project acknowledges that boys often prefer to work in a different way to girls, and a sole diet of two-dimensional techniques and processes can be discouraging for some children. Sax (2007) writes about research from the world of science in which MRI scans of children's developing brains were studied over many years. The team of 12 neuroscientists in America, at Maryland's National Institute of Mental Health, found that there are over 100 distinct biological differences that make boys more emotionally vulnerable, physically active and impulsive than girls, as they grow.

Reflective exercise

Watch this revealing film about boys' engagement with Eva Rothschild's purpose-built sculpture, at London's Whitechapel Gallery.

www.whitechapelgallery.org/exhibitions/childrens-art-commission-eva-rothschild-boys-and-sculpture

Then listen to their thoughts and reflections on the experience.

www.youtube.com/watch?v=_3uZuCyIArE

Read Leonard Sax's book (2007) *Boys Adrift: The Five Factors Driving the Growing Epidemic of Unmotivated Boys and Underachieving Young Men.*

Reflection point

- How do you cater for gender differences in the experiences that you plan in art and design?
- How confident do you feel to organise physically active, tactile, messy or large-scale work?

(Continued)

(Continued)

- Look at the spaces available for making three-dimensional work in your classroom or school: can you change the layout of furnishings, work outside or book the school hall for your 3D art and design sessions?

Figure 4.4.2 A boy making a sculpture outdoors.

On the following pages, you will find a quick reference guide to give you a fast and easy way to look up the key processes for 3D work, as well as best-fit uses in the classroom context, and an explanation of key learning opportunities (see Table 4.4.1). Before you do that, let us just reconsider the pedagogy and importance of 'play'.

The role of 'play' in three-dimensional work

Do you know the old story of the child who is given an expensive birthday present, and then proceeds to ignore the gift in order to play with the cardboard box that it came in? This is an example of the child's natural propensity to be imaginative, inventive and engage with the sheer physicality of objects, and it is these qualities that we can draw upon to engage children when introducing 3D

Table 4.4.1 Three-dimensional processes

Process	Materials	Vocabulary	Contextual examples and resources
Modelling Concerned with manipulating soft materials that can be changed and molded by hand.	**Clay-work** • School clay/terracotta clay. • Cheese wire: for cutting chunks off the block. • Hands and fingers. • Rolling pins. • Kitchen utensils: for cutting; adding texture; press clay through a garlic press for a hairy or grassy texture. • Clay tools: for shaping and smoothing. • Textured material: for pressing patterns. • Barbeque or cocktail sticks: for drawing into the clay. • Slip: add watery clay to scored surfaces of two parts that you want to join, smooth together at the point of contact. Allow children to play with the clay to see how many ways they can manipulate it with their hands before using any tools. Show them how to pinch a pot, roll a long string of clay and create a slab, as with these few techniques they will be able to make anything they wish. Clay does not necessarily need to be fired in a kiln if you haven't got access to one. The important thing is that children have lots of experience in using this material to build their muscle tone, to develop fine motor skills, and to learn about changing states of materials problem solving.	Mold Pinch Pull Press Slab Wrap Layer Smooth Roll Stretch Cut Score Sgraffito Carve Shape Form Slip Coil Kiln Biscuit Glaze Carve Pottery Folk art	Rebecca Warren **www.matthewmarks.com/new-york/artists/rebecca-warren/selected-works** Annie Woodford **www.anniewoodford.co.uk/objects.html** Fischli and Weiss **cfileonline.org/exhibition-clay-fischli-weiss-venice-biennale** Sharon Brill **www.sharonbrill.com** Other examples could include Joanne Cooke or Brendan Hesmondhalgh, who use the theme of animals. Or look at the use of clay and ceramics in history and crafts in Britain and across the world, such as the Terracotta Army or ancient Greek pots.
	Salt dough Combine 2 cups of flour, 1 cup of salt and 3/4 cup of water; mix well. Roll out on a lightly floured surface. Cut into desired shapes and make holes for hanging. Preheat oven to 300 degrees Fahrenheit (150 degrees Celsius); bake for 30 minutes; allow to cool. Decorate with poster paints or tube paints.	Pummel Stretch Cut Shape Craft Colour	**http://traditions.cultural-china.com/en/16Traditions265.html** **www.allfreecrafts.com/homemade-gifts/objets/salt-dough-crafts**

(Continued)

Table 4.4.1 (Continued)

Process	Materials	Vocabulary	Contextual examples and resources
	Modelling clay • Modelling clay needs to be warmed to slightly above room temperature before using, otherwise it is too rigid to work with. • Make models for stop-motion film making.	Roll Blend Relief Bend Curl Model Spread Animation	Barbara Reid **www.barbarareid.ca/portfolio** Nick Park **www.youtube.com/** **watch?v=OmNymPocKro**
	Papier mache • Create a structure using plasticize or construction methods and cover this with layers of glued paper. Lay newspaper on a clear table top and use a handful of cellulose paste to cover this until it is damp, then tear strips and apply to the structure, criss-crossing the strips to give added strength. Finish with a layer of tissue paper to add colour and detail. • Line a bowl or container with clingfilm before covering with around eight layers of papier mache, building in pattern, colour and texture by adding coloured tissue paper, threads, sequins, etc. When dry, remove the bowl and peel the film.	Cover Harden Air-dry Structure Form Shape Hollow Layer Smooth Surface Detail Design Pattern Colour Folk art Craft Decoupage	Resources **www.papiermache.co.uk** Mexican folk art **www.mexican-folk-art-guide.com/** **papier-mache.html#.WAJQ4DKZP-Y** Demonstration video **www.youtube.com/** **watch?v=cpAKNS6tvO4**
	Plaster-impregnated bandage • Can be used as a final layer instead of papier mache. • Cut bandage into small pieces and leave in a tray: this is the dry area. • Have a small amount of water in a bowl: keep this as the wet area.		How to use plaster-bandage **www.youtube.com/** **watch?v=1JQrhKOaZ2Y**

	• Dip one piece of bandage at a time into the water, rub gently between fingers and thumbs to release the plaster; apply to the sculpture, criss-crossing as above. Smooth the surface as much as possible whilst still wet. • This can be painted afterwards to add detail and colour. **Aluminum foil** • Wrap and press foil around objects to create forms and impressions of shapes, textures and pattern. • Try to make a small sculpture or object that stands up, by tearing/scrunching just one square of foil from a roll. • Wrap foil around wire sculptures to form areas of volume. • Scrunch foil into long flexible strips that can be bent and joined together easily to create organic forms or chunky jewellery. • Aluminum foil can be painted with PVA glue mixed into poster paint.	Scrunch Bend Decorate	Foil figures **www.dolvinartknight.blogspot.co.uk/2014/01/foil-figure-sculpture.html**
Construction An additive process, which involves using joining techniques to build and create structures.	Wire Paper Rolled newspaper Recycled materials, such as cardboard, plastic, etc. Foam Wood Matchsticks/cocktail sticks Bamboo Foil Willow sticks Fabric	Rigid Attach Bind Intersection Spatial Structure Substance Solid Torn	Chris Gilmour **www.chrisgilmour.com** Sue Webster and Tim Noble Anthony Gormley **www.antonygormley.com** Anthony Caro **www.anthonycaro.org/frames-related/Gallery.htm**

(Continued)

Table 4.4.1 (Continued)

Process	Materials	Vocabulary	Contextual examples and resources
	Bubble wrap Corrugated card Masking tape Packing tape Zip-ties Coloured electrical tape String Scissors Wire cutters Glue Use any combination of the materials listed above, plus others that you can add, to create structures and models. Models or sculptures that move are 'kinetic art', which is designed to move and interact with the space in which it is displayed. It can be mechanically driven or affected by natural elements, such as the wind. Create a structure with wire and wrap this in kitchen foil to add substance and form.	Gap Open Closed Volume Relief Balance Movement Marquette Geometric Mobile Constructivism Cubism Assemblage Arte Povera Kinetic art	Thomas Heatherwick **www.heatherwick.com** Es Devlin **www.esdevlin.com** Architecture **www.architecture.com/Explore/** **Architects/** **InspirationalArchitects.aspx**
Carving A reductive technique, where material is removed to create structure or details.	• **Soap sculpture:** carve bars of cheap soap with dining knives. • **Plaster of Paris:** mix powder with water to achieve a creamy texture; pour into empty paper cartons, such as juice cartons; peel away paper once the plaster is set, and sculpt the block with sandpaper. • **Wood:** children, especially in Key Stage 2, can be taught to safely use chisels and knives to carve into soft wood, such as lime or balsa wood.	Sculpt Statue Figure Cut Grooved Design Decorate Engrave Etch Whittle Safety goggles Protective	Simon O'Rourke **www.treecarving.co.uk/about** Henry Moore **www.henry-moore.org/collections/** **henry-moore-works-in-public** Grinling Gibbons **www.youtube.com/** **watch?v=zJ6tgxNU_gc**

Topic	Description	Vocabulary	References
Installation art This can be made by arranging materials or objects in a specific, or exhibition, space.	• Use already existing objects or specially made sculptures to create an environment. • Children can arrange objects themselves, design the surrounding area, use projections or computer generated images on multiple screens within the space. • Installations can be a good way to communicate the exploration of a theme or issue, as the viewer's opinion and thoughts matter in interpreting the experience. • The viewer physically and emotionally interacts with the work because of the nature of the immersive experience, which is very different from other forms of art.	Concept Space Reference Projection Interior Exterior Design Ideas Impact Experience Interact Physical Craft Presentation Construct	www.tate.org.uk/learn/online-resources/glossary/i/installation-art Yayoi Kusama www.victoria-miro.com/artists/31-yayoi-kusama Random International: Rain Room (2012) www.random-international.com/work/rainroom
Land art This is where landscape and art are closely linked, through using natural materials as media.	• Children can react to environmental concerns through making art and designing with natural materials. • Use stones, leaves, shells, different tones of earth, sand, leaves, sticks, water, etc. to create shapes and patterns on large and small scales. • They can work in groups to facilitate dialogue on the topics they are exploring. • Children can be made more aware of the natural world by creating designs for garden areas, and researching the structures, colours and shapes of plants and flowers. • Make miniature gardens, or a mini-garden in a bottle.	Regular Irregular Think Question Opinion Touch Sound Smell Hear Look Heavy Damp Sharp	What is land art? www.tate.org.uk/learn/online-resources/glossary/l/land-art Richard Long Richard Smithson Andy Goldsworthy Sam Ovens www.samovens.co.uk www.urbangardensweb.com/category/creating

techniques using play as a strategy. Have you considered your own attitude towards the notion of play in a learning context? What is your perception of play as a learning strategy? The word itself has connotations of frivolity and, perhaps, of wastefulness which uses up precious learning time. Nothing could be further from the truth, as research shows that 'play' is in fact a very serious business. Lester and Russell's 2008 report, 'Play for a change', concluded that the increase in structured, or utilitarian play, and the emergence of technology-based play, has led to some confusion over the nature and meaning of this fundamental childhood activity. A more recent review by Gleave and Cole-Hamilton, 'A world without play' (2012), states that play is unequivocally linked to the learning process and, as well as being wonderfully pleasurable and emotionally satisfying, that it is:

> *crucial to the processes of learning and development. Play is varied and flexible and there is no 'right' or 'wrong' way to play; encompassing an endless range of play types, which could be active or subdued, imaginative or exploratory, involve others or carried out alone.*
>
> (2012, p4)

A playful attitude is an essential element to foster creative learning in art and design. You might like to refer to Chapter 1, where we first looked at the pedagogy of play and learning through self-invested enquiry and curiosity, and apply these to your understanding of the place of play in the art and design curriculum, before trying out some of the materials and methods in the above table for yourself.

━━ Case study ━━━━━━━━━━━━━━━━━━━━━━━━━━━━━━━━━━━━━

Our artist-in-residence, Al Johnson, discusses what it means to her to be a sculptor, and gives some good advice to get you started in using 3D materials and techniques.

Al Johnson

I am a sculptor: I love the physicality of sculpture, its presence in a space, its reality. I love the complications of making sculpture, the variety of materials that can become sculpture, the physical demands on the sculptor. I even like the slow progression of sculpture: some of my works have taken years to complete. I can, however, understand the possible reluctance of teachers to engage with this process, if they are dealing with classes full of enthusiastic children, a demanding curriculum, limited time, restricted space and small budgets. It is tempting to keep art deskbound and two-dimensional, but making sculpture can meet many aspects of the curriculum. Sculpture is closely related to physics and mathematics, encompassing measurement, weight, volume and dynamics. (I wish someone pointed this out to me at school, when art was my star subject but science and maths were such a slog.) There are also strong links to technology, including the quality and functionality of materials, construction techniques and problem solving.

Clay

Sculpture in the classroom doesn't have to be big or heavy or even permanent, but it does offer another way to explore and understand the world. Working with clay is a useful and accessible way to start with sculpture. I have found that clay has almost magical properties for some children who find language difficult. The process of manipulating the clay, and finding form with it, can release creative energy and develop confidence. I worked with a ten-year-old who had difficulty responding in class and articulating ideas, yet made an astonishing sculptural self-portrait, which he could explain and discuss. Self-hardening clay will make permanent works that can be air-dried

Figure 4.4.3 Clay bears, each molded from a single piece of soft clay.

Figures 4.4.4 and 4.4.5 Student working with the theme of 'abandoned village'. The pieces were fired in a kiln and displayed with tea-lights for dramatic effect.

and painted. Traditional terracotta clay, which is much more tactile and satisfying, can be used for temporary works, which you might recycle by rolling back into blocks and rehydrating by adding water, before sealing in a plastic bag and reusing on another occasion.

Construction

Temporary sculpture can be collaboratively made on a large scale. A variety of cardboard boxes will give you giant lightweight building blocks (shoe shops and electrical retailers will often supply

(Continued)

(Continued)

these). At the end of the session the results can be filmed or photographed, and the boxes recycled. Children can work in groups in different areas of the school, such as the hall or playground, to develop different kinds of structures. For example, in one school the pupils made a wall across the hall using the boxes like dry-stone-walling, creating archways, doors and windows.

This needed complex (and noisy) negotiation, and an understanding of the properties of the material they were using. You might ask them to make balancing structures, starting with large boxes at the base and working up, then reversing with the smallest at the base to compare how well the structures work.

Figure 4.4.6 Papier mache monsters constructed from recycled material, masking tape and papier mache, with a final layer of tissue paper to add colour and detail.

Aesthetics

Sculpture is of course not just about scale and balance as 'aesthetics' are significant; could they make a structure that is visually pleasing as well as stable? Sculpture has multiple viewpoints, so ask: Does the structure work from only one viewpoint, or from multiple positions? How would it look from above? Would it need other elements, such as colour or pattern, to achieve unity? Discussions about aesthetics can be explored further in the classroom: pupils could be asked to bring something in from home that they find beautiful, to develop an exploration of varying attitudes to aesthetics and taste.

Making sculpture has enormous potential: perhaps because it is playful, and the outcome is not prescriptive, it avoids the fear of drawing that many children develop.

Visit Al's website: **www.aljohnsonsculptor.com**

Further reading

Briggs, P (2015) *Make, Build, Create*. London: Black Dog.

Caan, S (2011) *Rethinking Design and Interiors: Human Beings in the Built Environment*. London: Laurence King.

Useful handbook on sculpture for teachers.

Garner, J and Vercoe, J (no date) SWMLAC and DfES: **www.discoveryzone.org.uk/sculpture%20handbook.pdf**

Online resources at Tate: **http://bit.ly/2oPWqdz**

Find artists specialising in sculptural methods: **www.sculpture-network.org/en/home/artists.html**

4·5
Craftwork and making

Introduction

Education and training in craft is of wide-ranging importance. It produces makers of the future, prepares those with craft skills for the wider creative economy and beyond, and develops the haptic and creative skills so important for all young people and their learning.

(Crafts Council, 2013)

As a nation, craft techniques and skills are an indispensable part of Britain's heritage and cultural background, as well as leading us to have an international reputation as a major creative hub in the world economy (Department for Culture, Media and Sport, 2016b).

The Warwick Report (2015) 'Enriching Britain: culture creativity and growth' argues that the British cultural and creative industries should be seen as inseparable from one another and are of paramount importance in terms of Britain's future economic security and its status in the world. The report also highlights, however, that barriers and inequalities in access to cultural and creative opportunities exist which, sadly, can start at school if art and craft activity is not valued enough. The report recognises this challenge by stating:

While acknowledging the very important ways that social inequalities limit access, the report also notes that much debate about inequalities is built upon a narrow definition of arts and culture, seeing it through hierarchies of taste or public funding and operating with what has been called a 'deficit model'.

(2015, p9)

The significance of arts education has been highlighted in recent reports such as this one, and gives voice to the alarm at the apparent current decline in English schools.

In January 2016 the then Minister for Culture, Ed Vaizey, stated:

> *The creative industries are one of the UK's greatest success stories, with British musicians, artists, fashion brands and films immediately recognisable in nations across the globe. Growing at almost twice the rate of the wider economy and worth a staggering £84 billion a year, our Creative Industries are well and truly thriving and we are determined to ensure its continued growth and success.*
>
> (DCMS, 2016)

With such a clear message of affirmation from the government it is rather surprising to find that many schools are continuing to reduce the amount of time that children spend on 'making' and on creative subjects, where they can find their personal preferences and talents (NSEAD, 2016; Williams, 2014). The Crafts Council's report 'Studying crafts 16' (2016) shows a dark picture of the take-up of craft and design subjects at secondary level, meaning that young people who come out of the school system now are unlikely to have experienced handling, creating, designing and making. There is a danger that they might not even have a basic understanding of what they are missing, which has obvious implications for future generations who will miss out on skills being passed on to them. It is possible that there is a perception amongst some people that handcrafts are rather old fashioned, pointless and detached from today's realities and the needs of contemporary living. For example, if your idea of 'crafts' is that it involves making items such as corn-dollies, or recreating 1970s-style crocheted toilet roll holders, then you might like to think again. In the twenty-first century the range of crafts and the workplaces that craftwork has impact upon is also staggering, as described by the Crafts Council:

> *From master goldsmiths to makers who build film sets and props, from the small batch production of designer makers to one-off ceramic masterpieces, and from centuries-old traditions to cutting edge digital making. Makers contribute to sectors as diverse as engineering, medicine, technology, architecture, fashion and design.*
>
> (2014, p3)

In 2009, Craft Scotland developed a successful campaign to attempt to challenge stereotypical views on crafts and making by launching an advertisement to be shown in cinemas. The campaign was entitled 'The "C" Word', which was intentionally provocative and sent powerful messages that portrayed crafts as highly desirable and contemporary.

Reflective exercise

Watch the video clip of 'The "C" Word': **www.vimeo.com/6864925**

Look at the Craft Scotland website: **www.craftscotland.org**

━━ Reflection point ━━━━━━━━━━━━━━━━━━━━━━━━━━━━━━━━━━━

What has surprised you about what you have seen on the two links in the Reflective exercise?

- On the Craft Scotland website, in the section called 'About Craft', it is suggested that you will probably own some craftwork yourself. Think about a piece of work that you possess and try to work out why it is so important to you. It might have been handmade by someone you know or love, or hand crafted by an expert, but the sense of touch, crafting and skilful handling will no doubt be a part of the reason it is important to you.
- What practical 'making' activity do you enjoy, or would you like to try in the future?
- How could you incorporate your own craft interests into your teaching?

━━ Case study ━━

Sadia was a Year 3 teacher as well as deputy head of a junior school, who had a passion for knitting. The children in her class had transferred from the nearby infant schools and, in addition, there were children who were new to the area. Sadia was keen to develop a sense of community in the class to ensure that the children settled well and felt comfortable in each other's company. She had also observed that many of the children had poor fine motor control and some were unable to do everyday tasks, such as tying knots or gripping pencils. Sadia started an optional lunchtime knitting club and invited the children to join her for the weekly session. She soon had a steady attendance of nearly half of the class. She kept a lively interest by setting up knitting challenges, such as to knit woolly dog collars for a local rescue centre, and encouraged a wide range of children to become enthused by introducing new materials for knitting, such as video tape and plastic bags pulled into strips. Sadia said that both she and the children could relax and get to know one another in this supportive environment, whilst at the same time she was sure that they were learning and developing key skills for life. Over time she had taught the whole class to knit and, once they were independent in the skills, she suggested they knitted whilst she read to them at daily story time.

Figure 4.5.1 Final year teaching students learn to knit.

Analysis

This example shows how Sadia understood the value of the craft of knitting, not only in relation to the haptic and manipulation skills the children were learning, but the social aspect too, which had a positive impact upon their ability to bond as a group. The children responded positively to the imaginative challenges that Sadia gave them, which helped them to see a purpose for the activities. Inviting them to experiment by knitting with unusual materials encouraged them to think about creative alternatives and new possibilities open to them, whilst involved in the actual 'making'.

Practical activity

Learn how to do finger knitting

www.youtube.com/watch?v=X8y4bGgFQCw

Hint: use bulky or thick yarn when working on this craft with young children.

Crafts and well-being

England's Crafts Council are also working to raise the profile of crafts and making, and in their 2014 manifesto 'Our future is in the making' it was noted that craft enriches society:

> *Beyond economic value, education in and through craft contributes to cognitive development and engages learners. Through engagement with materials and ideas, it develops creativity, inventiveness, problem-solving and practical intelligence. And making fosters wellbeing: It is a vital part of being human.*

(p3)

There is much recent research to endorse this statement (Burt and Atkinson, 2015; Yair, 2011; Devlin, 2009) which adds further validation and justification for including plenty of opportunities for your class and for yourself to engage in craft activities.

The Crafts Council manifesto calls for the following five changes to be made to government policy.

1. Put craft and making at the heart of education.

2. Build more routes into craft careers.

3. Bring craft enterprise into education.

4. Invest in skills throughout careers.

5. Promote world-class higher education and research in craft.

Reflective exercise

Read the manifesto by following this link: **www.craftscouncil.org.uk/content/files/7822_ Education_manifesto@14FINAL.PDF**

Figure 4.5.2 These hilarious and characterful sock creatures are very simple to make and effectively displayed by children who have woven them into their school's wire fencing!

In the classroom

Any student teacher or experienced teacher who is slightly unconfident about art and design, or who feels that they are 'not good at drawing' as discussed earlier in the book, can often find a way into successful creating and making through craft activity. The same exploratory and experimental pedagogical framework applies with craft work, just as it does with all the other processes that we have looked at. It can be quite tempting to use the 'here's one I made earlier' approach when teaching crafts, but before you succumb to asking children to work from a template or within a rigid structure that you have set, just remind yourself of the reasons why you have planned the activity in the first place. Hopefully on that list you will have mentioned some of the following.

- Creativity and imagination.
- Innovation.
- Practical skills.
- Physical skills.

- Thinking through making: haptic/tactile.

- Learning about materials: what they can and can't do.

- Learning about design and developing a sense of aesthetics.

- Concentration and commitment.

- Risk taking and working with mistakes.

- Patience and resilience.

- Community bonding.

- Understanding world traditions, culture and heritage.

Table 4.5.1 gives you a list of craft techniques that can be easily incorporated into your curriculum. The very best way to engage with the various processes listed here is to collect the appropriate resources and have a go yourself, before you try it with your class. You could think about setting up a craft evening with your friends or for staff in your school after work one day, or hold a fundraising craft evening for parents, such as a 'Stitch 'n Bitch' night, where everyone joins in to either teach or learn a new technique (often both) over a glass of something delicious and with some homemade treats to eat.

Find out how to set this up: **https://blog.etsy.com/en/how-to-throw-your-own-craft-night**

Making and craftwork can be a wonderful way to promote resourcefulness and sustainability, and to encourage children to recycle and 'make do'. Rather than describe how to do these techniques, I have added the best of the internet's instructions and video tutorials so that you can learn by example.

━━━ Further reading ━━━

Hanaour, Z (2006) *Making Stuff: An Alternative Craft Book*. London: Black Dog.

McMurdo, M (2016) *Upcycling: 20 Projects Made from Reclaimed Materials*. London: Jacqui Small Publications.

Woodley, M (2013) *Red Ted Art: Cute and Easy Crafts for Kids*. London: Square Peg.

TextileArtist.org favourite recommendations of craft books (for adults): **www.textileartist.org/textile-artist-books-our-recommendations**

Table 4.5.1 Craft techniques and resources

Craft and making techniques	Resources needed	Instructions/online tutorials	Notes
Batik	Washable gel glue Flour Wax and batik kettle Tjanting Wax crayon Kitchen paper Cotton fabric Acrylic paint (mix non-washable PVA into poster paint) Dylon Paint brushes Bucket for soaking Dryer or iron	**www.thatartistwoman. org/2008/07/kid-friendly-batik. html** **www.youtube.com/ watch?v=8hi3cG4RxNE** **www.youtube.com/ watch?v=ohJxPCte_FM** **www.auntannie.com/ SurfaceDesign/CrayonBatik/**	Glue batik Flour batik Hot wax batik Crayon batik Look at examples of batik from around the world: **www.batikguild.org.uk**
Decoupage	Collage material, images and photos Scissors/craft knife Tweezers Foam Wooden support or old furniture, etc. Glue Glue brushes Varnish	**www.thecraftcorner.co.uk/how-to-3d-decoupage-1-w.asp**	Foam pads as a support for decoupage can be a good way to introduce children to this craft technique.
Felt-making	Towel Bamboo place mat Netting Washing up liquid Soap Cloth Wool fibre	**www.youtube.com/ watch?v=jNMs2LSXq70**	It looks satisfyingly simple on this tutorial.

Flower pressing	Flowers Heavy books Flower press	www.funnyhowflowersdothat.co.uk/pressing-flowers www.redtedart.com/how-to-press-flowers	Look at examples of historic festivals, where flowers are used to decorate, such as Derbyshire's Well-Dressing, www.projectbritain.com/welldressing
Fusing fabrics and applique	Fabric swatches Plastics and netting, such as fruit sacks PVA glue Needles Threads Paint Scrim Baking parchment Iron	www.colouricious.com/?v=79cba1185463	This website is a huge resource of textile artists to look at and inspiring ideas for textile projects. There are excellent video tutorials of the different techniques, which show demonstrations in a clear way. www.thespruce.com/quilting-4127498
Knitting and crochet	Knitting needles Yarn	www.learn2knit.co.uk/howtoknit.php	Take your time by following the written instructions; crochet instructions are on a separate tab.
		www.youtube.com/watch?v=jTAV-S7Ziys	Learn along with the video tutorial.
Knotting	Yarn, cord, string, etc. Beads Twigs, etc.	www.free-macrame-patterns.com/learn-macrame.html	This website shows you a huge range of knotty designs for making macramé.
		www.youtube.com/watch?v=nN9mWxPAkZM	This simple video shows you exactly how to create a range of knots.

(Continued)

Table 4.5.1 (Continued)

Craft and making techniques	Resources needed	Instructions/online tutorials	Notes
Metal and wood	Wire Copper Embossing tools Foil Wire cutters Soft wood Sandpaper Willow withies Seagrass Tape Hacksaw Hammer Nails Safety wear	**www.artistshelpingchildren.org/ metaltincansartscraftsideaskids. html** **www.artistshelpingchildren. org/artscraftsideaskids/ woodworking-techniques.html**	Look at the work of designer Thomas Heatherwick **www.heatherwick.com** Contemporary making and design artists: **www.themaking.org.uk/index.html**
Pottery and clay: hand-building	See Table 4.4.1 on page 105 for a list of resources and information for clay work.	**www.lakesidepottery.com/ HTML%20Text/Methods%20 of%20Handbuilding.htm** **ceramicartsdaily.org** **www.claygroundcollective.org**	
Paper craft Papier mache		**www.craftideas.com/how-tos/paper/2012/summer/ paper-crafting-techniques.html** **www.favecrafts.com/Techniques/19-Paper-Craft-Techniques** **www.instructables.com/id/ How-to-make-a-Paper-Craft-Paper-Craft-Basic-Techni** **www.mexican-folk-art-guide.com/ papier-mache.html#.WBIhEaOZOqA**	There are many examples of papier mache crafts from around the world. Have a look at Mexican folk art for inspiration.

Stitching and embroidery	Binka fabric/sacking/canvas/hessian Fabric swatches Needles Threads	**www.dmccreative.co.uk/ Education/How-To/Stitching- Guides/Embroidery-Stitches.aspx www.thesewingdirectory.co.uk/ embroidery-stitches**	Look at examples of American quilting: www.allpeoplequilt.com/magazines- more/american-patchwork-and-quilting
Tie-dye	White cotton squares/t-shirt/pillow cases, etc. Procion dyes Buckets Scissors Fixative, such as salt Gloves Elastic bands or plastic string Pegs and drying line Rags for mopping up spills	**www.instructables.com/id/ How-to-tie-dye-an-old-white- shirt-or-a-new-shirt- www.ritstudio.com/techniques/ creative-techniques/how-to-tie- dye-using-the-bucket-method**	
Up-cycling	Old clothes and fabrics Buttons and beads Scissors Needles and cotton Unwanted furniture and household items Joining materials such as PVA, staples, tape, etc.	**www.upcyclethat.com/dog- sculptures/6583**	Teach children about sustainability and recycling. Cut old clothing into pieces and join them up in unconventional ways: use sleeves for a scarf, cut trousers to make them into a skirt, make a skirt into a hat. Use tightly twisted plastic bags, fashioned electrical wire, etc. to create bangles, necklaces and other types of jewellery.

(Continued)

Table 4.5.1 (Continued)

Craft and making techniques	Resources needed	Instructions/online tutorials	Notes
Weaving	**Paper strip weaving** **Plastic bag rugs** Plastic bags Large rubbish bags or sturdy ribbon Rectangular piece of cardboard a little larger than the size of rug you wish to make. Metre stick Pencil Scissors **Weaving on a loom** Cardboard Scissors Ruler Yarn Plastic large eye needle Masking tape Beads and button Twigs	**www.youtube.com/watch?v=GOKN4L2Axg4** **www.youtube.com/watch?v=eX_E4qiecVE** **www.thriftyfun.com/tf517076.tip.html** **www.artbarblog.com/create/weaving-kids** **www.instructables.com/id/how-to-weave-on-a-cardboard-loom** **www.youtube.com/watch?v=-ByYJ5G4-Hc** **www.craftstylish.com/item/2546/how-to-weave-on-a-cardboard-loom/page/all**	There are many different materials that can be used for weaving, including paper and recycled plastics. Cut, plait and twist old clothing or other flexible materials, such as bubble wrap or cellophane to create more choice for using in the weavings. Look at weaving in a historical context, as well as in other areas of the world, where there is a rich tradition and a strong economic value: **www.silk-road.com/artl/silkhistory.shtml** **www.wildtussah.com/history-weaving-2/** **www.weavedesign.eu/weaving-history** There are many ways of creating your own piece of fabric or beautiful textile hanging. Add in beads, buttons, sparkly materials or tinsel, or natural materials to make these into highly original artworks.
Yarn wrapping	Yarn Sticks or twigs	**www.auntannie.com/FridayFun/GodsEye** **www.hodgepodgecraft.com/gorgeous-yarn-craft-wrapped-sticks**	Learn about traditional crafts of world cultures.

4.6

New media and technology

Introduction

For many contemporary artists, the way forward in art and design is to embrace and engage with the digital world, which in some ways seems in opposition to the philosophy of crafters, traditionalists and makers. Technology, science and the digital world, however, are intrinsically intertwined with fundamental art and design principles. Through art and design, there are so many expressions of scientific and technological advances that this book could not even scratch the surface with examples. The important thing for us to remember here is that science and art are finely tuned into one another and should not be seen as separate entities, as they are often portrayed in educational terms. The worlds of science, technology and art and design cross over at many levels, and links should not be underestimated in relation to the status of each of the subjects. Nicky Morgan, Secretary of State for Education in England from 2014–16, made it clear that she believed that the two areas of arts and science were far apart, and attempted to discourage young people from taking arts subjects by claiming that pupils were 'held back' by focusing on arts instead of maths and science (Garner, 2014). I wonder what Leonardo da Vinci would have thought of that? This great master of the Renaissance was a scientist, mathematician and an artist. He is certainly known for his art today but, in fact, he was an inventor and a visionary: we know this through the example of his designs for a helicopter, long before humans had even imagined the possibility of flight. Da Vinci was an anatomist and an explorer and he possessed the most insatiable curiosity that pushed him towards activities that we might think macabre, such as dissecting human bodies in order to find out what they looked like and how they worked; the basis for our understanding of human anatomy today (Sooke, 2013). The drawings he made of these investigations are objects of great beauty, so the aesthetics are equally as important as the information in this circumstance. Advances in science and technology would simply not exist if it was not for imaginative risk takers, creative minds and artistic thinkers to push ideas into reality.

Technology and art

Advances in technology seem unstoppable these days, and how we engage with the world is affected by this drive. Can you imagine what it would be like to be separated from your mobile phone? How do you feel if you leave it at home by mistake? Do you feel as though part of you is missing? I suspect the answer will be 'yes'. Most of us are now used to being instantly connected to our friends and having information at our fingertips all of the time. We are already seeing very young children entering school being able to swipe on a screen, but unable to turn the page of a book. In today's world we are surrounded by technology, our lives are becoming more reliant on the use of digital devices and, as artists are very often ahead of the game when it comes to innovation, it is perhaps not so surprising that there are many instances where the two worlds of art and technology are brought together with extraordinary results.

Reflective exercise

Artist research

You can see examples of these types of innovations by looking at the many TED Talks, which disseminate and celebrate current thinking in technology, entertainment and design. Look at this website to find art and design-related talks.

www.ted.com/talks?sort=newest&topics%5B%5D=Design&topics%5B%5D=art

The IK Prize at Tate was established in 2014 to reward professional development which celebrates the marriage of artistic practice, creativity and digital media. The website is another place you can look for inspiration and see how contemporary artists are embracing the latest technological developments.

www.tate.org.uk/search?q=IK+prize

Look at the research of designer, Maurizio Montalti, who investigates the potential of natural fungi to design sustainable products for the future.

www.dezeen.com/2015/01/21/movie-officina-corpuscoli-growing-products-materials-fungus-biotechnological-revolution

Media artist, Professor Mika Satomi, won the prestigious SMARTS prize in 2016 for her collaboration with designer Professor Wolf Jeschonnek in the EU funded project 'Artificial Skin and Bones', which investigated new aesthetic possibilities for prosthetics. Have a look at the important work that this collaboration has produced.

www.aec.at/aeblog/en/2016/06/23/artificial-skins-and-bones

Reflection point

- Have your perceptions changed in relation to how the practical application and understanding of the processes of art, craft and design impact upon our daily lives and our existence?
- Have you developed an understanding of the close relationship between arts, technologies and science? Can you imagine one existing without the other?
- Reflect upon what the future might hold for the children in your class, or those you have met on placements: do you understand why education in art, craft and design will be an essential part of their learning to help prepare them for that future?

New media in schools

New technologies have impacted on every area of the school curriculum, including art and design. Change has occurred at a rapid pace: as recently as 2000 one art education textbook suggested that every primary school 'should have a computer and a camera'. Today there are more computers than classrooms, as many tablets as tables and, by the time they reach Year 6, few children will need to borrow that school camera; they're too busy snapping away on their smartphones and sharing images on social media, and more likely to be designing PowerPoints than mixing powder paints.

The extent to which digital technologies have become part of children's everyday lives was difficult to predict and is impossible to underestimate. It's widely perceived that children's everyday experience of ICT means that they are more tuned in to technology than their teachers: *You can't teach ICT any more*, one Year 6 teacher recently told me, *you can only facilitate it*. So if children are already so computer-literate, why should teachers still strive to incorporate new technologies into their art lessons? What are the aims and purposes of ICT in the art curriculum and how can children learn about art and design through ICT? This section explores these questions and concludes with a selection of practical activities for children in Key Stages 1 and 2.

Why use ICT in art and design?

While we're all aware that young people can easily become glued to computers, the increasing use of small-screen devices means that we're more uncertain than ever about what it is they are actually doing. The chances are that it's several things at once. That ten-year-old slumped on the sofa is probably ploughing through a chapter of the latest *Artemis Fowl* adventure, while simultaneously FaceTiming their friends and listening to Taylor Swift. But while it's true that children are often confident users of computers, there is a danger that they can too easily become passive consumers of technology, rather than active makers. ICT activities in art and design can help to address this issue by taking advantage of children's love of new technologies while offering them opportunities to problem-solve, experiment and explore possible solutions.

Structuring learning

The main thing that we as teachers need to remember is to set children a balance of specific and open-ended tasks. Just as we might begin a sequence of art lessons by encouraging children to explore paint or clay, we can let them begin exploring art and design software in a similarly unstructured way. Some will already have experience of certain programs and will want to remind themselves of the basics, while others will be impatient to make a mark on their screen. Either way, it's good to allow them a little time to play, but set aside a limited time for such exploratory activities. If you have ever casually experimented with an art and design program such as Photoshop, you'll have found it relatively easy to create interesting patterns, effects and compositions. You may also have found that, having squiggled the cursor across the screen a few times to create these effects, it can be difficult to develop your ideas in a purposeful way. Left alone for too long, children often resort to scribbling digital sketches of familiar cartoon characters, in much the same way that they might on a piece of scrap paper, before losing interest, motivation and direction. Paradoxically, the fact that computers offer almost endless options for experimentation makes it very difficult for children to decide what to do next.

It's at this point that the teacher needs to step in with a precise plan. By setting specific art and design tasks in ICT we can encourage children to problem-solve, to think about the effects they want to achieve and to decide which tools and resources they will need to achieve their aims. In order to plan for such experiences, it's helpful to reflect on the ways in which the curriculum for ICT, or 'computing' as it is now referred to, reinforces and extends learning in art and design.

Visual elements

A useful way to begin to think about the connections between the two subjects is to reflect on the visual elements of art and design that are common to all artworks: line, tone, colour, texture, form, shape and space (see Chapter 2). Each of these elements (with the exception of form, which describes three-dimensional objects) can play a role in digital artwork. You might, for example, challenge children to concentrate on linear patterns by drawing twisting lines across their screens that overlap to create complex compositions; or you might encourage them to design repeated patterns of regular shapes, exploring the negative shapes that emerge from the spaces in between them; you might provide opportunities for them to explore combinations of lighter and darker tones and colours. Children can even experiment with creating 'textures' on the screen by layering marks and patterns (we call these 'implied' textures: they look rough but feel smooth).

Visual language

ICT also reinforces learning in art and design by borrowing subject-specific imagery and terminology. Much of the language we use in 'real' art lessons can also be used in digital art lessons and it's important to relate what children do in ICT to the paintings, drawings and collages that they will have made previously. When children see an icon on a screen that represents a pencil, paintbrush or paint bucket, they should be able to anticipate how they might experiment with the tool. For example, it won't take children long to notice that the software offers them options for using each tool in a different way. They could begin by varying the size of the brush they 'paint' with, before experimenting with different levels of opacity of colour, in much the same way that they would try adding water to paint to make it more translucent. Similarly, by the time they reach Key Stage 2, children should be familiar with some of the commands that are common to various software packages, such as 'file', 'edit', 'copy', 'paste', etc.; it's useful to remind children that, even if an art and design software package looks a little intimidating, they bring a range of existing knowledge and skills in ICT to the experience.

Practicalities

Having started children off with some open-ended, exploratory tasks teachers should then help children to progress on to more structured activities. If you're fortunate enough to be teaching in a well-resourced room with multiple PCs, begin by instructing children to log on to their PC and open the software package you'll be using. Your subject leader for computing should be able to advise you on which software options are available to you. The activities that follow assume you're using Photoshop, but there are some free online equivalents that feature a similar range of tools and functions and some activities can be completed on even the most primitive of painting programs.

Teaching strategies

Whichever activity you try, there are one or two things to bear in mind from the start of the lesson. First, once your children have successfully logged on and are ready to start, ask them to switch their monitors off. It's a sad truth that however interesting a teacher you may be, you'll never be as interesting as a computer. If children have a screen to look at then they'll look at it rather than you. Second, once you have everyone's attention, demonstrate the beginning of the activity on your interactive whiteboard. Go through each step slowly and ask children to describe what you are doing, before repeating the demonstration more quickly, this time asking individuals to guide you through each step. Alternatively, ask one or two children to demonstrate and provide a running commentary on each step they take. Third, it may be that some children will appreciate a written reminder of the steps they need to take; however, as is the case with most art and design activities, most children find that it's better to learn through *doing*.

Practical activities: have a go!

Here are three sequences of lessons for you to experiment with and to use with the children in your class. The activities are aimed at Key Stage 2 (though you'll see some aspects are accessible to younger children) and are designed to build upon children's previous experiences of the traditional art processes of drawing, painting, printmaking and collage. The lessons also offer children opportunities to explore three visual themes (composition, repetition and juxtaposition), in ways that will help them to realise the rewards of a partnership between art and design, and ICT.

Practical activity

Composition

Composition is best described as 'the way things are put together', and effective compositions often feature a range of shapes and forms that help to create a sense of balance and depth. Here are some guidelines to help children to make digital compositions of each other in 'action' poses.

- During a games lesson or break time, use a digital camera to capture shots of your classmates 'in action': playing football, basketball, etc.
- Load the images onto a PC and select those you think capture your classmates' movements in the most dynamic ways. Now you'll need to remove the backgrounds to isolate the figures.
- In Photoshop, use the 'lasso' tool to trace carefully around each figure on the screen: if you find this challenging, try removing sections of the background one at a time to leave the figure standing alone, then 'edit' and 'copy' the figure.
- Head online to locate an image (covered by Creative Commons licence) that will provide a background for your composition, e.g. a stadium. Make sure the image is relatively large (more than 500MB) and save it to your PC.

(Continued)

(Continued)

- With your 'background' image open, 'paste' the figure you copied from your photograph. You'll need to locate the 'transform' tool to adjust the scale of the figure in relation to the background (try holding 'ctrl' and pressing 'T').
- Create a dynamic composition by adding more figures. Experiment with the relative size of each figure in order to create a sense of space in your composition and finish by 'flattening' the layers of the image: this will enable you to use the image in other applications.

Practical activity

Repetition

Art and design software offers opportunities for quickly creating complex patterns. The first activity makes use of the most basic of 'paint' programs and can be completed by younger children, while the second is designed to challenge older children to experiment with more complex patterns.

It might seem strange to begin an ICT lesson by heading back to the twelfth century, but the patterns created by medieval craftsmen are a great source of inspiration for digital designs. The British Museum has a wonderful collection of tiles collected from sites such as Rievaulx Abbey in North Yorkshire, while New York's Metropolitan Museum features a range of Islamic designs on its website: **www.metmuseum.org/toah/hd/geom/hd_geom.htm**

Key Stage 1

Paint is the simplest of art software programs, yet it offers young children opportunities to quickly create some interesting patterns.

- Begin by selecting a colour and using the 'rectangle' tool to create a rectangle, before choosing a new colour and using the 'polygon' tool to create a triangle (when children are a little more confident they can create further shapes, but begin by limiting them to these two).

Figures 4.6.1 and 4.6.2

- Now click and drag the 'select' tool over the two shapes, go to 'edit' and select 'copy' then 'paste'. The copied shapes will appear in the top left corner of the screen.
- The shapes can be dragged around the screen into a new place: they can also be rotated or flipped by using the 'image' option at the top of the screen.
- Once children are confident with these operations they can experiment with making the pattern more complex. Remind them that they can save different versions of their images to demonstrate how they have explored different options.

 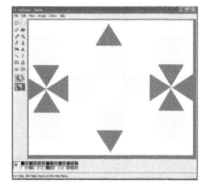

Figures 4.6.3 and 4.6.4

Key Stage 2

Older children will enjoy experimenting with options for image manipulation which are offered by software programs such as Photoshop.

- Use the 'image' function of a search engine to locate an image of a hexagon; save it as a new file then create a second file of a larger size.
- Copy and paste the hexagon into the larger file so that it has plenty of space around it, then use the 'paint bucket' tool to fill the shape with colour.
- Next use the 'rectangular marquee tool' to draw a rectangle above the hexagon and fill it with another colour.
- Now make sure that you can see the 'layers' palette, then go to the 'layers' menu at the top of the screen and duplicate the 'rectangle' layer. This will give you a second rectangle, though you won't be able to see it until you move it away from the first one.
- Hold 'ctrl' and 'T' on the keyboard and you will see that you can now rotate this layer around. Rotate it and place it on another side of the hexagon, then repeat until you have six rectangles. You can use the arrow keys on your keyboard to fine-tune the placement of the shapes.

(Continued)

(Continued)

 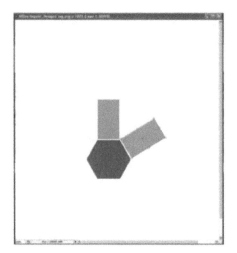

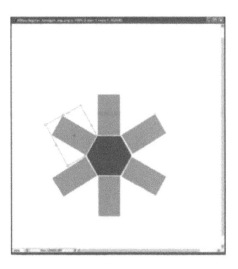

Figures 4.6.5, 4.6.6 and 4.6.7

- Next, use the 'polygonal lasso' tool to draw a triangle in between two of the rectangles, fill it with another colour then do the same as you did before to create five more identical triangles, each placed between two rectangles.
- Now go to the 'layer' menu and 'flatten' your image: this means you can now select all the layers at once.

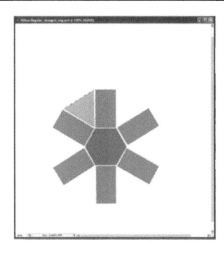 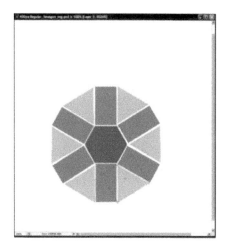

Figures 4.6.8 and 4.6.9

- Use the 'polygonal lasso' tool to trace around the whole of your design, then 'copy' and 'paste' it, moving it to a new place. Do this several times and experiment with creating a range of repeated and overlapping patterns.
- Finally, you can quickly change the colours of the design by using the 'image'/'adjustment'/ 'hue & saturation' options on the main menu at the top of the screen.

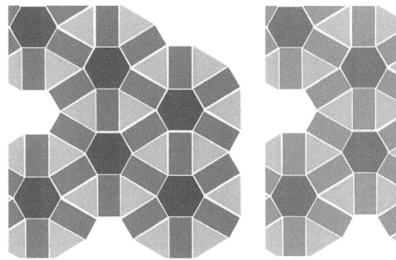 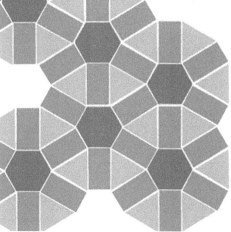

Figures 4.6.10 and 4.6.11

(Continued)

(Continued)

Extension

Once you're confident with the tools, you can explore countless other combinations of shapes, colours and patterns: imagine how much longer it would have taken twelfth-century tilers to complete their designs!

Practical activity

Juxtaposition

This lesson is inspired by the work of artist John Stezaker, who creates intriguing juxtapositions of facial features: **www.saatchigallery.co.uk/artists/john_stezaker.htm**

Children will need to work in pairs for the activity, each with their own portrait photograph uploaded to a PC.

- Begin by photographing your partner: choose someone who looks really different to you. Take several pictures of each other and upload them to your PC.
- Choose the two portraits you like the best and open them in Photoshop. Use the 'lasso' tool to select half of one of the portraits; you could try 'slicing' the image straight down the middle, or experimenting with curved lines. 'Edit' and 'copy' this part of the image.
- Move on to the second portrait and 'paste' your selection on top of it. You should now be able to see half of one face and half of the other, though you may need to move one layer around and experiment with changing its scale.
- In order for the juxtaposition to be really effective you'll find you need to experiment with different photos to find the most striking combination.

Extension

Older children can extend this idea by juxtaposing images from different sources. Trace the images as described above, then use the 'brightness' and 'contrast' features to reduce them to silhouettes and combine them into a single image.

Further reading

LDOnline, 'Integrating the arts with technology: inspiring creativity'.

National Center for Technology Innovation and Center for Implementing Technology in Education (CITEd) available at: **www.ldonline.org/article/30245**

Find out all about Leonardo da Vinci: **www.leonardodavinci.net**

Discover recent events in the world of technology: **www.nesta.org.uk/project/digital-arts-and-culture-accelerator**

Process and practice: conclusion

Professional development

I hope you will plan to use each section of this chapter for staff development and training over an extended period in your school. As staff changes occur within a school, it is important to keep revisiting the different processes, so that staff skills and good practice are maintained. At the time of writing there is a renewed interest by OFSTED in examining the purposefulness of non-core subject areas, and your school development plan should reflect the possibility that an inspection will investigate learning that is taking place in art and design. By planning strategic staff development, that covers the processes and practicalities in this chapter, you will be well on your way to providing excellent teaching and learning in this subject. There are many ways that you can continue to develop your skills and knowledge, some of which are mentioned in the Further reading in each section, and there will be more information for you on how to do this in Chapter 6.

Chapter summary

This chapter has essentially been a guide to get you started with knowledge of the basic processes, materials and techniques that you will find most useful for teaching art and design in primary schools. We have underpinned this with theory that highlights different 'ways of knowing' that is facilitated by practical activity. We have situated practical work in art and design within the theoretical context of experiential learning, and developing children's procedural and tacit knowledge. As you develop in skills and confidence, you will be able to extend and expand your own knowledge and understanding of these processes by experimenting with, and developing, some of the ideas you have found here. In the next chapter, we shall explore the nuts and bolts of planning and assessment so that you can transfer the knowledge you have gained so far straight to the classroom. Before we move on, though, I have one more treat for you. Let me introduce you to sculptor, Al Johnson, who we have already met in the section on 3D and the material world. She shares her experiences of being an artist throughout this book: she is, in a way, our artist-in-residence. This will help you to see aspects of art and design learning from another perspective and, in this section, she discusses her use of materials and techniques, with a focus on using found objects.

Case study

Al Johnson

Discussions about sculpture often focus on materials and techniques, perhaps because the media and systems of sculpture are less familiar than those of painting. The question most often asked of sculptors is 'how did you do that?' You can consider how sculpture is made, and then translate this into practical sessions in the classroom to develop brilliant experiences that will be unique for many children. Most children love to learn new hands-on skills, particularly if there is an element of perceived risk. They are often happy to wait in line for the thrill of (supervised) use of a glue gun, or for the delight of sawing up sections of wood with a tenon saw.

The range of materials available to sculptors has increased exponentially. Traditional sculpture materials were limited to those that could be carved, like wood and stone, those that could be

(Continued)

(Continued)

modelled, like clay and wax, and those that could be poured into moulds, like bronze. Sculptural materials now include plastics, rubbers, a huge range of metals, including welded and forged steel, textiles and found objects. Many contemporary sculptures combine a range of techniques and materials. My installation, *Land of Laundries*, combines traditional media, recycled materials and found objects. The work is a consideration of the theories, superstitions and stories that seem to have developed in order to assess the skills and personality of the laundress. The work has seven pairs of arms trapped in pillories, each engaged in a single task: soaping, pegging and folding. The arms are plaster life casts of my own arms, and the pillories are constructed from timber benches discarded by a swimming pool. The white linen that links the arms was gathered from charity shops and markets and is embroidered with superstitions and anecdotes.

The idea of the found object (real objects being reused in sculpture) is now so commonplace that we hardly question it. Picasso added handlebars to a bicycle seat to make the sculpture, *Bulls Head*. You might collect objects in the school or playground and alter the way they are perceived: a yard broom can become a giant's tooth brush; a pencil can draw a line, but if you put enough pencils end to end, can they be a line? What objects can be changed temporarily: Wrap a broom up in pink shiny satin and question, is it still a broom, or is it made functionless? The surrealist, Méret Oppenheim, covered a teacup, saucer and spoon in gazelle fur in 1936. It still has the form of a tea-cup, saucer and spoon, but you can't use it, so maybe it has become something else entirely.

The art world was scandalised when in 1915 the French artist, Marcel Duchamp, bought a new snow shovel from the local hardware shop, hung it in his studio and renamed it, In Advance of the Broken Arm. Perhaps young children, happily creating junk sculpture from discarded cartons glued together and painted, are benefitting from Duchamp's radical approach to what sculpture can be.

Figure 4.0.3 Land of Laundries: plaster life casts, timber and embroidered textiles.

5

Planning, assessment and progression

Chapter objectives

This chapter will help you to:

- Understand planning, teaching and assessment in relation to content, skills and knowledge development.
- Understand how to plan age appropriate, progressive art and design experiences for children.
- Differentiate for individual and special needs.
- Understand what is meant by mastery of the subject.
- Ensure pupil progression in art, craft and design.

The following standards especially apply within this chapter.

4. Plan and teach well structured lessons.
5. Adapt teaching to respond to the strengths and needs of all pupils.
6. Make accurate and productive use of assessment.
7. Manage behaviour effectively to ensure a good and safe learning environment.

Introduction

Throughout this book we have journeyed towards deepening your understanding of what is so special about learning in and through art, craft and design. Through the reports, research evidence, theoretical perspectives and case studies that you have encountered so far, you have hopefully developed a real understanding of the rich variety and great value of the subject. We have looked at embedding principles for good learning, and in this chapter we shall see how to apply those principles to ensure that the children you teach are offered high quality art and design education through well focused planning, teaching and assessment strategies.

In this chapter, we shall consider how to plan well and how to organise learning in art and design; this will give you more weaponry for creating space in the curriculum, so that sufficient time is allocated and children are given the opportunity for deep learning in this area. Planning and assessment for art and design can often appear to have a slightly different look from other subjects, and this is because the intrinsic qualities of the subject are a bit different from all of the other subjects that you will teach. To expand on this point, we shall explore the inclusive nature of the subject. We shall look at ways to enable you to provide learning opportunities in art that can be easily accessed by children of all abilities and needs, at their own levels. You will also need to have a good understanding of what assessments to make. This is key to ensuring progression for each child, so that children leave primary school feeling enthusiastic about the subject and confident in their own capabilities.

Time allocations for art and design

Ensuring quality means that we need to plan and teach art experiences that build upon one another over a period of time in a sustained way. This can be difficult to achieve for some schools where the pressure is on to raise attainment in core subjects alone. Art and design is often one of the subjects that loses out to external pressures, as we have already discussed, so the skills, competencies and knowledge that are outlined in the previous chapter (Processes and practice) are sometimes taught rather superficially. This is especially true where art is planned into the curriculum as a bit of a treat, for example as something that might happen on a Friday afternoon, if and when children have 'worked' hard all week, or as part of a movement in schools known as 'golden time' (and only then if children are seen as deserving enough). It is not unknown for children who need a boost in subjects such as English and maths to be withdrawn from art (and other curriculum areas) for additional input in those core subjects, which means that they often miss key learning in the social, creative, emotionally and physically engaging activities that art and design can provide for them. Arrangements such as these also risk promoting a non-inclusive ethos, as children can miss out on being able to complete their artwork if they are withdrawn from class at a time when everyone else is doing just that. Equally, they might be excluded from golden time for a variety of reasons, but it is often exactly those children who most need the kind of education that gives them new ways to communicate and express themselves, which is made possible through the language of art.

Sometimes learning in art and design is squashed into a week's worth of activities, known as an 'art week': this might happen in the summer, after exams have been completed. Although compressing learning into one week can allow teachers to plan exciting activities and experiences for a dedicated period of time, this method of organisation for the art curriculum does not provide children with the slow and steady progression of skills and understanding that they need. Art weeks, therefore, work best when they are planned *in addition* to normal subject time across the three terms of the year.

These scenarios show how strategic planning for whole-school organisation of art and design is necessary to ensure children's entitlement to a broad and balanced curriculum is fulfilled, and that progression in skills and knowledge is developed over time.

═══ Case study ═══

Kath is the head teacher of a one-form entry primary school in an urban area on the outskirts of a large city. The catchment area is such that the demographic is very mixed in terms of children's ethnicity and social status, with 12 per cent of children eligible for free school dinners. Kath is conscious of the fact that although, as individuals, children make fantastic progress during their time in her school, this is not always reflected well in SATs results, and she admits that she feels under immense pressure to focus learning towards the core subjects in her organisation of whole-school planning. She says: *The trouble is it's just no good forcing children to learn in only a few key areas; they have to have a well-rounded education, and at our school we want our children to have the best and most enjoyable experiences within their learning. That means showing them new ways of looking at things, being able to solve problems and being creative.*

Kath, in her fourth year as a head and having taught in primary schools for 20 years, is firm in her belief that art and design will not be sidelined under her management. She structures whole-school planning to include art and design, taught as both a discrete subject and through links with other subject areas. Kath states: *I know many colleagues who bow under the strain of ensuring constant improvement in league table results, but we must be mindful of children who will be growing up into a world that we can't predict, and they are going to need skills and understanding that will allow them to function in that world. Visual literacy, to my mind, is the skill they are going to need in the future: in fact they need it right now! Learning in art and design brings a multitude of transferable skills to children's development and this is why we prioritise the subject in my school.*

═══ Reflection point ═══

- How is the art and design curriculum organised in your school, or what planning structures have you come across in your placement experiences?
- Have you observed art and design being taught by other teachers? How did those lessons resonate with your own principles and values for good practice?
- What examples of class planning for art and design have you seen? Did the planning account for children's original ideas and creativity?

Analysis

It is important to take a critical look at your past and current experiences of art and design teaching in schools, so that you can start to decide what is good and, conversely, what is not so useful for teaching and learning in this subject area. You might raise questions about the development of children's skills and knowledge, which ideally should progress slowly and steadily. If, for example, the subject only shows up once a year as an 'art week', this cannot happen.

You might now be able to think critically about practice where outcomes are predetermined, or driven by the need to fill a display board. By now, you should have started to develop a strong justification and rationale for creative and open-ended practice, and for maintaining a place for the subject in your teaching timetable.

Get organised!

Before you make decisions about what will be on your plan, it is essential for you to consider the broad structure of how you will teach it. Each school will have their own long-, medium- and short-term planning design, and a good one will ensure that children cover all of the processes over each key stage or phase of learning, as well as meeting a wide range of work by different artists, craftspeople and designers. They should also be offered opportunities to experience different genres from the world of art.

Stages of planning

Planning in art and design is just the same as other subjects, in that the learning is split over a period of time into palatable chunks. Units of work are defined by topic or theme, and then broken down into project work.

Long-term plans are usually the domain of the art subject leader in a school, who can plot experiences across the years to ensure children have a full coverage of the art curriculum. Where there is strong and effective subject leadership in a school, the art co-ordinator will usually be more than happy to assist class teachers in developing medium- and short-term plans.

Medium-term plans are those that stretch across a term or half a term, so these are very important for structuring learning across and within a project.

Short-term plans are more detailed weekly, daily or individual lesson plans, depending on your individual requirements, but these are essential for becoming well organised (especially in the early stages of becoming a primary teacher). You can use short-term plans to:

- make lists for resources that you will need;
- plan timings for different events within the lesson;
- write a few key questions to keep the learning well focused: make bullet points of these for quick and easy access;
- note key vocabulary that you want to introduce or use;
- make notes regarding individual children who might need specific interventions;
- evaluate children's learning;
- design next steps for learning.

If you are a student or trainee teacher it is likely that you will also need to make a note of related teaching standards on your plans.

Practical activity

Structure learning for a medium-term plan

- Use the diagram in Chapter 3 (Figure 3.6, page 58) which explains the stages that contribute to the learning journey. You can use these to help you break your project into manageable, progressive 'chunks' over a few sessions or lessons.
- Have a look at the diagram in the same chapter, which shows the basic elements of subject content of 'Materials, Processes, Visual Elements and Contextual Understanding' (Figure 3.5, page 57). Think about how the features of the learning journey that you will plan can be included at points during each session.

The 2014 National Curriculum is underpinned by four key aims, which are clearly related to subject content, as outlined here.

1. Materials

Aim: exploring ideas and recording experiences to produce creative work.

2. Processes

Aim: gain competence in art, craft and design processes and techniques.

3. Visual elements

Aim: review and evaluate work using the unique language of art, craft and design.

4. Contextual understanding

Aim: know about artists, craft makers and designers and their historical, cultural and social contexts.

- Draw or create a map using the progressive stages of the learning journey, together with the elements of subject content, that will enable you to plan an art and design project over a series of lessons, from beginning to end. Alternatively, use the following medium-term plan template in Table 5.1 to help you plot out the learning over a few sessions.

Once you have decided upon your medium-term plan it will be easy to divide up the learning into separate sessions: for example, over a five- or six-week period, or over a week or a few days. The sessions you have outlined on this plan can then be broken down further into smaller units.

A single lesson plan (see Figure 5.1) will help you to keep learning focused, especially if you are teaching something for the first time, or feeling a bit unsure of how the lesson will turn out.

(Continued)

(Continued)

Table 5.1 Medium-term planning model

Art and Design: Medium term planning			Term:			Year/Class:		
Topic:			Teacher:					
Week/ Session / **Stage of learning**	**1** Provocation and ideas: RESEARCH/ PLAN/ SKETCH	**2** ↑	**3** Making and processes: EXPLORE AND EXPERIMENT	**4** ↑	**5** Review and evaluate: EDIT/ADD/ CHANGE/ DEVELOP	**6** →Display and celebrate	**SEND/EAL/ Individual Differentiation**	**NOTES**
Learning aims: Skills and concepts								
Techniques								
Contextual examples								
Materials and resources								
Assessment opportunities								
Notes								

Use the following single lesson planning sheet to double check that you have everything you need for a successful art and design lesson. The circular format should help you to keep Kolb's 'experiential learning cycle' in mind at each stage of your project (see Chapter 4, Figure 4.0.1).

Term/Date:	Sequence in scheme: (e.g. three of six)	Title of session:	Prior learning:
Timescale: (e.g. two hours)	Organisation: (e.g. group/ individual/pairs etc.)	Scale of work: (e.g. large/small)	Teacher Standards:

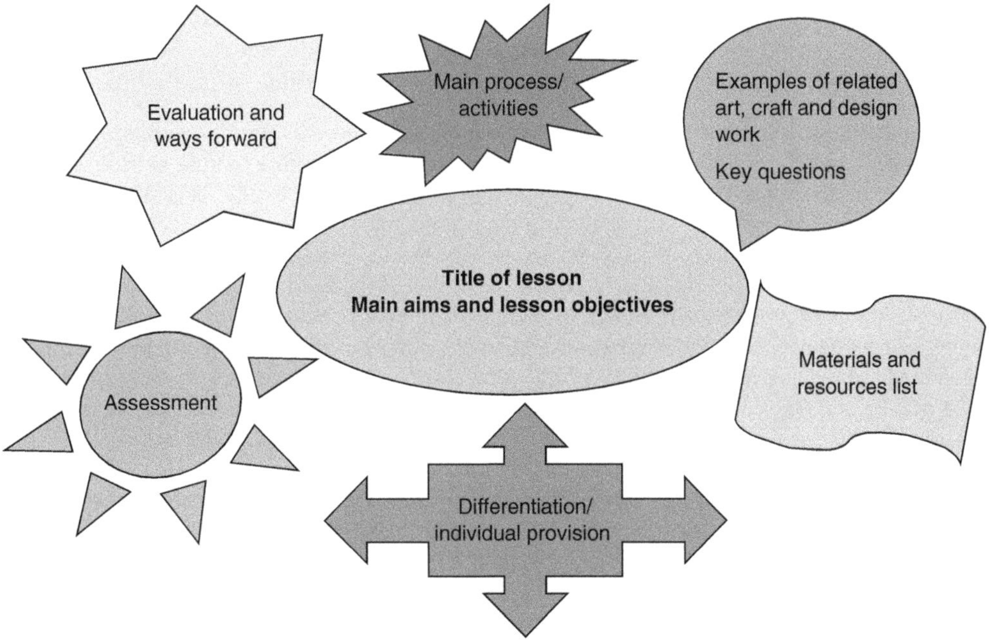

Evaluation and ways forward

Main process/ activities

Examples of related art, craft and design work

Key questions

Title of lesson
Main aims and lesson objectives

Materials and resources list

Assessment

Differentiation/ individual provision

Figure 5.1 *Single lesson plan design template.*

Choosing what to teach

There are as many topics and themes to choose from as there are artists to look at. Sometimes it can feel a bit overwhelming to decide upon what you might teach over the course of a year, a term, or even a short placement. It is usually a good idea to link artwork to current learning in other subjects so that children are able to transfer learning across different domains, as well as make the connections that we know exist. For example, if you are teaching about resistant materials in science and DT, you might devise a project that incorporates a process such as batik, so that children can see how this works on a practical level. (You could have a look at Chapter 7 for further inspiration in relation to learning in and through other subjects.)

Termly topic themes can be a useful starting point for developing art and design ideas, as many schools organise the curriculum by a rolling programme of 'big' topics over a period of time, such as a year or two. These types of topics tend to be open to interpretation, so are therefore good for developing enquiry-led processes. You might find topic examples such as space, identity, eco-warriors, endangered animals, superheroes, etc., lend themselves well to learning in creative subjects such as art.

―――― Theory focus ―――――――――――――――――――――――――――

Funds of knowledge

Once you get to know your children well it will be easy to devise art projects that they will be excited by and respond to in a positive way. González et al. (2005) advocate that we use children's 'funds of knowledge' to create situations that will facilitate good learning.

But what are funds of knowledge? This is a term that was introduced by Norma González, Luis Moll and Cathy Amanti, and it is significant because it advocates that teachers can use children's existing knowledge and home life experiences, which they have gained from their families and cultural backgrounds, to make learning in school more meaningful and inclusive. The researchers worked with disaffected school children in Mexico who were seen as disadvantaged and low achievers. By observing the children in their home environment, they discovered that these children had an enormous range of practical skills and a vastly underestimated depth of understanding in terms of literacy, mathematics, scientific concepts and creative areas of learning. The school curriculum was found to be inappropriate for this group of children's learning needs, as its aim was geared towards narrowing their learning to fit into a conventional system: their own life experiences were not appreciated or valued to achieve this aim. The children who were observed by the researchers could think quickly and make instant decisions. They were proficient at mental maths, and able to recognise a good deal when they saw one. They were able to understand the environment and how to work the land to their advantage. The researchers discovered many of the household objects, artefacts, types of food, clothing, festivals and traditions that were familiar to the children and their families could be utilised back in the classroom to facilitate feelings of self-esteem and value within the group. All this research is enormously valuable to us because it highlights how we can so easily make assumptions about the capabilities of children we are teaching; especially those who do not conform to our expected norms. It is also relevant because it demonstrates that we should consider children's funds of knowledge as factors when planning topics, so that children themselves will feel a personal investment in the work, rather than always imposing topics or themes that we assume they will find interesting.

National priorities: safeguarding and behaviour management

A key aim of the DfE's 'Strategy 2015–2020 World-class education and care' is one *that allows every child and young person to reach his or her potential, regardless of background*, as stated by former Secretary of State for Education, Nicky Morgan (2015). In order to reach their potential in art and design you will have to establish some firm rules around how children behave in the art classroom, and do this with the children themselves so that they 'own' the rules. We have already discussed how art lessons can be relaxing and freeing, but this does not mean that you can let go of high standards of good behaviour for learning: in fact, you need to do quite the opposite. The term 'safeguarding', which has become a national priority, links directly into this. OFSTED (2011) states that the definition of this term mirrors Morgan's aim for education and in addition it is noted that reasonable steps should be taken to ensure that children both *are* safe, and *feel* safe. Safety must always come first and by establishing a respectful attitude towards each other, the learning environment, resources and outcomes in terms of artwork, you will teach your children important life skills that feed into the 2015–2020 Strategy for Education's system goals and 12 priority areas. Staying safe is the main reason why behaviour has to be managed in the first place. Behaviour management has been one of OFSTED's national priorities since the 'Importance of teaching' White Paper was published in 2010, but it is perhaps more useful to use the phrase 'behaviour for learning', which allows you to focus more on enabling children to take responsibility for their own behaviour. This 'bottom up' approach for behaviour management sits well alongside the pedagogies and theories we have explored in former chapters. I hope that by providing stimulating and interesting art and design projects, which children are enthusiastic about and motivated to do, you should not have to worry too much about poor behaviour in art lessons, but to be on the safe side you can remind children of the shared rules that underpin behaviour for good learning at the start of every lesson.

For tips on managing children's behaviour, read this article by Paul Dix: **www.theguardian.com/society/joepublic/2010/feb/09/pupil-behaviour-management-tips**

Managing differentiation

Just as in any other subject, you will almost certainly have children in your class who have varying degrees of interest, attainment potential and attitudes towards art and design. Some children will struggle to express their ideas visually and some might exceed all expectations and display great talent and ability; other children will fall somewhere along the line between these two extremes (Tomlinson, 2001). Heise states that within groups of children there are individuals of varying *racial, ethnic, cultural and socio-economic backgrounds; physical, emotional and academic abilities; different dominant languages; with different degrees of parental support, learner styles and preferences, and interests* (2007, p1) and we have to be able to account for some or all of these in any one classroom. So, where do we begin to ensure all learners are valued and challenged within our art and design lessons? It might be comforting to know that art and design is one of the easiest subjects in which to develop an inclusive curriculum, where children have a chance to develop learning at their own pace and to achieve at their own level.

Cultural diversity

Art is an intrinsic part of our human experience: people of every culture have engaged with artistic practice of one kind or another since the beginning of human history. By observing and learning about art from different cultures and around the world, and by planning art projects where children have an opportunity to explore their own identity and cultural backgrounds, you can promote tolerant attitudes and cultural understanding. This type of learning in art and design can be used as a tool to break down prejudices and cultural barriers: it can explode stereotypical ideas and myths in relation to gender, culture and ethnicity by encouraging children to understand others who hold different perspectives on life from their own.

Barriers to learning

Engagement in arts subjects can often give children who are less successful in certain areas of learning an opportunity to achieve well and feel proud of their work. Children who experience physical, social, emotional or academic challenges can be helped to feel enabled, empowered and motivated to participate through inclusive strategies, which you have planned to focus on their individual needs. Children with English as an additional language and non-English speaking children will find that they are able to communicate through visual means, as art has the potential to transcend spoken language barriers.

More able

Page (2010) states that more able learners can become labelled as gifted, talented and creative, but they can equally be criticised as underachieving or as having special needs. Page says that this can be due to schools and teachers being unaware of how to appropriately cater for these learners' needs. Children who display a high ability or talent in art, craft and design are often able to think beyond the limitations of the tasks set: they might find tasks too easy. They might have a natural ability to express themselves and communicate through visual means; they might be able to learn quickly, and adopt new techniques and materials easily; they might have good fine motor skills and show confidence in trying new ideas without fear of failure. These children are likely to achieve a 'mastery' level earlier than others but should be carefully managed so that they are indeed stretched and challenged and not just given more of the same, which might slow their progress or even put them off.

Reflection point

Tomlinson (2001) states that: *At its most basic level, differentiating instruction means 'shaking up' what goes on in the classroom so that students have multiple options for taking in information, making sense of ideas, and expressing what they learn* (2001, p1). It is therefore essential for you to get to know the children in your class on many levels.

Ask yourself the following question in relation to the points below: How well do you know the children in your class ...?

- As individuals, and how they operate within groups?
- What is their learning profile and skills level?
- What is their emotional resilience like?
- What are their physical abilities?
- Do you know about their cultural backgrounds?
- How much do you understand about their personal interests?

By learning about the children and considering these points you have, of course, already begun the assessment process. With good knowledge of the children, both as individuals and as group members, you will be able to devise art projects and lessons that tap into their needs, celebrate their diversity and acknowledge their preferences.

Once you have identified children who will need particular types of support you can use the four key curriculum elements suggested by Tomlinson (2001) of 'Content', 'Process', 'Product' and 'Environment', which could help you to focus the provision in your differentiated curriculum.

Content: this refers to the input, and *what* the main aims for learning are. It can include both practical and intellectual knowledge, as discussed in Chapter 3. You can vary the way you manage your input, whether it is through showing related images, using demonstration, taking children on visits or outside, using technology, etc. Consider how particular individuals will access the way you present the learning to them.

Process: in this context it means *how* children go about making sense of the content. You might, for example, use observation and dialogic strategies to gain a deeper insight into an individual child's responses.

Product: the output, or how children demonstrate their learning. A variety of types of 'products' might appear at different stages of the process, including sketches or unfinished work. Offering a range of processes, materials and techniques for children to explore and experiment with will allow them to apply and demonstrate their learning at all the different stages of a project over a few sessions.

Environment: the learning environment should be a flexible, respectful, safe space that enables inclusive access to resources, and opportunities for collaboration and independence. The learning environment need not be bursting with colourful displays as some children (for example those who have Autism Spectrum Condition) might prefer a non-cluttered or very plain environment in which to work. (See Chapter 1 where we looked at the environment being the 'third teacher'.)

Mastery in art and design

The 2014 National Curriculum for England regards 'mastery' of the subject as a goal for children's achievement. It states that in Key Stage 2, children should:

> *improve their mastery of art and design techniques, including drawing, painting and sculpture with a range of materials [for example, pencil, charcoal, paint, clay].*

(DfE, 2013)

This indicates that children should already be at least some way to being 'masterful' by the end of Key Stage 1. Do you think this actually possible? What does this mean in reality? It certainly does not mean that by the time they arrive in secondary school they should be drawing like Leonardo Da Vinci and painting like Picasso.

A quick look at an online thesaurus shows us that the word 'mastery' equates to attributes such as: finesse; genius; dexterity; proficiency; virtuosity etc.

The Collins English Dictionary (2012) definition of the word says much the same thing:

noun: (pl) masteries

1. Full command or understanding of a subject.

2. Outstanding skill; expertise.

3. The power of command; control.

4. Victory or superiority.

There is a problem here though, as these literal definitions of the term have the potential to distract us from what we know to be good teaching and learning for children in art and design. If we truly value that children should be able to develop their own ideas, experiment and explore, and be free to express themselves visually, how might we be able to specify whether they have mastered the process, or not? The other little difficulty is that we are assuming that there is an end to this process, which occurs once the child has become an expert or is in full command of the art and design techniques they have engaged with. This will, of course, never happen: we only have to look at the great artists of the past to know that they never stop learning or pushing boundaries, even once they have mastered something. So we must be careful not to set ourselves up for failure by expecting perfection from children's artwork, nor (importantly) must we set the children up to feel that they have failed.

More positively, we can view the idea of mastery in a slightly different light. We can view this as helping children to develop to the best of their potential as individuals whilst they are in our care and value them for what they can do now, as much as what they can become in the future. How each child masters the ideas, materials, techniques and processes that they will encounter in art and design learning will be an individual achievement: it will happen at different ages and stages so it is, once again, crucial that we know our children as the unique human beings that they are. This leads us very neatly on to how we ensure progression occurs and to look at the tricky area of assessment in art and design.

Assessment and monitoring progression

Many primary teachers have great difficulty with the notion of assessing art and design, so if you are worried about this please be reassured that these feelings are not unusual. The idea of 'assessment' is often aligned with rigorous checking of what children know and can do, compared with their peers. In core subjects you may well have folders full of tick sheets and comparison charts, where you record every little step that children make so that you can measure the impact of your teaching. If you are teaching in a year group where external exams are part of the process, you will be keeping records that affirm that you know about every misplaced full stop or spelling mistake, and you can address this immediately by planning next steps for the child to give them more practice, or to embed new concepts that they had not quite grasped. Often these assessment methods can be implemented by testing children, or by reading and marking their work, which allows you to see exactly what or where the gaps are in their understanding. You cannot, however, apply the same methods to assessing children's artwork. Assessing artwork takes a very different set of skills on your part: it is a complex procedure that takes confidence, time and, to a certain degree, intuition. Yes: intuition. Art, design and creativity does require an ephemeral and unmeasurable aspect of assessing, which is far away from what we generally understand assessment to be about in primary schools.

Theory focus

Many theorists have acknowledged intuition as a feature of reflective practice. For example, Donald Schon's stance is that teachers reflect *in action*, as well as *on* their actions (1983), so teachers not only think and evaluate after their lessons, but they act and make decisions *in the moment*, in response to particular circumstances. This intuitive act is made possible due to their deep understanding of theory, pedagogy and subject matter, as well as having a belief in the potential of each child as an individual. Atkinson and Claxton wrote about the role of intuition and tacit knowledge within education in their book *The Intuitive Practitioner*, and Claxton defines this as another 'way of knowing' (2000, p40). This involves the teacher being able to make immediate sensitive and useful judgements without the involvement of justification, which comes later in reflecting *on* action. Dann (2002) points out that since national summative assessments have taken precedence for learning, the role of teacher intuition has been marginalised, and in fact, if anything, it has been made to be almost unacceptable, due to difficulties to do with standardisation and accountability. Dann, however, acknowledges that the use of intuition does exist in situations where formative assessment is implemented because that is how teachers operate on a human level: for us, formative assessment is the key to progression in art and design learning.

Theory focus

Assessing learning, rather than assessing outcomes, is a priority when considering progression in art and design. This requires you, as the teacher, to accept that children accelerate in their learning at different rates and at different stages of their lives. In any one class we are dealing with children who are developing at different times, in different ways, with different life experiences to bring to the mix. Assessment in art and design should never be seen as the outcome alone, because that is not evidence to validate the learning that has occurred. Instead we need to think about how we can develop children's progress through formative methods such as discussion, questioning and observing, in association with practical outcomes. Once again, knowing and understanding your children well are your best tools here. This type of formative assessment is known as 'assessment for learning' which, according to the Assessment Reform Group (2002), is:

> the process of seeking and interpreting evidence for use by learners and their teachers to decide where the learners are in their learning, where they need to go and how best to get there.

(p1)

The reform group devised a set of ten principles for formative assessment, and these were based upon a large-scale review of research evidence, undertaken by Black and Wiliam (1998). The principles state that assessment:

(Continued)

(Continued)

1. Is part of effective planning.
2. Focuses on how children learn.
3. Is central to classroom practice.
4. Is a key professional skill.
5. Is sensitive and constructive.
6. Fosters motivation.
7. Promotes understanding of goals and criteria.
8. Helps learners know how to improve.
9. Develops the capacity for self-assessment.
10. Recognises all educational achievement.

All of these principles lend themselves easily to teaching and learning in art and design.

The Scottish Curriculum for Excellence website helpfully explains this a little further, and gives us some guidance on the types of questions to ask ourselves when using formative assessment.

- How well is the child doing?
- What progress has s/he made?
- What does s/he need to do now?

Figures 5.2 and 5.3 A child's observation drawing on a field trip to a farm is directly transferred to classroom work, showing an understanding of movement in drawing, as well as shape, colour and texture.

Reflective exercise

Read more about the research here.

www.oecd.org/edu/ceri/34260938.pdf

Self and peer assessment

Facilitating self-assessment and peer-to-peer assessment is a principal strategy to enable children to articulate their learning and understanding, and for them to develop a metacognitive approach towards their learning. This is known to increase children's involvement in their work (Brown and Harris, 2013) and gives them a sense of empowerment within their own learning. Children can learn to become 'critical friends' to help each other to progress and to view their own work with some objectivity. Constructive criticism is a good balance between your encouragement, and children's review and evaluation of their own work, and the work of others. It will instil confidence and permit children to begin to set their own goals and challenges. You can use a 'two stars and one wish' approach, to ensure that the feedback has positive elements, as well as suggestions of areas for development.

Summative assessment

At certain points of the year you will want to provide a summative account of the children's learning: for instance to provide feedback to parents, and for handing over to the next teacher. In primary schools this is the only time you are likely to need to make summative assessments, as art and design is not a subject that is graded or tested for public examinations. If you have documented formative assessments well, summative assessments will be a simple process to perform.

What are we assessing?

Your planning will already have given you a focus for making assessments.

If you have used the planning templates suggested in this chapter you will already have defined aims and learning objectives for a scheme of work and single lessons. Assessment, therefore, should have a focal point which stems directly from this. Peer-to-peer and self-assessment can also be built in to the assessment process as this gives you vital information for your own judgements.

Here are some key areas for making assessments in art and design.

- **Learning aims: skills and concepts.** A balance of technical skill and conceptual understanding will ensure that children make progress to become proficient in the use of tools and equipment, as well as being able to use these to express their ideas and emotions through visual mediums.

  You can assess: children's level of skill, their grasp of concepts and their awareness of links between concepts, skills and materials. For example, if you have been teaching children to use tonal values through observational drawing, or photography outside on a sunny day, you might assess whether they retain this concept and use tone again in later work. You can also assess their ability to understand and use appropriate vocabulary and the correct terminology associated with art and design.

- **Provocation and ideas: research/plan/sketch.** Children should be able to make images in which they record observations and experiences, and keep notes on what they have seen and learnt about art and design. They should communicate ideas, practise techniques and try these out towards a conclusion. They should be given opportunities to work with others and collaborate to develop new ideas.

  You can assess: their enthusiasm to engage in these activities, how well they collaborate with their peers and their willingness to develop both group work and personal ideas and plans. They might, for example, show resilience and persistence in working through problems, by making different versions of a model or by sketching ideas in many ways in the decision-making process.

- **Making and processes: explore and experiment.** Children should understand the qualities and uses of different materials and media, and be increasingly able to choose their own materials to suit the task. They should be given opportunities to make decisions that enable them to use materials imaginatively and to develop personal responses to original stimuli.

  You can assess: how children respond to these challenges; how well they are able to communicate their ideas; how willing they are to take creative risks in experimental work; and whether they are progressing in their ability to use materials with increasing care and skill. You can also look at how independent they are and at their level of confidence.

- **Review and evaluate: edit/add/change/display.** Children should become increasingly articulate in talking about art, craft and design. They should be able to think critically when looking at their own work and the work of others; they should be able to explain their actions and discuss how they might change or develop their work.

  You can assess: their ability or confidence to give opinions and to accept feedback, whether they can recognise similarities and differences, and if they can make connections between their own work and the work of others. You can also look at the care and attention to detail they have used to bring the work to a satisfying conclusion.

Children should make clear progress in all four areas over time. This can be recorded so that their development is documented for summative use later on.

Record keeping

Recording progress in art and design should reflect the fact that this is a visual subject area. Individual portfolios are a simple way to keep track of what children have experienced during their time in school, and their own efforts in responding to those experiences. Sketchbooks provide good evidence of how each individual child progresses in their ideas. Children can be encouraged to record their own progress over the course of a project through documenting the process, perhaps by taking photographs of their work and uploading these to their own electronic platform, or to a class file.

Keeping a portfolio of children's drawings is a wonderful way to monitor progress, as these clearly show leaps of development in terms of skills with materials, as well as conceptual understanding.

It is good practice to look at these with the children every so often so that they are aware of their own progress.

Figure 5.4 This five-year-old demonstrates keen observation skills: that the sitter is holding a baby in front of her. He has made an additional drawing to the side of the original to show this.

Figure 5.5 This girl, aged seven years and 11 months, has drawn the figure from a front and side view. It shows the child's developing ability to draw what she observes, rather than what she thinks the subject looks like. It also reveals her interest in detail and pattern.

Figure 5.6 This boy, aged nine years and nine months, shows the child applying his understanding of the use of tonal value. He has included contextual imagery in this drawing, by the addition of background information (i.e. the seating underneath the figure).

Figure 5.7 This drawing made by a boy aged eleven years and three months shows an awareness of shape and tone, which he has employed to denote the form of the figure. We can look at the hands and feet to see the great level of detail that he has observed.

There are several theories of how children's artwork progresses, and these are often linked to child development theory. You can research the different perspectives by looking at the work of Viktor Lowenfeld and Betty Edwards, which is outlined on this website.

www.bit.ly/2mCOUql

You might also be interested in the work of Maureen Cox, who researched the use of children's development in drawing from a psychological perspective: see the Further reading section for more details.

▬▬ Professional development ▬▬▬▬▬▬▬▬▬

A very good way to ensure breadth and balance across children's learning experiences in school is to open conversations between the teaching staff around planning and progression. The notion of assessing children in art and design can be a contentious issue, so this makes it a very interesting INSET topic, perhaps for a twilight session.

If your school is doing this for the first time, you will need to organise an audit of existing practice. This will give all staff a starting point from which to develop a whole-school approach, or policy, for planning and assessment for progression in art and design.

Ask all class teachers to bring examples of children's artwork, along with current planning, to the session. Use a large space, such as the school hall, to lay artwork out in year group order before asking staff to view the work. Give out sticky notes and ask teachers to write comments and questions, and place these next to the appropriate pieces of work. Use these to initiate a discourse about the assessment of children's work.

▬▬ Reflection point ▬▬▬▬▬▬▬▬▬▬▬▬

Lead a discussion about the quality of work that you see.

- Can you tell whether there has been effort and enthusiasm put into the work?
- Does the work reflect the diversity of outcome that you should expect?
- Is it clear how skills and concepts develop over time?
- Is there evidence of a wide range of techniques, use of materials and subject matter across the years?
- Do the teachers think that the topics they have covered have been interesting to the children? What new ideas do they have for future planning?

▬▬ Practical activity ▬▬▬▬▬▬▬▬▬▬▬

Remind teachers of the learning journey professional development session from Chapter 3 and ask them to implement this concept in their class planning. Scan and send, or give out, the two planning models from this chapter for medium-term, and short-term planning (Table 5.1 and Figure 5.1).

┌─ **Practical activity** ─────────────────────────────────┐

Hold a 'festival of ideas' in the staff room. Teachers can work in small groups to develop new ideas to enliven the art and design planning across the whole school. Give each group an iPad for researching different artists and artwork for inspiration, as well as large sheets of paper and marker pens so that they can create mind-maps on which to collect their ideas. These can then be shared with the whole staff, one group at a time.

└──┘

┌─ **Practical activity** ─────────────────────────────────┐

Agree with the staff about how you will manage record keeping and assessment of children's work in art and design, then make sure this is written into the school policy.

└──┘

┌─ **Chapter summary** ────────────────────────────────────┐

This chapter has given you theoretical basis for planning and progression, and models for ensuring that your planning in art and design is based upon the principled approach that remains the philosophy of this book. We have considered many facets of teaching, including behaviour for learning and developing inclusive strategies. Art and design is different in nature to most other subjects, and by following the suggestions for planning and assessment here, you should discover that teaching this subject will make a lot of sense to you and to the children in your class. It is important that children are aware of what they are learning and why they are learning it: planning, assessment and progression should dovetail into a learning experience that will serve every child in terms of 'mastery' and in building confidence for the future.

└──┘

Further reading

Access Arts, online advice and guidance for planning: **www.accessart.org.uk/curriculum-planning**

Cox, M (1993) *Children's Drawing of the Human Figure*. London: Lawrence Erlbaum.

DfES (2004) 'Excellence and enjoyment: learning and teaching in the primary years, planning and assessment for learning'. Available at: **www.webarchive.nationalarchives.gov.uk/20130401151715/http://www.education.gov.uk/publications/eOrderingDownload/Designing%20opportunities%20for%20learning.pdf**

Goepel, J, Childerhouse, H and Sharpe, S (2015) *Inclusive Primary Teaching*. Northwich: Critical Publishing.

Incredible Art Department, 'Classroom management and discipline'. Article on behaviour in the art classroom. Available at: **www.incredibleart.org/links/toolbox/discipline.html**

NSEAD, online curriculum resources: **www.nsead.org/curriculum-resources/nc_england.aspx**

TDA (2009) 'Including pupils with SEN and/or disabilities in primary art and design': **http://dera.ioe.ac.uk/13784/1/artanddesign.pdf**

Thomson, P, Hall, C and Russell, L (2006) 'Promoting social and education inclusion through the creative arts'. Available at: **www.leeds.ac.uk/educol/documents/190288.pdf**

6

Beyond the classroom and into the future

Chapter objectives

This chapter will help you to:

- Discover the importance of visual literacy.
- Look at the role of galleries and museums within children's learning.
- Investigate working with artists.
- Find out what to do if you want to be an art and design subject leader.

The following standards apply within this chapter.

1. Set high expectations which inspire, motivate and challenge pupils.
2. Promote good progress and outcomes by pupils.
8. Fulfil wider professional responsibilities.

Introduction

A fundamental part of learning in this subject is that children are taught to discover the world of contemporary art, along with the history of art, crafts and design from all around the world. You might have already noticed that many of the activities and practical suggestions in this book link to specific works of art or artists, and this is to reinforce that looking at existing work is integral to any project you might undertake with your class. This is so that children are introduced to our rich cultural heritage and artistic traditions right from the start, and are then able to contextualise their own work within an extensive legacy of what has gone before them. Art and design learning does not exist within a vacuum and throughout the centuries artists have been inspired to create new work by observing examples by their predecessors and peers, and allowing themselves to become influenced by these to produce their own new work.

For children, understanding the different ways that artists, craftspeople or designers think and work can give them an insight into worlds that might be different from their own. To do this they need the skills that can be developed through 'visual literacy': this can open doors and show them new ways of being, which might enable them to find their place in the world. We have the power at our fingertips, and on our whiteboards, to expose every child to the globalised cultural heritage that is available. In this chapter, we shall look at potential curriculum enrichment that is made possible through intro- ducing children to contextual studies, both in the classroom and in gallery and museum situations. We shall explore what it means to invite artists to work with your class in school, and how this can be a unique learning experience for the children and for yourself. Finally, if you have been inspired enough by the concepts explored in this book, you might like to think about taking on the role of subject leader for art and design in the future. This chapter will offer you some guidance and advice on what that might entail and where to go for further information and guidance.

Visual literacy

In Chapter 5, Kath, the head teacher from the case study, talked about the need to emphasise visual lit- eracy within education, because this is one of the key skills that twenty-first century children will need to acquire. Her point was related to the fact that today's children will grow up into a workplace that is very different from what we know and understand right now. Already, machines are taking over many manual and service jobs, and people in the future will have to construct a range of jobs that machines cannot do. An article in *The Telegraph* (2016) reminds us that we are not immune to the impact that the development of thinking robots and artificial intelligence will have on the workplace, as this will affect how we view things now, and how we will manage our lives in the future (**www.telegraph. co.uk/news/science/science-news/12155808/Robots-will-take-over-most-jobs-within- 30-years-experts-warn.html**). Becoming visually literate will give children the thinking skills they need to access a whole range of new possibilities, most of which we cannot yet even imagine.

=== Theory focus ===

What is visual literacy?

Elliot Eisner, one of art education's most central theorists of recent times, stated that:

In order to be read, a poem, an equation, a painting, a dance, a novel or a contract - each requires a distinctive form of literacy, when literacy means, as I intend it to mean, a way of conveying meaning through, and recovering meaning from, the form of representation in which it appears.

(1997, p8)

The distinctiveness that Eisner talks about is visual literacy: a language that we use when 'reading' something that we are looking at. It is an indispensable skill to enable us to engage not only with the world of art and design, but with life in general. Have you heard the saying that 'a picture can paint a thousand words'? This demonstrates that the language of images facilitates communication, where words are just not enough. The artist Georgia O'Keefe said: *I found I could say things with colour and shapes that I couldn't say any other way, things I had no words for*, and the painter Edward Hopper stated that: *If I could say it in words there would be no reason to paint*. This signifies that the language of images is as important a language to learn as any other literacy, whether text-based, numerical or digital, such as coding. In our increasingly image-saturated world it is essential that children are taught to read, understand and critically interpret images that they encounter: this can be achieved by introducing them to a wide range of artworks, both in the classroom and beyond.

Visiting galleries and museums

Looking at art with children should not be a case of you lecturing them with your great knowledge of artists and art history, as no matter how well informed you are, children will not be very interested in your own expertise. Keeping children's own responses at the centre of any dialogue can reap wonderful discussions and imaginative interpretations. Utilising your local galleries and museums can be excellent professional development for yourself, as well as giving children direct experience of observing and interpreting artworks. In this section, primary teacher and gallery educator Edward Dickenson shares his experiences of working with schools at the Ben Uri Gallery in London. He gives some excellent advice and support to help you guide children towards interpreting artworks and images.

The role of galleries and museums in children's learning

Edward Dickenson

A trip outside the classroom offers children a valuable variety of learning experiences, not least because it is a break from the formality of desk-based work. Galleries and museums contain a wealth of treasures in their collections which can inspire, delight, confound and challenge, and you will find the vast majority of these institutions, both large and small, have dedicated learning teams who can help your children access the objects and art in their collections.

For some children a school trip might be their first visit to a cultural institution, and you can offer an invaluable opportunity to demystify what can often appear strange and inaccessible. Giving children the chance to see art in the flesh, explore historical objects and speak with experts from outside their familiar experiences can have a real and lasting impact. Not only can this foster a

(Continued)

(Continued)

lifelong interest in arts and culture, but it can also expose a world of artists, craftspeople, curators, technicians and volunteers, and the livelihoods this fostered interest can lead to.

Figure 6.1 Looking at, questioning and discussing artwork.

Planning a visit

As with all school outings, memorable gallery and museum trips must be planned carefully and supported with lead-in and follow-up activities. Large institutions might have a broad selection of workshops to choose from, which need booking up ahead of time, whilst smaller venues often make up for a more limited collection and fewer amenities by offering your class a more person-alised experience. Don't be afraid to ask about the availability of bespoke visits and workshops, regardless of the size of the place: establishing a relationship with a museum helps the facilitator to prepare which means there are often learning resources ready and waiting to support you and your children, both before and after their trip. Whilst national institutions might offer more established programmes of learning workshops, search locally, too, for smaller galleries and museums as they are often actively looking to attract schools with exciting free sessions. Staying local also makes organis-ing a trip far easier; a half day with minimal transport often means you can get out and back with little disruption or cost. Look at your long-term plan and think about which teaching units would best benefit from a gallery or museum visit. Is there a particular medium which is difficult to do in your school? Perhaps a gallery near you specialises in pottery workshops, or you have a local print studio which offers screen printing. Keep cross-curricular links in mind as well; you'll find many venues can support pretty much any area of the curriculum and have a great deal of experience doing so. You could make a serious case for art gallery visits supporting the study of a wide range of subjects in your school.

Contextualisation

In general, galleries and museums offer children the invaluable opportunity to get up close with art and culture, and to explore what art is and can be. No art is created in a void: galleries contextualise paintings, showing them alongside the artists' peers, inspirations and followers, creating conversations where before there was merely one voice. Make an effort to get to know some of the history of the artist and medium being studied, as this really brings the works to life for your class (if in doubt, see what resources galleries might have to support you with this). Contextualise the art as a product of what came before and after it; this could be as a continuation of, or as a reaction to, the work. To this end there are simple techniques with which you can broaden your teaching by exploring artworks. Whilst this is best done in front of the actual works, you can easily replicate the process with a whiteboard or reproductions in school.

Ways to read paintings

By exploring a work of art, children can develop critical, analytical and visual skills. The more time they spend looking at art, the greater their enjoyment and understanding of art can be. Whilst many paintings tell stories and include multiple layers of information, it is important also to draw out personal opinions, observations and ideas in order to keep art relevant, interesting and, above all, exciting. This section outlines a few techniques to engage children which can be applied to most works of art. It does not attempt to be a definitive guide by any means, nor should it be merely confined to examining paintings, but the hope is that it will promote discussion, understanding and enjoyment by encouraging children to spend a little bit longer in front of a work of art.

Art is often described as a universal language, available to all, yet many feel bemused, alienated or indifferent to it. As a visual medium, art can be taken in or dismissed at a glance, but to promote deeper exploration you can ask a wide range of questions in order to help children start to unpick what lies in front of them. Wherever possible, surround them with different works of art. Put posters of works up and encourage discussions about how they feel about them, whether that is positive or negative, and why. Five to ten minutes could be set aside each day to look at a new piece of art and share opinions. Art terms (e.g. abstract, figurative) could be put up on wall displays or made into a word of the week. The more practice children have discussing art with your support, the more competent they will become. Whilst it is important to inform yourself as much as possible about when, where and by whom a painting was made, you do not need to be an expert. Place art into context: pin it to a timeline and consider the differences in the artist's time to our own.

When discussing artwork, display it as large and as clearly as possible. If you can display it on a whiteboard that allows you to zoom in on particular details, do. Similarly, colour copies could be made and distributed amongst groups. Start with lower order questions that encourage quick answers. Consider the core questions:

- **Who?:** Who can you see in this picture? What can you tell about them?

- **What?:** What is happening?

- **Where?:** Where is this set (indoors, outdoors, urban or rural, country/part of the world)? What clues suggest that?

- **When?:** What time of day/year? What period of history?

Always encourage children to justify their responses: *Why* do you think that? *Which part* of the painting makes you think that? Explore puzzles and queries by looking for clues. Pore over every inch of the canvas and consider the artist's intentions. Is it likely she/he meant that? What else could she/he have been trying to say, or show? By continually justifying their answers, children are starting to consider higher order questions that draw upon their own opinions and experiences. Follow on from this by considering the following:

- **Why?:** Why might the figures in the painting be behaving in this way?

- **How?:** How does this painting make you feel? Why? How has the artist made you feel this way? How have the colours she/he has chosen affected you?

Figure 6.2 Josef Herman (1911–2000), Refugees, gouache on paper, c.1941, Ben Uri Collection.

What follows is an example of how you might read a painting with a class of children, starting with short, lower order questions and building up to higher order questions that draw further upon individual experiences and opinions. In this way, children don't just learn about a painting's story, they discover it.

The work used as an example is Josef Herman's *Refugees,* painted in *c*.1941.

Introduce the painting but don't reveal the name of the artist or the image's title. Information too early on answers questions that a class can work out collectively, and it can colour individual interpretations of a work.

Give children a challenge to look at the painting for 30 seconds and try to memorise as much of the image as possible. Then remove or cover the painting and ask the class to rebuild it verbally by calling out all the different parts they remember.

Reintroduce the image and begin to ask the questions that follow. Bear in mind that some of the answers aren't definite because they are open to interpretation. What is important is that exchanges are quick and meaningful. Don't tell children the answers or assume understanding; keep them on their toes by making them justify themselves. They'll soon start to see what's expected and will take less of a passive role in looking at the painting.

• Who can you see in this picture?

There are four people in the foreground of the painting, we assume a family: a man, a woman, a child (either a boy or a girl) and a baby wrapped up and held close to the woman's chest. A menacing giant black cat stalks across the roofs of buildings behind them. This family doesn't appear to have any bags; their possessions consist of the clothes on their backs and a single rolled blanket.

• Where might we be? Where in the world? How can you tell?

We are in a street outside: there is a town in the background, possibly meaning the figures are on a road. Are we in Eastern Europe? The architecture (spires and Orthodox church) suggests so. The absence of streetlights might mean it is a poorer town, a more rural area or perhaps the artist felt urban lighting might be a visual distraction.

• What time of day is it? What time of year? Can we tell which year it might be?

It's night as we can see the moon, possibly winter as they are wrapped up (it could either be snow on the ground, or moonlight). Their clothes don't seem very different to today but there is no sign of modern technology (streetlights, cars). This could almost be any time in the last 100 years. Could this even be a scene from today?

• What is happening? How do the people feel? How can you tell?

The man is holding something rolled up (a blanket, or possessions?) and holding his arm out. When might you make that gesture? Is he explaining something? The woman is holding her baby close: it might be crying as its mouth seems open. She looks to the man (her husband?), her eyes looking down slightly: is this concern? She's looking at the road, not at the man's face. The child has his/her hand in their mouth: is he/she nervous/cold/hungry? His/her eyes are wide, indicating fear. In the background an enormous cat walks on the rooftops (we see the shadow it casts), with a mouse in its mouth (the mouse is dead as it is dripping blood).

- What information does the title *Refugees* give you? Have you heard this word before? Where? What does it mean to you?

The people (a family?) are on the run, chased from their homes. They are carrying the things they need but they don't have much. They are looking for somewhere safer to live.

- What questions do you still have? What is puzzling you? How might we work out the answers?

The cat is far larger than real life: we can tell it is actually there and not superimposed because it is casting a shadow on the roofs. Is this a fantasy? Everything else seems realistic so is the cat a symbol for a threat, something dangerous, persecution? If I told you this was painted in *c.*1941, who might the threat be? Does the mouse stand for something, too? Does it represent those who are in danger: Jewish people in particular?

- How does this painting make you feel? Why? How has the artist made you feel this way?

Where do warm colours appear and where are the cold ones? The large eyes of the family draw you in, focusing your attention and helping you to empathise with the characters. All the figures, including the cat, are facing in one direction so the painting is given a sense of movement. We know we are on a journey.

Analysis

The artist, Josef Herman, fled his native Warsaw as a young man at the behest of his family, leaving a large number of close relatives behind. Entering the UK via Glasgow, where *Refugees* was painted, he created art that remembered those he had left. There may be two clear reasons for Herman choosing to paint a family here: first, the presence of children makes the scene seem all the more threatening and dangerous, engaging us emotionally as we worry for their safety; second, the fleeing family also represents the artist's own Jewish family back in Warsaw, who sadly failed to escape to safety and died in the Warsaw ghetto, something Herman did not yet know when he painted this. The tall white spires are a style found in Warsaw, the city of Herman's birth; not Glasgow, where this was painted. This further suggests Herman is looking back at the life he has left behind, implying that the people in the painting might also be Polish Jews fleeing persecution from the Nazis. The cat represents the danger they are running from, the dead mouse in its jaws a reminder of what will happen to them if they are caught. It also echoes the Nazis' treatment of those they deemed undesirable, suggesting that there is a natural hierarchy amongst humans. Hitler believed that some people were born inferior and should be treated as such, just as a mouse would be by a cat. Although *Refugees* was painted in *c.*1941, there is a timeless quality to the painting: the family could be one from today, the cat representing not the Nazis but whatever other danger they are facing.

Open-ended enquiry

Wherever possible, maintain a sense of mystery about the painting you are exploring, allowing the children to build up their own justified observations and opinions, whilst holding back on more established knowledge (artist, date, known subject matter, title of work) until later. Definitive answers will close down children's thinking and limit lines of enquiry. Build up a breadth of potential readings: even seemingly silly answers can have their value. Just ensure you discuss whether certain readings are more likely than others, and why.

Start to look at other artwork and consider how you could adapt this approach to suit your class and the unit you are teaching. Many figurative paintings like *Refugees* tell clear stories, but more abstract art can still offer a wealth of information. Remember to pose questions like: How does it make you feel and why? Shape, colour and composition all play their part in affecting how you respond to a work and this can often be deeply personal, drawing upon your own preferences and life experiences. And whilst learning to explore an image is enjoyable and empowering in itself, it also sets children up for creating their own works of art and speaking about their peers' in thoughtful, critical ways.

Leading a gallery trip

As you become more comfortable with exploring art critically with your students, you might want to consider self-guided tours around museums and galleries. Most institutions just ask that you call in advance to give numbers and times, and then you are free to tailor a visit to your children's own needs. Make a preliminary visit and note where the particular works are, that you'd like to look at. Bear in mind that spending a good 15 minutes on each one, with transitions between the works,

Figure 6.3 Leading learning in a gallery.

means that covering about four works in detail in one hour is a reasonable expectation. Speak with the learning team or check online beforehand to see if there is any extra information that they might be able to give you. Many larger venues will be fine if you carefully sit your class on the floor in front of a work, although bear in mind that other learning groups might be passing through, too. You might even end up with a crowd of visitors enjoying your session.

Professional development

Whilst workshops are a common output for gallery and museum learning departments up and down the country, there are more involved partnerships that you could explore. Many institutions hold CPD training for teachers, so sign up to a variety of learning mailing lists to receive updates. If you are finding that particular training dates are continually difficult for you to attend, speak with a member of the gallery as they may be keen to alter the events to ensure as many teachers as possible can attend.

You might also want to consider larger projects such as Arts Award, the National Gallery's Take One Picture, Children & the Arts' Great Art Quest or Kids in Museums' Takeover Day. These organisations have dedicated teams who can help you decide if the projects will be suitable for your school, and work as great advocates to ensure that senior management receive all the reassurance needed that the children will get an enormous amount out of the projects. Art education can and should be broad and deeply supportive of the curriculum, and there are projects run nationally that help every child find value in creative learning; not just those who have already decided they are artistically inclined. Approach your local galleries and museums to find out what their offers are: you are likely to find that unexpected and exciting learning experiences are closer than you thought.

Artists' stories

Edward Dickenson's reassuring guidance above should help you to feel more confident in looking at artworks, then questioning and leading discussions about them with children. Much essential information about artworks and artists can be found by researching them online, but it is not often that we actually get to hear the artist's own perspective. This book's own artist-in-residence, sculptor Al Johnson, explains exactly what it is like for her when her artwork is viewed and responded to by her audience. Later in the chapter, we shall meet Alistair Lambert, another artist who works with primary schools, who will offer yet another insight.

Case study

Exploring meanings

Al Johnson

Art is, by its nature, a non-verbal language. We are all constantly reacting to imagery that surrounds us: much of it demands us to think in a certain way by being loud, brilliantly coloured and fast moving. Allowing children some space to react to art that is silent and stationary has enormous value, and can allow for a variety of responses. I have worked in gallery settings encouraging both children and adults to find their own path through paintings and sculpture, and am constantly surprised by their ability to explore and analyse an image and to allow full rein of the imagination. Art is understood on many levels: visually, intellectually and, importantly, in relation to the personal experience of the viewer. I made *Downed*, a sculpture that references the fragility of a crashed WWI biplane, from timber, steel and textiles. Red knitted garments, deconstructed and re-stitched, stretch over the wooden structure and beyond it, creating a textured pool on the floor. My intentions with *Downed* were layered: to reference the cultural shifts in the perception of women in the early twentieth century, moving from domestic sphere to munitions factory; to consider the concept of the flying machine itself as the bird of freedom remade as a warplane; and to explore the nature of historical and contemporary warfare.

Figure 6.4 Al Johnson (2007), Downed: knitted and woven textiles, timber and forged steel.

I have shown this work in a variety of galleries, but also in settings where I have been able to talk to visitors, to generate discussion and encourage response. During a discussion at the National Gallery about this work, a small boy was sitting on the floor close to the edge of the 'pool' of red knitting that surrounds the sculpture. He was intrigued by its texture and was clearly finding it difficult not to touch it. When I asked what he was thinking about, he said the sculpture reminded him of his grandma. Clearly, his train of thought was at some distance from my intentions for the work, but I have always remembered his reaction because it was a response that was very personal: it was about the importance of the senses (of touch in particular), an indication of how objects function as a trigger for memory and about the nature of memory itself.

Memory and meaning

A friend who is a Reception teacher wanted to encourage this kind of lateral thinking and kept a shoe box in her classroom, full of postcards of paintings. Each day one child in turn chose a card, which was put into a special frame for the day, and they had two minutes to say why they

(Continued)

(Continued)

had chosen the image. The responses were wide ranging and encompassed stories, family memories, holidays and references to moments or events that were special to them. The specifics of the image were not the point; in fact children often chose images that might be considered dull or bland by a more sophisticated audience. Sometimes they could not quite explain why they had chosen a particular painting, just that they liked it. It is really exciting to encourage children in that moment of discovery, of finding the art that touches them and gives rein to their imagination.

Reflective exercise

- How will you plan to develop visual literacy in your daily or weekly planning?
- What have you learnt about interpreting art from the examples in this chapter?
- What have you learnt about talking to children about art?
- Make a list of all the beneficial concepts and skills that children will learn by talking about art.
- Have a look at your long-term planning to see where a gallery or museum trip would fit in and begin to plan a visit for your class.

Artists in schools

Whilst going to visit galleries is one way of putting children in touch with real artwork, another more direct way is to arrange for them to meet an artist, or invite an artist to work with your school. Having an artist work with your class can be a wonderful way to shake up the curriculum and stimulate children to learn and express themselves in creative new ways. This can also provide a good opportunity to give children a glimpse into the world of work and an insight into professional practice, as well as allowing you as the teacher to gain new skills and understanding. It also enables children to actually meet an artist, and to realise that they are real people. Working with an artist gives children an insight into what art can become: they learn that art can happen anywhere and at any time, and that it is something they can control and manifest themselves, which is very empowering for children. For some children, it might switch on the light and allow them to become our 'creatives' of the future.

Planning together with your artist is fundamental to having a positive experience, so you should discuss expectations, find out what resources you will need to supply and how you can support the process during the project.

It is important to remember that a professional artist will not necessarily have had any formal education in pedagogy and theory for teaching children (as you have), so they should be treated as any visiting guest, rather than being left to get on with it whilst you mark your books. Your role is to be as actively involved as possible, so that you provide a positive role model for children and show that you value the experience. Good preparation and clear, realistic aims will help you to avoid possible frustrations, as outlined by Sharp and Dust (1997) whose research highlighted potential benefits and frustrations that featured in many 'artist-in-schools' projects. Table 6.1 is a helpful guide for when you consider bringing an artist into your school.

Table 6.1 *Hosting an artist-in-residence: pros and cons*

Children	Teachers and schools	What can go wrong?
• Gain insight into the profession. • Learn about process within art-making. • Develop new strategies for making their own artwork. • Develop skills and learn techniques. • Benefit from positive role models. • Develop confidence in expressing themselves. • Experiment and take creative risks. • Experience different approaches to learning. • Feel included. • Benefits children with special needs.	• Enriches the curriculum. • Contributes to CPD. • Helps to introduce new themes. • Develops ways to use art across other subjects. • Involves parents and wider community. • Promotes positive image of the school. • Makes links with other schools. • Helps to focus on personal and social issues. • Develops relationships between staff and children.	• Lack of support for the artist. • Confusion over aims of the project. • Teacher resentment over the artist's role. • Lack of pupil commitment. • Involving too many pupils. • Too much pressure. • Lack of opportunity for feedback and evaluation.

Adapted from Sharp, C and Dust, K (1997) *Artists in Schools, A Handbook for Teachers and Artists*. Slough: NfER.

▬ Case study ▬

Artist-in-residence

Many of the points that Sharp and Dust (1997) make are borne out by the experiences of our second artist, Alistair Lambert. Alistair has been working with schools and community groups for many years and now sees this as part of his own practice: many artists do see presenting workshops or working with children in this way, and find it affects their personal work in a positive way. Alistair works with one school especially on a regular basis, as their artist-in-residence, amongst many other commissions and projects. He describes his role as one of a specialist, who brings distinctive skills and unique ways of working to the school and to the children he works with. He is perceived in a different way from other visitors to the school, as 'the artist'. He says that there is an expectation by the school, parents and children that something wonderful and special is going to happen, which he finds very freeing and which allows him to push the boundaries way beyond what might normally happen in an art and design lesson. During one residency, he worked on a project with the theme of 'nature', as part of an art week with a primary school which was used to keeping neat and tidy work and displays. The art co-ordinator had organised a very complicated week of activities and seemed anxious that there would be nowhere to display any of the project work that was about to take place, but Alistair's ability to solve problems and think creatively and quickly meant that this would not be a challenge for him. He decided to work outdoors and use the playground pergola to create a jungle with the children. The resulting work was an installation that the children could climb into and experience physically.

(Continued)

(Continued)

Figure 6.5 Children's own work formed this jungle installation.

The scope of ambition here projects art into another realm for these children, so that the artwork is not just a display but becomes a real and unique thing.

Alistair says:

> *The teacher who was organising arts week had developed a massively complex plan for the week, where everyone had certain activities to complete, which is not really how I work: I always just come up with an idea and think, Yes, that sounds brilliant, let's do it! It's the ability to come at things from different angles and see things in different ways. But most of all, my enthusiasm is for the actual making and getting them to share what I experience, and to feel the joy of making and finding out what happens. I do have a plan, as there are 30 children who need to be kept busy. But once I have the plan I like to see where it takes us. Sometimes I get a bit anxious about whether I have planned enough, but in the end what I have is the ability to go with the moment, so to do that, I make sure I have interesting materials around me and that everything is well organised. It is then easy for me to believe in the inevitable creativity of the children to make something! Once they start and they get into the mode of working, one thing leads to another, they have more and more ideas, and*

we always end up with something great. I think that many of the schools I work with don't fully understand the value of what they are getting by employing an artist, until the end of the project. And then they suddenly see why this is of such enormous importance: because something extraordinary and unexpected results from it which they cannot ever get in other areas of the curriculum. Sometimes I meet children I have worked with and they remember little tiny details of something they have made. It makes me very happy to think that the work must have had a lasting impact on them.

Reflective exercise

What Alistair says about trusting children to be creative and to come up with their own ideas resonates well with the theoretical perspectives that you have read about in this book. By trying out the practical activities throughout these chapters, I hope that you have developed a new understanding of what it is be an artist, what it means to be an art and design teacher, and why this subject holds a very special place in the primary curriculum. Reflect upon the theories and pedagogical perspectives that you have encountered in this book.

- Which theory do you identify with the most?
- Revisit the personal values that you determined in Chapter 1 and see how they correspond with your favourite pedagogical framework.
- What kind of art and design teacher do you want to be?

Subject leadership in art and design

Perhaps by this point you are feeling so enthusiastic about art and design that you want to lead the subject in your own school. Your personal drive and vision for change is ultimately going to stand you in good stead for educating colleagues to develop high standards of teaching and learning in art and design. As subject leader you can seize every chance to share your understanding about the importance of art and design and initiate a new energy for the subject, which will soon become infectious: take every opportunity to share your enthusiasm and show willingness to help other staff who might be much less confident, or worried about teaching the subject. You can do this both formally and informally, by using the activities from earlier chapters in this book to lead staff meetings where you can share ideas, or promote and demonstrate certain processes. You can help colleagues informally by talking to them individually to help them link topic work through art and design activity, and to help them plan creative art and design projects. You can help yourself, too, by keeping information and resources in electronic folders, which you can forward to the staff. Web resources that demonstrate techniques, materials and ideas for learning in this subject, along with gallery information and artists' websites, are especially useful.

Action for change

If your school needs a big art and design update or boost, try to be realistic about what can be achieved and when: an initial audit of practice across the school and a survey of teachers' skills levels will give you a very good starting point. You might also look at the resources available in the school to see what needs replacing or changing. For example, take a look at the state of paintbrushes and paints: insist on offering children good quality materials, beautifully presented, as this will give children the impression that these resources are worth caring for. Once you have all the information you need, arrange to speak to your head teacher to negotiate a budget for making necessary initial improvements, and then maintenance.

It will be impossible to make many changes very quickly, so thinking strategically is the best way forward: split goals into short-, medium- and long-term action plans. You will need to have a frank but tactful conversation with the head teacher to present a long-term strategy of your vision for change, so being armed with an action plan, which shows a thoughtful and manageable system, will be invaluable. See Tables 6.2, 6.3 and 6.4 to prioritise actions for your own situation over five years. This is a realistic timescale if you have a major job on your hands.

Professional development

You will probably not be surprised that I am going to suggest a gallery trip for this section. I suggest you choose a gallery that will be interesting to you, so that it will encourage you to take your class in the future. Take a sketchbook with you to make notes, jot down ideas and, of course, draw. Go with friends or colleagues to see something contemporary, if you can, and try the following activities.

Before you go, have a look at the National Gallery's Take One Picture website to give you ideas of how to use art to inspire work across the primary curriculum: **www.takeonepicture.org.uk**

Once you are in the gallery:

- Find out about the education/schools programme on offer at the gallery.
- Look at the space in the gallery: What does it feel like to be in that space? How is the physical and emotional atmosphere affecting you? How have the works of art been organised in the space? What is your reaction to the work? Do you feel surprised/challenged/uncomfortable/satisfied, etc.?
- View the exhibition with an open mind: look for works that you could use with a theme that you might teach in the future.
- Choose one work of art that you are drawn to and complete a sketch of it.
- Make notes about how you could use this work with children. What practical activity could be introduced? Write three questions you would use to engage children with that piece.

Chapter summary

In this chapter we have broadened the notion of art and design as a classroom-based activity and repositioned our aim: to give children a balanced and holistic education in the context of the real world of artists and art practice. Throughout this chapter you have developed an understanding of what it means to be visually literate, and that this is not a 'should have' for children, but a 'must have'. Visiting museums and galleries offers opportunities for children to develop visual literacy, and to engage and participate in cultural heritage and contemporary debates that affect us all. We have had two very interesting perspectives from artists who work with children, and these have been honest and revealing. They have also been helpful in that you can consider your own philosophical position for planning art and design activities or projects.

Lastly, we have looked at what the role of subject leader for art and design might entail. It could be an interesting exercise to remember your own starting point on first picking up this book and realise how much you have learnt, and how your confidence and skills have developed as you have progressed through the pages and activities. Can you recall what it is like to be that unsure and unconfident teacher of primary art and design? Now, you have the motivation and enthusiasm, and the commitment to creativity and visual expression needed to champion this wonderful, facilitating subject. If this is you, you will make an ideal and much needed, proactive subject leader for art and design.

Further reading

Bowden, J, Ogier, S and Gregory, P (2013) *The Art and Design Primary Coordinators Handbook*. London: (Belair) HarperCollins.

Charman, H and Ross, M (2004) 'Contemporary art and the role of interpretation'. Tate Papers no. 2 Autumn. Available at: **www.tate.org.uk/research/publications/tate-papers/02/contemporary-art-and-the-role-of-interpretation**

Freedman, K (2003) *Teaching: Visual Culture Curriculum, Aesthetics and the Social Life of Art*. New York: Teachers College Press.

Renshaw, A (2005) *The Art Book for Children*. London: Phaidon.

Roland, C (online) *Looking At and Talking About Art with Kids*. Available at: **www.artjunction.org/archives/looking@art.pdf**

Cape UK: **www.capeuk.org**

Working with artists in your school: **www.artistsinschools.co.uk**

Table 6.2 Short-term plan

Short-term

Target	Action	Resources	Cost (Low £, Medium ££, High £££)	Outcome
Learn about staff opinions and confidence to teach art, craft and design.	Questionnaire. Observe displays. Look through children's sketchbooks to identify the variety of skills and techniques being used across the school.	Paper, printing.	£	Develop a starting point for INSET.
Organise and audit the resource cupboard.	Inventory of current supplies. Organise and label central resources. Make a list of resources needed. Track use of material. Order new materials.	Restocking low inventory, new equipment and resources.	£££	Monitor and update resources.
Meet with the head teacher to discuss findings from questionnaire and observations.	Work with the head teacher to agree budget. Plan staff meetings and INSET.	Completed staff questionnaires, notes/pictures of observations.	N/A	SMT involvement Budget agreed.
Review the school's art policy.	Discuss with staff. Update and publish policy.	Current art policy, paper, printing.	£	Staff meeting to agree targets.
Visit other art co-ordinators in the borough.	Make new contacts with other schools and art specialists in order to help enhance the study of art through exposure to new ideas and methodology.	N/A	£	Create support network.

Table 6.3 Medium-term plan

		Medium-term		
Target	Action	Resources	Cost (Low £, Medium ££, High £££)	Outcome
Observe the teaching of art throughout the school.	Use PPA time to observe art being taught in each class.	N/A	£	Develop starting points for INSET.
Set up assessment policy: portfolio.	Review children's sketchbooks and portfolios.	Completed staff questionnaires, notes/pictures of observations	£	Monitor assessment procedures.
Staff are provided with information, techniques and ideas for projects.	Create a folder of resources for staff: all teachers able to access ideas and techniques.	Ongoing. No cost.	£	Staff are proactive and enthused to try new ideas.
Team teach.	Support, plan and teach with identified staff.	Resources for practical work. Staff time.	££	Staff confidence increased.
Art club.	Advertise to specific year group: Key Stage 1/Key Stage 2. Agree rota system for staff/parents to help out.	Parents of art club members to contribute (optional) donation for materials.	£	Profile of subject raised.
Staff meetings and INSET days.	Plan strategic skills development in line with School Development Plan.	Resources as required.	£	Develop subject knowledge and skills amongst staff.

Table 6.4 Long-term plan

	Long-term			
Target	Action	Resources	Cost (Low £, Medium ££, High £££)	Outcome
Create links with local artists.	Contact local artists. Exploit skills of parents with art skills to contribute. Publicise and celebrate these connections by documenting collaboration and publish on school website.	Recycled materials, scrap schemes, general art resources.	£££	Children receive specialist input by someone working in the field. The status of art is increased.
Annual staff monitoring of portfolios of children's work.	Staff to discuss collection of artwork children have engaged in over their time in primary school.	Photographs of children's artwork. Digital folders. Staff meeting.	£	Monitor assessment procedures. Children and staff are able to witness progression.
Staff INSET in a gallery or museum.	Encourage staff to use at least one of the new things they have learnt from this experience in the following art and design lessons.	Local or national gallery. Travel costs.	£	Provide a fresh perspective on how art can be taught. Staff should leave feeling more confident and inspired to teach art.
Annual visits to art galleries.	Ensure that all year groups have at least one annual visit to an art gallery or museum.	Galleries may provide free online resources, risks assessments.	£££	Learning is taken outside the classroom where children can appreciate art in its intended form.
Bi-annual art exhibition of children's work.	All staff involvement. Organise dates. Ask PTA for support (refreshments etc.)	Recycled materials, scrap schemes, general art resources. Display materials.	££	Celebration of achievements. Children should feel confidence and a sense of pride. Teachers inspired and motivated to teach innovative art projects.

7

The broad and balanced curriculum

Chapter objectives

This chapter will help you to:

- Explore how learning in art and design can be present across all subjects.
- Understand how to use practical and haptic elements of art and design to motivate children to learn in other subject areas.
- Ensure that children have meaningful and deep learning experiences.
- Help you to find starting points for teaching art and design.

The following standards especially apply within this chapter.

1. Set high expectations which inspire, motivate and challenge pupils.
2. Promote good progress and outcomes by pupils.
3. Demonstrate good subject and curriculum knowledge.
5. Adapt teaching to respond to the strengths and needs of all pupils.

Introduction

This final chapter of the book will give you an insight into the value that excellent practice in art and design can bring to facilitate good learning in other areas of the curriculum. We have already acknowledged that the school curriculum often forces children (and teachers) down a certain, narrow route that ends with testing, but most of us realise that our lives outside of the school walls are not that simple: we cannot just section areas of our lives off and deposit them neatly into boxes named 'English', 'maths', 'geography', etc. In real life everything we do and feel has much more complexity, and we naturally piece things together to find a meaning in our existence. Life is, after all, entirely cross-curricular. Jonathan Barnes writes about this in his book, *Cross-Curricular Learning 3–14* (2011) where he states that:

> it is important for the child to enjoy being a child, to enjoy learning now and for its own sake and not primarily for some future role that they may or may not take on in the adult world.

(p2)

Enjoyment and learning should go hand in hand when teaching primary aged children so that they are inspired to carry on *wanting* to learn. It can, indeed, be one of the great privileges of being a primary teacher: to have time to get to know the children over the course of a year, to see them develop in many ways and to nuture their individual interests and talents. It is a great privilege for me, too, to have contributions to this chapter from many esteemed colleagues who are experts in their own subject areas, all of whom recognise the true value that art and design brings to their respective subjects. Whilst we do not cover every single subject that primary schools teach, it is hoped that there is enough here to inspire you to form your own routes into cross-curricular teaching, with art and design at the core. The following sections will inspire you to bring art and design into all your subject teaching to motivate and enable the children in your class to enjoy a life of learning.

7.1
Art and ... maths

Robert Watts

Introduction

This section explores the potential for cross-curricular work between maths and art and design. It begins with a brief justification for cross-curricular learning, before identifying some of the principles for linking art and design with maths. It concludes by exploring several visual examples to show how children have explored the deeply rooted connections between the two subjects.

═══ Theory focus ═══

Multidisciplinary

In recent years, maths and English have increasingly come to dominate the primary curriculum at the expense of foundation subjects such as art and design. Under pressure to raise standards in core subjects, teachers have allocated more and more time to literacy and numeracy at the expense of creativity. Were we to try explaining this turn of events to Leonardo da Vinci, however, he'd probably scratch his head, furrow his brow and wonder why this was. Surely, he'd argue, these subjects should not be *competing* for space on the timetable? He would almost certainly point out that children's learning in literacy should help them to articulate their responses to the visual world, while their growing understanding of *number* should encourage them to appreciate the beauty of mathematical principles. Rather than compete for space on a crowded timetable the subjects should, Leonardo would conclude, integrate harmoniously for children to engage with, interpret and value the world around them.

Leonardo's extraordinary capacity for multidisciplinary knowledge and understanding earned him a place in the title of Ivor Hickey and Deidre Robinson's *The Leonardo Effect* (2013). Hickey and Robinson argue that teachers should embrace opportunities for cross-curricular learning.

(Continued)

(Continued)

Rather than be restricted by a timetable of divided subjects, children should be encouraged to ignore traditional subject boundaries, and be given opportunities to indulge their imaginations and to learn independently or collaboratively with their peers. Given the opportunity you will find, as many teachers do, that there are a wide range of meaningful connections between subjects, and none more so than between maths and art. We sometimes perceive the two subjects to occupy opposite ends of the primary curriculum: children who excel in maths are often expected to be disinterested in the arts, whilst those with a creative streak are often perceived to struggle with numbers. With a little reflection and thoughtful planning, however, you can help children to understand that maths and art can be taught in a harmonious way: one that centres on the meaningful connections between the two disciplines.

Why link art and design with maths?

There are several reasons why teachers should explore the ways in which art and design can support and enrich children's learning in maths. First, by making meaningful connections between maths and art, teachers can help to broaden children's perceptions of the nature of both subjects. Maths, some children might think, is all about getting their sums right, learning their times tables and carrying out repetitive activities that have little relevance to their daily lives. Yet many mathematical principles, such as the properties of shapes and their relationships to one another, can be understood in purely visual ways. Through linking maths with art and design, teachers can challenge children's preconceptions of maths and remind them that learning in the subject can happen without making any calculations or writing a single number sentence.

Second, by placing an emphasis on the visual qualities of maths, teachers can offer both visual and kinaesthetic learners a wider range of opportunities to engage with the subject. Whilst some children might find it easier to listen to explanations, remember mathematical facts and articulate their learning through words, others will need to *see* what the maths looks like, or to use real objects to explore their learning. Although we often see children in Early Years settings and Key Stage 1 using real resources, such as cubes, to understand maths, as children grow older such resources tend to remain hidden away in the classroom. Art offers older children a way of building upon their understanding of mathematical concepts in a visual way that makes sense to them.

Finally, by emphasising its links with art and design, teachers can help children to appreciate the beauty of maths. You might be surprised to learn that in the 2014 version of the National Curriculum for England there is only one solitary reference to beauty: it can be found in the pages devoted to maths, rather than art and design. The relationship between beauty and maths is deeply rooted: 2,000 years ago in ancient Greece, for example, people were aware of the ways in which the proportions of architectural structures were partly dependent upon mathematical principles for their beauty. Yet there is also a mathematical element to the beauty of the natural world: slice an apple in half and you will discover that its pips are arranged in a perfect pentagon; count the petals of a flower and you will find that the number in each layer corresponds with the Fibonacci sequence; if you look at the natural world you will find endless evidence of rotational and reflective symmetry.

In the classroom

In this section, we'll look at some examples of children's work inspired by the beauty of maths. Evidence of the potential of cross-curricular links between maths and art can be seen at Ashley Primary School in Walton-on-Thames, Surrey. Uniquely, school staff place the notion of 'harmony' at the centre of all learning; a notion that encompasses the visual, the mathematical and the environmental, as deputy head teacher Jackie Stevens explained:

> We have a curriculum like no other here at Ashley. We know of no other school that engages and inspires their children through the wonders, miracles, symmetry and geometry of the world around them in the same way that we do. From the four-year-olds in our Reception classes to the Year 6 children, embedding the principles of harmony into their learning to help them understand more fully the world in which they live is becoming more and more part of everyday learning at Ashley.

Have a go at some of the following activities with colleagues before trying them out in your maths class.

Number patterns

Children can explore number patterns in the context of the natural world, such as the example of a fractal tree (Figure 7.1.1). At Ashley School, children learn about the value of natural environments, such as the coral reef, by exploring the mathematical patterns that can be found. In this activity children began each design with a single straight line, before splitting it in two, repeating the process and changing the colour to create beautiful patterns, doubling or halving numbers. Jackie added:

> It's through this link that the children have investigated coral. As a result they used fractions to create these wonderful depictions of what lives and breathes beneath the seabed. Looking closely at the results reveals the maths involved.

Figure 7.1.1 Fractal tree.

Rotational symmetry

Reflective and rotational symmetry are other areas of the maths curriculum that naturally lend themselves to work in art and design. In this activity children use compasses to create circles, before marking six points around the circumference as the starting point for creating beautiful symmetrical patterns. At Ashley School, teachers take advantage of the opportunity to make meaningful cross-curricular connections, this time with children's learning in RE. Jackie continued:

> Here are some examples of hexagons created by some of our Year 6 children. Whilst exploring Islamic art and architecture they discovered that Allah could only be portrayed though the beauty of geometric patterns. The children created a piece of collaborative art with tessellating hexagons; each hexagon is different to show the importance of diversity.

Like their work on fractal trees, children's patterns may initially look identical but eventually look distinctive and original.

Figure 7.1.2 Studying art from around the world lends itself to understanding concepts of maths and design.

Problem-solving

Problem-solving activities offer opportunities for children to use and apply the maths they are learning to 'real life' situations. In this example, the 'handshake game', children could begin by imagining people arriving at a gathering and meeting each other. When there are only two people in the room, there will only be one handshake. When there are three people there will be three and when there are four there will be six. But how many handshakes will there be when all ten people have arrived in the room? Here you can see how one group of children explored this problem in a visual way by creating a complex pattern of circles (representing people) and lines (representing handshakes).

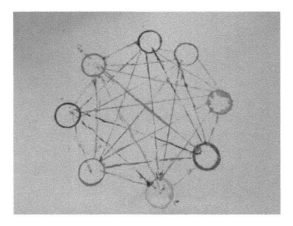

Figure 7.1.3 Problem-solving through art.

Pattern and shape

Tangrams are a wonderful way of experimenting with shape and space in maths, art and design. Specifically, tangrams offer children opportunities to explore relationships between a range of regular shapes such as squares, triangles and parallelograms. Templates for various tangrams can be easily located online and, in this activity, children used wax crayons to make rubbings of textured surfaces before applying watercolour over the rubbings: the wax resisted the watercolour, which resulted in some beautiful patterns. Children then did the same with their tangrams, before cutting out the individual shapes that form the tangram and re-arranging them into new compositions.

Figure 7.1.4 Exploring relationships through shape and space.

Tessellation

In this final activity, children built on their previous experiments with tangrams to explore ways of creating repeat patterns using computer software. Taking a scanned or photographed image of one of the shapes from their tangram, children used art and design software to copy and paste the shape, repeating the process several times and carefully positioning each shape to create a repeat pattern. Like the other activities in this section of the book, this is an idea that can be simplified for younger children and extended for older learners. Whatever their age, children will develop their understanding of the relationship between maths, art and design and of the unique range of opportunities for learning offered by this combination of subjects.

Figure 7.1.5 Computing skills are used to develop repeating patterns.

7.2

Art and ... physical education

Jonathan Doherty

Introduction

Physical education (PE) shares many common features with art and design in primary education in supporting the holistic development of children's knowledge, skills and understanding. Art and PE alike are concerned with first-hand, sensory experiences: they both require personal expression, representation of ideas and responsiveness to problems; they both involve processes of investigation, exploration and discovery; they both refine practical skills in the use and control of materials and equipment (Callaway and Kear, 1999). The following definition by Doherty and Brennan (2014) captures both the learning dimension and the 'physical' nature of PE:

> Physical education, as part of the whole education process, is a field of endeavour that is concerned with lifelong physical, intellectual, social and emotional learning that accrues through experiencing physical activities in a variety of contexts.

> (p11)

This definition is one that could easily and equally be applied to art and design.

── Theory focus ────────────────────────────

In both subjects, it is impossible to separate the physical self from the thinking self: mind and body become one. Richard Shusterman (2006) coined the term 'somaesthetics' to capture the philosophical significance of the body's role in aesthetic experience and its roots in aesthetic tradition.

(Continued)

(Continued)

The development of physical and perceptual skills is fundamental to both art and PE. For example, fine motor skills are refined when involved in activities such as moulding clay; holding or manipulating a pencil or brush requires hand preference to become secure; strength in the shoulders and hands is developed when children use art materials; a relaxed pincer grip when drawing and painting requires development of the small muscles of the forearm to control the fingers, and to provide dexterity for accuracy and fluidity (Tredgett, 2015); making sculpture and craft work helps to build symmetrical body strength, which requires children to transfer information across the midline of the body (Macintyre and McVitty, 2004).

Sensory learning

Activities in both art and PE involve the processing of visual information: observational drawing, for example, requires developed ocular-motor systems so that the eyes can flow quickly and freely across a page and direct the hand. Perception is the bridge between our conscious mind and the external world (Doherty and Hughes, 2014) and involves three key qualities: being observant; being sensitive; and being discerning, which are essential for engaging in visual pursuits. This perceptual-motor ability continually develops through the primary years due to increasing brain development during this phase of children's lives. Art and design's practical activities directly involve all of the senses: touch, for instance, is important for the information it provides through skin receptors about pressure and movement, and is needed when applying paint to paper; proprioception is the sense of where the body, or body parts, are situated within a space and is important in feeding back information during activities such as light or heavy mark making, or constructing models or sculpture; the vestibular sense gives information on body positioning, such as whether we are upright when sitting, or if balance is maintained centrally. Hannaford (1995) believes that it is through sensory experience that we represent images in our thinking and show creativity. We use all of our brain to do this: shapes, colours and patterns are processed in the brain's occipital lobes; emotional responses in the limbic systems; and movement in the basal ganglion of the limbic system. Together, these shape our thinking and increase our knowledge.

Dance: art and movement

All areas of physical education require these skills, but dance is the area that calls for individual aesthetic response and creativity most of all. Dance requires children to engage emotionally and intellectually to sensory experiences and to appreciate quality and beauty in ways that are personal and imaginative to them: exactly like art. Dance is a way of knowing that integrates all aspects of being human: kinaesthetically, emotionally, intellectually and socially. Cone and Cone (2005) state that dance exists as both art-form and movement-form. It combines functional movements with those that display expression and imagination. Through dance, children develop non-verbal communication, aesthetic appreciation and artistic expression. Children experience the processes of creating, performing and evaluating through dance, and realise what it means to be an artist (Doherty and Brennan, 2014). Dance provides an ideal medium to compose and combine a variety of actions, to learn dances from different times and places and to express feelings, moods and ideas in response to stimuli.

In the classroom: Pieter Bruegel

The artwork of Dutch painter, Pieter Bruegel, provides an ideal stimulus for combining art and PE. In Figure 7.2.1, *Children's Games* (1560, painted oil on wood canvas), he wanted to show the games he knew that children played. The painting shows an incredible 80 games that children play in the town square.

Figure 7.2.1 Kinderspiele (Children's Games) by Pieter Bruegel. KHM-Museumsverband, Vienna.

I have used this in dance lessons with Key Stage 1 children successfully for many years. I suggest printing good quality colour images, laminating them and having enough for children to work in groups of three to four.

- Let them spend time looking at the picture and discussing it. You can provide some initial prompts to scaffold their thinking: What games can you see in the painting? How many games do you recognise? Can you name them? Which games use equipment and which don't? Would you say more games are played in pairs or small groups than are played alone? Why might this be?

- After a short time, let the children choose a favourite game they can see in the painting and set them the task of representing this in movement. Let them select several more 'games' from the picture and put aspects of these into their dance.

- You might then ask the groups to perform their dance, while the rest of the class watch and provide an evaluation of the dance.

- You can follow this up in the classroom by discussing the painting and how games have not really changed since it was painted.

- Point out the artist's use of the colour red to lead the viewers' eyes around the artwork.

- Ask the children to draw an action scene reminding them to use colour in the same way. Use pencils and oil pastels before finishing off by adding a wash of diluted brown tempera paint or watercolour, which they could sponge or paint over their drawing to produce a resist effect.

Building a foundation of movement

Understanding movement is fundamental to expressive subjects in schools. Jensen (2000) described this as *the choreography of systems* because complex movement production activates multiple learning systems in the brain. It involves the pleasure and reward systems (thalamus); balance systems (vestibular); visual systems (occipital); sensory-motor (cerebellum); emotional attunement (amygdala) and the memory systems (parietal and temporal lobes). Each has its own trigger. For instance, our attentional system is activated by movement, contrast and shape, so mind and body really do work together. Movement (in relation to dance) is often classified into four categories (Davies, 2001):

- **What:** body actions, shape, articulation, design and fluency.

- **Where:** size, extension, zone, level and direction.

- **Who:** the relationships of body parts to the whole body: this involves relationships with both objects and people.

- **How:** the dynamics of weight, space, time and flow.

Contemporary art: performance

Children will, with support, develop their ability to observe, analyse and make judgements on the dances they see. By teaching them appropriate language, they can record sophisticated responses to dances, which can be written or drawn. Knowledge of the body and how it performs, with concepts such as balance, form and rhythm, are easily transferred to art, as can be seen in the work of artist Heather Hansen, who combines dance with drawing to produce performance art. Her large charcoal drawings show how movement and creating art are inextricably linked as it is the movement in her work that really brings them to life. You could replicate her techniques by taking drawing materials to a dance session, and asking the children to draw as they dance. Explain that you are not looking for them to draw pictures, but make marks that they think best represent the movements they are making whilst dancing. 'Dance my design' is a simple activity where children draw a pattern on a large piece of paper during a dance lesson. Say to your class: Watch this movement. Now show that to me by drawing. You can vary the patterns to include twisting patterns drawn slowly, or try jagged patterns drawn fast.

Look at Heather's website: **www.heatherhansen.net**

This section has aimed to show the strong links that exist between PE and art. It has shown how movement is at the core of physical and artistic education and has as much to do with the natural physical development of the child as the intellectual and brain development. We have explored the idea that dance, through similar processes of composition, improvisation and exploration, as well as observation and analysis, affects children's physical and perceptual skills, and that children's enjoyment and

Figure 7.2.2 *Children work in pairs to explore movement through drawing.*

Figure 7.2.3 *Capturing dance movement on paper.*

Figure 7.2.4 A child's drawing that explores movement.

motivation to learn is enhanced when these two dynamic and exciting subjects are taught together. It has focused on dance as an expressive medium and given ideas for you to try with your class. Drawing, painting, clay modelling, printing and sculpture can all be inspired through dancing.

Reflection point

Observe a dance lesson during your PPA time.

- If possible, do this exercise with colleagues. Take some drawing materials with you and observe children during a dance lesson.
- What movements can you see in their dance? Describe them. Draw them: is the dance convincing?
- Is there variety in movement? Is there variety in the marks you have made?
- What shapes can you see in the movement? Can you draw those shapes?
- How does watching this dance make you feel? What ideas or feelings do you think the dances were trying to express?

Practical activity

Have a go!

- Capture everyday movement in art: study animal tracks, tyre tracks or footprints in sand.
- Use black felt tips in repeating patterns on white paper to give the illusion of movement.

- Use a pencil and a ruler to repeat a line that is rotated each time to give a blurred movement effect.
- Encourage children to compose 'action words' to describe their dances (e.g. curvy, pointed, zig-zag, floppily, spiralling, twisting, swooping, floating, rising, accelerating, wriggling, writhing). Dance these. Draw them to show the movement involved.
- Combine three action words together into a sequence.
- Create a word wall in your classroom with movement words under the categories of 'What', 'Where', 'Who' and 'How' the body moves.
- Organise children into small groups with the task of creating a group body sculpture. Children can take this idea further and represent ideas such as bravery, happiness or trust in their sculpture.
- Body machinery: form a group to represent people in action in a body sculpture.
- Try drawing a crowd at a football match!
- Dances from other cultures offer further exploration of the body and its movement: read the story of *Rama*. Provide photographs of Indian dance hand gestures. Children can then explore how parts of hands touch each other. Then experiment with ways of opening and closing hands at different speeds and tensions, and make up hand clapping rhythms as part of composed dances.
- Depict colour in dance: actions of stretching, bright, lively movements and quick jumps depict yellow. Red can represent wide jumps or travelling actions. Purple, the regal colour, might be accompanied by high level movements and slow measured walking actions. Children can make up their own dance patterns to other colours of their choice.

Practical activity

More drawing

Learn to draw movement.

www.theguardian.com/artanddesign/2009/sep/19/learn-to-draw-movement

7.3

Art and ... music

Alastair Greig

Introduction

Creative practice encourages the ability to establish concrete links between subjects, to ask questions and to provide an imaginative environment for children to feel safe in experimenting with artistic practices. Of course, we all want to encourage children to be creative in music making as well as in art, but often the concepts associated with music, such as standardised notation, can interfere with the process and instil anxiety in primary teachers who are not specialised in the intricacies of representing sound on manuscript paper. Such outcomes can be difficult to analyse without the benefit of extensive study and understanding of post-Second World War, contemporary, classical music. In this chapter, we shall examine a number of significant musical works from that period, opening up possibilities for appropriate adaptation within any primary classroom, and connecting art and music in a manner that is secure and clear.

Whilst we could spend an entire series of books examining music of the past 70 years, and looking at how we could link these with art to use the ideas with primary aged children, we must seek to address less obvious ties between the two subjects. For example, we can start by looking at pieces of art from the past, and how we can use paintings as starting points for musical discovery and, of course, vice versa.

Art or music?

Look at the image in Figure 7.3.1. Is this a piece of art or a musical score? In effect, it is both. Many composers have used graphic notation to express sounds and ideas in this way, as it would be impossible to represent the same thing using standard western notation. This provides us with a most appropriate starting point to explore the links between art and music. The score, after all, is the visual representation of the composer's intentions and only becomes music once performers begin interpreting the series of signs and symbols from the paper.

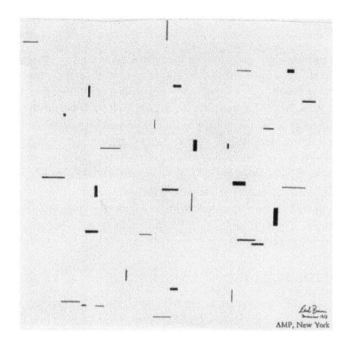

Figure 7.3.1 Earle Brown, December 1952.

The composer, Earle Brown, has provided musicians with a series of rectangles and lines left hanging in space as if they were part of a mobile sculpture, rather like those by artist Alexander Calder. What he has left out is significant, particularly for our purposes. A conventional music score would always have a clear indication of which instruments are to be played at the start of the manuscript, as well as a time signature and a key signature to explain which set of notes to use, and so on. This score has none of these and leaves such decisions to individual musicians and the conductor, which therefore involves them in the process of creation. Each rendition of the work will be unique, dependent on choice of instruments, notes, durations, environment and many other factors. The parallels between this open-ended approach (which was considered radical and innovative at the time), and what takes place when children create music are striking.

The pragmatic nature of the composition, making it performable by any combination of instruments, plays directly into the question of which instrumental resources are available for the teacher and class. For instance, you could explore sounds created by children using body percussion or their voices, or assign the shapes in the score to specific sonic objects and work towards a performance of the music. You might decide to approach this in another way entirely, which would be better suited to your class, but the *flexibility* is there to make those differences work. Now you know that musical exploration of this kind took place many years ago and is documented in the annals of music history, it allows you to plan a series of lessons combining art and music with the added confidence that this is a legitimate pursuit of composers working in the professional environment. It will also enable children to understand how music is created, communicated and appraised.

Chicken or egg?

Does the score or the sound come first? This is a question for the creative planner to ask and to find their own solution. In this example, I make no apology for starting with the realisation of visual symbols that will, later on, form a score. Swiss artist Paul Klee's famous opening to the *Pedagogical Sketchbook*, written in 1925, where he proposes: *An **active** line on a walk, moving freely, without a goal* (Klee, 1955) can be followed up by planning a series of mark making activities for children, such as exploring straight lines, curves, density and pressure, shapes and so on. The outcome would be a piece of artwork and a musical score, but without pre-conceived sounds. Before applying sounds to the visual image, it would be helpful for children to explore individual timbre of whatever sonic resources the school has hidden away on the music trolley, but these are probably percussion instruments (pitched and non-pitched). This activity should be free, exploratory play without a specific goal but with pure experimentation. This will allow the children to gain confidence with the instruments, and formulate an aural memory of possibilities.

Bring art and music together

These two aspects of art and sound work could then be combined, affording the children ample time to explore and choose specific sounds that best match the illustrations within their graphic scores. The ideal way to achieve this would be to divide the class into groups of between four and six children, each contributing to the others' musical creations. Dependent upon the age phase of the class, I do not think it is necessary to play the original catalyst, *December 1952*, to the children, or to launch into an explanation of the history of music post-1945, as this would be superfluous and merely tick the box marked 'I must impart knowledge because I am a teacher'. You, the teacher, need to know this information so that you have a reasonably secure theoretical foundation upon which to construct your plans, but do your children need to know that Brown conducted a performance at the Ferienkurse in Darmstadt, Germany in 1964? I think not! If, however, you wish to begin a music lesson with pre-existing works of art as stimuli for the above process, you would find many examples to use in the work of the aforementioned Alexander Calder, Jackson Pollock, Mark Rothko, Paul Klee or Wassily Kandinsky, to name but a few.

Kandinsky and Schoenberg

Generally speaking, colour is power, which directly influences the soul. Colour is the keyboard, the eyes are the hammers, the soul is the piano with many strings. The artist is the hand which plays, touching one key or another, to cause vibrations in the soul.

(Wassily Kandinsky, 1914)

Two giants of twentieth-century art and music, the Russian pioneer of abstract art, Wassily Kandinsky, and the reluctant revolutionary composer, Arnold Schoenberg, knew all about links between art and music and made them explicit in their theoretical and artistic works, details of which can be read in their correspondence (1984). Kandinsky produced a stage work in 1909 entitled *Der Gelbe Klang* (The Yellow Sound) illustrating his theories on colour. The same year saw the composition of Schoenberg's '5 Orchestral Pieces', the third of which is called *Farben* (*Colours*).

This piece was said to have inspired Schoenberg's theoretical *Klangfarbenmelodie* (*Tone Colour Melody*) where timbre, the 'colours' of instruments, could replace pitch as a defining element in music. Do forgive the history lesson, but I think it important to note that if two of the major figures in their respective art forms deem it appropriate to explore connections between music and art, then it's perfectly acceptable to use this in a primary classroom although, perhaps, we should approach it appropriately for the age phases concerned.

Practical activity

Have a go

Figure 7.3.2, taken from *Point and Line to Plane,* illustrates the connection rather succinctly. Here, Kandinsky transforms the second theme of Beethoven's Fifth Symphony, first movement, into a visual form using points and lines. There's a lesson here, methinks.

Take a well-known melody of your choice, perhaps something familiar to children, and play a simple recording of it to them. Ask them to use points (dots) and lines to create a visual representation of what they hear. This could lead to all kinds of musical and artistic lessons, choosing different pieces of music and creating visual realisations utilising colour, shape, lines, textures, marks and so on. The reverse process works too: mix up the graphic 'scores' and ask the children to create musical realisations of their peers' work.

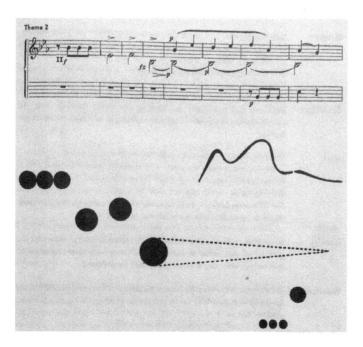

Figure 7.3.2 Punkt und Linie zu Fläche. Kandinsky, W (ed), Gropius, W and Moholy-Nagy, L (1926) Berlin: Bauhaus.

Subject knowledge and practice

Despite the imposing name of *Klangfarbenmelodie*, this is a concept that can be adapted for children. Using percussion instruments, you could ask your class to explore and discover new ways to play instruments, thus experimenting with timbre. The resulting sounds could then be combined using one child as conductor to direct who plays, when, for how long and where. The finished piece can then be turned into a painting, sculpture or collage created by the class. An imaginative and open-ended series of practical lessons could easily be organised, in both subjects, all with an extremely secure theoretical base. The children do not necessarily need to know the origin of your thinking at this stage, but a brief mention in your plans would satisfy National Curriculum requirements. Of course, the end results of the music may not feature heavily on your relaxing playlist, but that is not what this is about. Here, we are engaging children in the process of creativity, allowing them to experiment in a safe and conducive environment, work together and increase their subject vocabulary through group work and interaction with one another, thus building self-esteem and confidence through performing and sharing their work.

Divergent thinking: the music of John Cage

John Cage was famous for composing a piece consisting of silence, and for many other innovative and exciting compositions and events. His work is worth looking at for a cornucopia of potential lesson ideas. Take, for example, the opening of his *Aria* for any voice range: sounds, pitched and non-pitched, are determined by the performer (singer), although Cage indicates pitch vertically and the colours suggest modes of singing. (To see the colours you will need to look online or print colour copies for the children.)

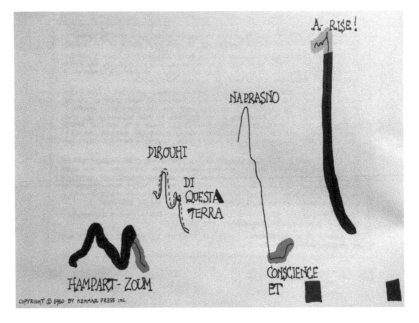

Figure 7.3.3 John Cage's Aria.

The freedom given to the performer, in this instance, is another theoretical foundation upon which to build lessons allowing the children to be free to interpret visual media in whatever sonic form it may take.

Further research on this composer would reveal his interest in altering perceived timbres of instruments, such as the piano. His experiments with 'preparing' the piano by inserting nails, screws and other objects between the piano strings resulted in extraordinary sounds emanating from such a commonplace instrument. I am not suggesting that you dismantle the piano in the school hall (although children and I have done this), but it does suggest that using instruments in unconventional ways is a means to facilitate musical creativity with your class and discover new modes of visual representation, which could be a fertile ground for visually artistic interventions.

Summary

We have only skimmed the tip of an enormous iceberg in this section. There are many opportunities for linking music and art together in your classroom, and I hope that you have seen how many subjects can co-exist during one imaginative and creative session: I also hope that this will inspire you to discover more links yourself. The one important point for you, as the teacher, is to understand how composers in the twentieth century experimented with music and sound, the results of which were not always considered beautiful but are always interesting, stimulating and will place the children's own creations within a context that is personally appropriate.

Further reading

Hayes, D (2010) The seductive charms of a cross-curricular approach. *International Journal of Primary, Elementary and Early Years Education,* Education 3–13. Available at: **www.tandfonline.com/loi/rett20**

Jan Molenaer's *Two Boys and a Girl Making Music*, 1629. The National Gallery's Take One Picture. **www.takeonepicture.org.uk/exhibition/2007/index.html**

Tate Kids: ideas for art and music: **http://kids.tate.org.uk/create/art_and_music.shtm**

7.4
Art and ... history
Karin Doull

Introduction

Humanities subjects and the creative arts are natural bedfellows. History investigates the human past: within that past, art and artistic expression play an integral part of experience. Visual images, ceramics, architectural decoration and 3D representations of human and animal forms provide powerful sources of evidence about people's lives, as Cooper (2012) suggests: *They are embedded in the narrative of history* (2012, p183). The art of a specific period can shape our understanding of that era, defining our view of significant characters and events. For example, we all *know* what Henry VIII looked like from the iconic portraits painted by Hans Holbein, conveying messages of the king's power and might. Every school library has a textbook on ancient Egypt, showing images of Nebamun hunting in the marshes, or Tutankhamun and Ankhesenamun on the golden throne. We use these to create visual reference points in our heads, building up a repertoire of different styles that allow us to locate these images in time. Whilst we share these sources, each discipline would approach them differently: artists will consider creation of the image or artefact, while the historian will seek to understand what they tell us of people's lives and ideas at that time. As Colllingwood states: *Art is a personally constructed interpretation and so reflects the culture that led to its creation* (Cooper, 2012, p183) enabling us to consider what aspects of time the artist chooses to emphasise.

Art can also be used as an outcome of historical investigation: children can demonstrate their understanding through the completion of a piece of artwork linked to historical enquiry. This might represent their perception of the significance of the person, theme or event explored. In considering controversial or emotive history, children can utilise art expression to demonstrate emotional engagement. A shared art project encourages children to contribute to both individual and group responses, resulting in a multiplicity of viewpoints that are often required for discussion when considering complex or emotive histories.

In both their thinking and their research, historians should, responsibly, unsettle their audiences, provoking them to think harder and deeper about the human condition.

(Jordanova, 2010, p4)

If we are to tie this thought from Ludmilla Jordanova to the suggestion of art educator, Henry Ward, that *issues-based and thematic projects have long been the staple diet of most art education* (**www. henryhward.com/art-as-cross-curricular-tool**) then we can see how combining history with art allows children to investigate hard and complex issues. By selecting a controversial historical theme, or one that encourages children to engage in emotive thinking, we create meaningful contexts for creative responses. Cowen and Maitles (1999) state: *Expressive arts ... was found to be effective in helping pupils to understand and feel like what it was like to be treated differently from others and in conveying personal responses to their learning.* Teaching emotive and controversial history, by its very nature, requires careful thought and preparation on the part of the teacher to help bring real past events to life and make the stories about people, *three-dimensional rather than actors in fancy dress* (T.E.A.C.H, 2007, p8).

═══ Case study ═══

It is important to ensure that historical investigation allows children time to discuss and debate issues in order to develop a good depth of understanding: it is all too easy to take a superficial view of a subject and skim over issues that should be challenged rather than simply accepted. This case study considers how student teachers worked with children to use art to express their understanding of the story of the 'Kindertransport'.

The Kindertransport was the name given to the evacuation of (mainly) Jewish children from Germany, Austria and Czechoslovakia to Britain on the very eve of the Second World War. After the pogroms of Kristallnacht on 9 and 10 November 1938, British public opinion began to advocate for the evacuation of Jewish children. The first transport arrived on 2 December 1938. The last left the Greater Reich on 1 September 1939, two days before the declaration of war. Transports continued to leave from the Netherlands until 14 May, the day the Dutch government surrendered to the Germans. In all, Britain accepted 10,000 children, saving them from death, which was the fate of 90 per cent of the Jewish children in occupied Europe. This is what is described as a 'redemptive story' as these children, although scarred and shaped by their experiences, survived. When considering a controversial and emotive subject such as the Holocaust, it is important to ensure that it is taught at a level that is appropriate for the age and emotional maturity of the children concerned.

This project focused on final-year student teachers planning a series of activities to help children understand the story of the Kindertransport, whilst using art to convey their responses. Tutors from the subject areas provided input, including a gallery visit, to develop students' subject knowledge and suggest possible lines of development or activities. The nature of the subject meant that it was most appropriate for the project to run with upper primary children (Years 5 and 6). The emphasis was on telling the story in a creative and imaginative manner.

Cross-curricular learning

Cross-curricular learning is potentially a very powerful learning tool, as it allows children to transcend subject boundaries, making clear connections between disciplines and broadening their scope of understanding. In order for cross-curricular learning to succeed, however, it is important that subject-specific learning intentions are identified. This ensures that *the integrity of each discipline is maintained* (Van der Merwe, 2007, p182). I wanted students to ensure that they focused on individual stories of real children. In this way they could come to see that *homing in on the single story of an individual figure from the period can be a means of learners identifying with the plight shared by many thousands or millions of people* (T.E.A.C.H 2007, p20). There must, however, be authenticity of the background story and information, as Yehuda Bauer suggests: *[W]e have to start with the history, and the history has to be placed in the proper context* (Bauer, 2004). Students also needed to ensure that they provided children with primary sources to work with, for, *if the sources used are not authentic then their histories are fiction* (Turner-Bisset, 2005, p27)

History learning intentions

1. Construct informed responses that involve the selection and organisation of relevant historical information.

2. Give some reasons for, and results of, the main events and changes in the periods studied.

3. Know that some events, people and changes have been interpreted in different ways and suggest possible reasons for this.

In art, students were encouraged to use 'found materials' as a basis for allowing children to explore these and then use them to create responses. The work of different artists was used as a visual stimulus, but specifically Katie Holten's *Excavated Tree (Flowering Dogwood)* as the exposed roots could symbolise the deep-rooted connections with family and culture for the children who were sent on the transport (**www.creativeconnexions.eu/cg/2013/01/katie-holten-excavated-tree-flowering-dogwood**).

Art learning intentions

1. Learn about the work of other artists, and to be influenced and inspired by art and events of the past.

2. Improve children's mastery of art and design techniques with a range of materials, with creativity and experimentation.

3. To use expressive art to reflect, visually respond and comment on emotive issues.

Students worked in a group to plan a series of activities over a day that would allow children to consider the historical aspect through expressive art. They began by using drama strategies, such as dressing up in 1940s outfits to introduce the history element, and providing children with the story of the Kindertransport. Some introduced the Kindertransport children through recreated suitcases, or by exploring the notion of 'journey'. Children developed ideas about the story and sequence of events by researching and making: art activities were used to help children show their responses.

Figure 7.4.1 Teaching students holding children's artwork on the theme of 'journey'.

In the classroom

One group of students undertook an extensive project to combine a number of elements within an installation using Katie Holten's *Evacuated Tree* as inspiration. The image of this solitary tree created a strong visual metaphor relating to ideas of isolation, identity and belonging. The students decided to create their own version with the children. They sourced materials for a trunk and base, cut some stylised branches from MDF and gathered actual cuttings of branches and roots. In the classroom the children painted the MDF branches and created a textured trunk with paint and crepe paper. Children assembled the piece, with roots and branches spreading outwards, and created train tracks, representing the journey to climb the trunk, with painted words to express the children's feelings. Each child then created a number of small items to add to the installation.

- Diary entries as scrolls detailing their feelings about leaving. These were added to the roots.

- Luggage labels detailing what they would take with them and why they wanted that item.

- Postcards sent back to families that were lodged in the branches. Children chose from a number of images that reflected the period.

- Transparency portraits of actual 'kinder'. Children used shading and tone to trace over photographs of children who had travelled on the trains.

Colour was an important element to convey emotion and pupils were presented with a range of options. The colour of the ribbons for the scrolls tended to be darker, representing loss and fear.

Figure 7.4.2 Diary scrolls tied with ribbon to symbolise the memories and emotional attachment.

Postcards were tied to the branches with brighter and shinier ribbon to represent more positive feelings. For the photo tracings, children could choose either single or multiple colours: some chose to use more than one colour to represent conflicting emotions about the journey. Students used open-ended questions to encourage the children to justify their choices. Why might you feel that way? What does this colour ribbon make you think of? How could you show that you feel both scared and excited? Students and pupils discussed the activity and explored ideas about the story of the event. Cooper would see this as an essential element in creative history teaching: *Collaboration is frequently seen as generating creativity* (2013, p24).

The completed installation demonstrated the children's understanding of the story of the Kindertransport through a variety of media. Whilst they had combined the two subject areas to investigate the question of what happened to these Jewish children, evacuated at the last moment before war, the learning of each subject remained discrete and distinct. This allowed the subjects to enhance and develop each other in a symbiotic way, creating an emotional response that was based on historical reality.

Figure 7.4.3 The finished tree is tangible evidence of the children's learning during the day's project.

Art is an expression of human experience; it allows students to acquire a type of historical understanding easily accommodating various perspectives and fosters a degree of empathy for historical actors.

(Suh, 2013, p138)

Further reading

Davies, I (ed) (2000) *Teaching the Holocaust: Educational Dimensions, Principles and Practice*. London: Continuum.

UCL Centre for Holocaust Education: **www.holocausteducation.org.uk/holocaust-education**

Holocaust Educational Trust: **www.het.org.uk/education**

Resources, such as factsheets linked to individual Kindertransport children, are available from websites such as **www.ajr.org.uk/kindertransport** and **www.kindertransport.org/history.htm**

7.5

Art and ...
geography

Anthony Barlow

Introduction

Geography is one of the humanities subjects in primary education, alongside RE and history. As such, these subjects *explore human experience* (Grigg and Hughes, 2013, p2) and amongst other things *promote deep thinking by stimulating debate, questioning and reflection* (ibid., 2012, p6). This section will look at how we can combine the two subjects of art and geography to enhance learning in both subjects, particularly through using art images to provoke and promote debate and questioning in a geographical context. I will argue that engaging with art images through the lens of geography and art might give multiple perspectives: seeing descriptive and instructional qualities, alongside aesthetic and artistic ones.

Personal responses

> Art is not confined to the way one person responds to it. It is the sum of subtle, private, individual, idiosyncratic feelings and we cannot know those, because they are shut away in other people's consciousness. So it might be that none of us know much about the world, though we know what we like.
>
> (Carey, 2005, p31)

Here I could paraphrase Professor John Carey's final statement in the opening chapter of his provocative book, *What Good are the Arts?* (2005), by substituting the word 'art' for 'geography'. It's a powerful idea that we all have 'personal geographies': personal responses to places, people and environments. This can be achieved through linking geography with art because personal response is the bedrock of artistic learning and expression. For Early Years and primary geographers, this statement is also a challenge for us to view our subjects differently, but at the same time it is a helpful way to reconceptualise our understanding of how we view these subjects. We can value this as teachers, and it can also help to highlight one of the important new subheadings within the 2014 Primary National Curriculum for England, which is that 'place knowledge', or situating ourselves within a place (i.e. pupils developing a 'sense of place') should be taken seriously. This can be achieved through active participation in outdoor learning, but also by using interesting art images that will spark children's curiosity and asking them to respond visually, through art.

Using images

Sometimes teachers might expect *correct* responses from pupils when looking at an image. After all, we have expectations and outcomes to meet, maybe we don't like surprises much, and we know what a right answer should be. In addition, we might be showing a picture which was created by a photographer or artist for a reason, right? But have you stopped to consider what a child's view might be? If children rely on a fixed view (i.e. that teacher knows best), it can prevent them from thinking for themselves, and they become afraid to suggest answers for fear of being wrong. When looking at images with children, it is very important to develop their capacity for enquiry and give them time to consider their response, for example by using strategies such as *think-pair-share* (Lyman, 1981). What children perceive, think or feel, and their view of their world as they see it, is as important as what we think, or know to be facts. This new approach to primary geography is sometimes called *everyday geography* or *ethno-geography* (Martin, 2008). This theory corresponds to post-modern art practice, which is underpinned by everyday experiences being key to both making and responding through visual media.

Key ideas

The aforementioned book by Carey, *What Good are the Arts?*, could equally have given me the title for this section: *What Good is Geography?*, as for some teachers there seems to be little purpose beyond that it is on the statutory curriculum, therefore it must be studied. A common mistake is that the learning is not rooted, or does not begin, within what children know already in their everyday lives and familiar environments, allowing connections to be made. However, this can be easily rectified as no matter where your own placement or school is situated, you can create meaningful connections. For example, if you are studying the Caribbean, and looking at images of pristine beaches, but your school is in an inner-city where children have never even seen the sea, there are still similarities and differences to be explored. Links between *there* and *here* can be made, allowing the social distance (Bogardus, 1925) between people, places and contrasting environments to be reduced. *There* can be brought towards the *here* and *now* of children's lives, reducing the physical and perceptual distance and promoting *understanding* rather than *otherness*. If you haven't watched Chimamanda Ngozi Adichie's TED Talk on 'The danger of a single story', I highly recommend it: **www.ted.com/talks/chimamanda_adichie_the_danger_of_a_single_story**

She explains her experiences as a Nigerian girl in England and talks about stereotypical perceptions and responses that others have shown towards her, as well as what Africa as a continent means to her.

Human-ities!

In primary schools where geography is judged inadequate by OFSTED (2011), it is stated that many pupils have weak core knowledge and a poor understanding of the world they live in. My own perception is that this might be because of a lack of developing relationships between people in geographical learning, where the 'human' aspects have been removed from the humanities. If you refer to the first chapter of this book and look at the work of Edmund Burke Feldman (1970), you would do well to utilise strong links with art and design to find a way of putting the human aspect back into teaching geography. Incidentally, physical aspects of geography are also often criticised by OFSTED as not a strong area either, and I am not arguing for an either/or scenario within the curriculum, but for *both* being taught *together*, and for using art to explore and express social, physical and emotional personal geographies.

Knowledge versus understanding

Catling (2015) has shown, in studies with pre-service teachers, that geography is still often viewed as *an information-based subject, with locational and world knowledge (information about countries and features) being dominant* (2005, p242). This *very narrow conception of geography* (Preston, 2014) is largely centered on *locational knowledge,* where the risk is that the learning is reduced to a pub quiz-style list of continents, capitals, oceans and seas. This view could be seen to lack real knowledge and understanding of 'place', as locations need to be contextualised and linked to prior knowledge. For geography, like art, to excel in the primary school it needs to appeal to the individual and the connections they make with the world: Carey's idea that it is about *personal response* and *subtle, private* and *idiosyncratic feelings* resonates strongly here. Standish states that:

> the notion that knowledge is rooted in the social context in which it was produced, denying the possibility for abstraction and shared cultural understanding, has undermined the view of geography as a body of knowledge and skills.

> (2009, p44)

This is where art and design can come into its own, to offer that sense of wonder through discussion and debate, by observing intriguing images of places from around the world. For example, look at those by Yann Arthus-Bertrand: *Earth from the air*: **www.yannarthusbertrand2.org**

Art is founded on embedded cultural knowledge, as Carey argues in his book, and can suffer the same fate as geography if teachers try to look for correct responses, or a certain set of knowledge, rather than enquiry and exploration. The following example shows how geography and art can work together to develop a deep-seated 'sense of place' that enables children to learn geographical concepts in a holistic and meaningful way.

Take one location

I live in London, and therefore have a certain understanding and 'sense of place' about the city. You, the reader, could live anywhere at all, and certainly not necessarily in our capital, but if you are teaching about London it can be all too easy to fall prey to stereotypes by showing children traditional symbols, such as the London bus or Big Ben. Using artwork can be a good way to introduce alternative viewpoints and, through discussion, can help to encourage a more open-minded perspective. Through looking at artwork, children learn that there are no fixed or correct answers that are directly right or wrong, and it will allow them to question, empathise and imagine, to help them gain a sense of place. An example is the work of artist, Stik, whose signature graffiti-style work can be seen in many London venues and draws attention to features of buildings that would otherwise be missed by the passer-by. Stik's work exists in many worldwide locations, so once again the notion of personal connections and social distance can be highlighted. See his work here: **www.stik.org**

London is a place that can be studied by any age phase through themes such as industry, landmarks, the built environment or rivers, people, etc. Studying specific cities such as London is essential to ensure curriculum coverage and to teach children about their own country, but this can also be problematic: how can we give children a real sense of place if we can't actually go to that place? If we are considering children's everyday geographies, this will be much more than just showing them a photo of a London landmark or of the River Thames. Making the effort to go beyond the

Figure 7.5.1 *Student teachers worked with Year 6 children on the theme of 'London and British Values: The Bake Off!' to produce cake sculptures, influenced by both London landmarks and the work of British artists.*

usual tourism stereotypes is key: look for a wide range of images such as those from contemporary artists, filmmakers and photographers to inspire thoughtful dialogue with your class. You can use your questioning skills with the images to build and extend learning. Try this popular list of enquiry questions to start with: *What is the place like? Why is this place as it is? How is this place connected to other places? How is this place changing? How would it feel to live in this place?* (Storm, 1989, p4).

For me, when using photographs or images to promote discussion and thinking, the 'what ifs ... ' are just as important as what the image actually shows. Allied with everyday geography, the process of thinking geographically is very important; exactly the same can be said for creativity through art: allied with everyday creativity, the process of thinking artistically is also very important (Craft, 2001; Eisner, 2002). The emotional aspect of geography is expressed as 'geographical imagination': a term developed by Doreen Massey:

> *It is probably now well accepted, though it is still important to argue, that a lot of our 'geography' is in the mind. That is to say, we carry around with us mental images of the world, of the country in which we live, of the street next door. All of us carry such images ... and talking about them is one good way in, to beginning to examine what it means to think geographically.*
>
> (Massey, 2006, p48)

Table 7.5.1 will help you to engage with geographical concepts through the lens of art images.

Table 7.5.1 Ideas for using art images in geography

Outcomes	Ideas
Consider the whole image.	Where can you see foreground/middleground/background? Can you see the horizon? Where is the sun in the sky? What does this tell you? What time of year do you think it is? Cut up the picture and ask children to reconstruct it. Ask them to think about positional and directional language. Give children half of an image (make a cut across a significant feature, e.g. the horizon). Use sticky notes for children to hide aspects of their image. Children then swap images with another child and write or draw what is missing.
Use specialist vocabulary.	How would you label or annotate the picture? Can you use a geographical dictionary to help you find vocabulary? What diagrams can we use or create that would compare with the scene? Use vocabulary word cards regularly with images: Which words match the picture/describe the opposites of the scene? Can you think of synonyms/antonyms that correspond with the scene? Play 'hangman' to develop geographical and art-related vocabulary related to the images you are using.

Practise skills.	Sketching, labelling, questioning, comparing and evaluating. Use software technology, such as Evernote, Sketch, or a simple transparent overlay in plastic.
Encourage comparisons with seemingly different scenes.	Enable comparisons and contrasts to broaden an understanding of contrasting localities. Compare a city/area they are familiar with to one which is unknown to them (e.g. London vs Manhattan), or different scenes of mountains (e.g. Grampians vs Rocky Mountains).
Taking their own pictures.	Discuss techniques involved: aerial views, side views, ground level view, bird's eye, etc. Offer children a challenge to take three pictures on theme, print them out, look at the differences and discuss what these images reveal (e.g. What would we want to improve or change about our environment?)
Ensure understanding of a 'frozen moment'.	A picture never tells the whole story: it is a moment in time, taken from a particular angle in a particular place. Show children one of your own images and explain what you cropped from the image, both in the moment and when you prepared it to be shown. Show them 'what happened next' images from natural disasters (e.g. Japanese tsunami in 2011: **www.theguardian.com/world/ interactive/2011/sep/08/japan-tsunami-before-after-pictures**) Explain how this can change how you view the image. Other good examples online would be: **www.beyondintractability. org/cic_images/talarico-brazil-pic3.png** or **www.bit.ly/2guRf16**

Adapted from Richardson (2009).

Summary

I hope that, through this short piece, I have shown that there are strong links between views of the world that are shown through artworks, and facilitating an understanding of the world geographically. Images should be discussed, debated and challenged. Children's views need to be taken into account so we can draw upon the skills that are part of art learning to develop these important aspects of children's educational experience. Children can then go on to make a personal response through creating their own artwork linked to their geographical learning. Michael Rosen once asked the question, *what is the use of education if children cannot find out who they are and what their place in the world is?* (BBC1, 2010) and through linking geography with art you will help children to do exactly that: to enable them to discover their identity within a sense of place.

━━━ Further reading ━━

Hawkins, H (2013) Geography and art. An expanding field: site, the body and practice. *Dialogues in Human Geography,* 37: 1.

Schultz, K (2011) *Being Wrong: Adventures in the Margin of Error.* London: Portobello Books.

Find out about postmodernism: **www.tate.org.uk/learn/online-resources/glossary/p/ postmodernism**

7.6
Art and ... science
Padraig Egan

There is grandeur in this view of life ... from so simple a beginning endless forms most beautiful and most wonderful have been, and are being evolved.

(Charles Darwin)

Introduction: the role of observation

You might know Charles Darwin as a scientist and theorist but he was also a talented artist with interests in the natural world. His famous drawings from the Galapagos Islands are not just studies of birds but works of art, which were beautifully crafted through observation. Darwin, like many artists, minutely observed the world around him: a skill which is innate to both artists and scientists, and a quality which is fostered in the Primary Science Curriculum (DfE, 2015). Darwin influenced many artists of his time, such as Claude Monet and Edgar Degas, who were inspired by his evolutionary ideas. He was a very creative person, whose observation skills were the foundation of his work in classifying the world by its species and recognising the significance of how we interact with each other. Furthermore, we can look to the time of the Renaissance which, as Bradburne (2001) suggests, is when the skill of *observation* became critical to artistic practice, and Leonardo da Vinci is mentioned as *the intelligent observer par excellence* (2001, p9). Observation from direct experience was key to Leonardo's achievements: he held absolute belief in the necessity for this and it fuelled his insatiable curiosity for everything around him. The outcome was an unparalleled understanding of the natural world which informed all his endeavours, including his art. So, it is within these traditions set by Darwin and da Vinci that children do not see learning in terms of separate subjects, but they try to make sense of the world through their observations and first-hand experiences. This is obvious to us when we watch children at play as, through this medium, children learn a plethora of concepts across all the different subjects, which seamlessly interlink with one another. In this section, we shall look at how art and science can be successfully interlinked to accelerate learning in both subjects. We shall also examine a case study which demonstrates how art and science can be successfully taught together within a school garden project.

Links between art and science in the curriculum

In the subject of science, children are encouraged to explore, observe and find out about things pertaining to the world around them (DfE, 2013). Examining things for scientific purposes is usually achieved through inquiry-based activities, which develop children's inquiry skills, such as observing, asking questions and looking for patterns (Sackes et al., 2009). These skills are key, as they lay down the foundations for developing scientific skills and attitudes needed for later life (ibid.). They are also skills that are highly valued within art education. Cremin et al. (2015) indicate that there is a synergy between science education and creativity, which allows teachers to contextualise children's investigative and exploratory engagement in meaningful ways. Therefore, art is deemed an effective pedagogical tool that gives children a context for exploring concepts in the science classroom (Ansberry and Morgan, 2007). Similarly, artists and scientists alike attempt to understand all manner of things through observation, classifying, measuring and making new connections. They share an innate curiosity about the world and how things work, just as children do. These can be viewed as a common bond which ties the two disciplines together. There are many examples in contemporary art where it would be difficult to specify whether the work is art or whether it is science. For example, you could have a look at the work of British artist Ann Veronica Janssens on the website of London's Wellcome Musuem: **www.wellcomecollection.org/exhibitions/states-mind-ann-veronica-janssens**

How do we teach the two subjects together?

With perceptions of art and science as diametrically opposed in some political circles and areas of society, it is necessary to be clear about their commonalities as well as where opportunities for meaningful collaboration exist. Selecting and gathering information, observing and recording, exploring, investigating and analysing, can all be classified as methods of inquiry common to both science and art. The daily classroom experience of many primary teachers is a science curriculum divided into topics (Howe et al., 2005) but this can lead to study of scientific concepts being sidelined over topic work, hence meaningful cross-curricular links with art can be missed. But, as we have discussed, the fundamentals of learning in art are also the fundamentals in the study of science, and it is not difficult to forge links between the two disciplines. One way to integrate science and art into the lives of children is by encouraging their natural curiosity, and by using the power of outdoor learning. Stunning autumn leaf colours such as reds, browns, greens and yellows will provide visual images that engage curiosity and lead to investigations in science and learning about the world with an artistic eye. Observing the natural world can lead to questions that form the basis of inquiry. For instance, Anne Osbourn's 2005 'SAW' project (**www.sawtrust.org**) links science, art and writing, and gives the example of a Year 4 child who was undertaking leaf rubbings as part of an art class. The child noticed that the veins on a leaf were opposite each other and that the leaves on the twig were arranged alternately, but when the veins were arranged alternately the leaves were opposite each other on the twig.

Teaching art and science in the outdoor environment affords opportunities to take children outside the classroom to learn about the natural world. The outdoors also provides us with scientific phenomena in visual form, which shows nature in an unusual way: the visual patterns on fungi, for example, can be intricate and beautiful. These wonders of the natural world act like magnets, attracting children of all ages with their intriguing representation of natural phenomena. They awaken curiosity and a hunger to learn more by using natural images from science as a starting point for scientific experimentation. By doing this, the diversity and interest can break down barriers between science and the arts, as exemplified in the following case study.

Case study

School garden

Mr Dillon, head teacher in a central London school, decided with his staff to construct a school garden to promote a cross-curricular approach to learning. Mr Dillon, a keen artist himself, used a contemporary art paradigm when planning the garden: for example, for a child to draw a flower it is better for that child to experience the flower, to explore it and discover its qualities using his/ her senses, to collect information about it. This approach also underpins the rudiments of science investigation, therefore opportunities for first-hand observation, exploration and analysis were considered when constructing the garden. The children were involved in the planning, planting and care of the garden, and once it was fully operational with plants, flowers and vegetables, etc., the children could observe the results of their planting and study them further. They looked at images of artworks with garden themes, including examples from around the world, and produced their own artwork in response, such as creating sculptural flowers which were inspired by aboriginal art. A bug hotel was constructed, which once inhabited offered children the opportunity to observe and sketch what they saw at proximity using magnifying glasses: the children subsequently returned to the classroom to draw the insects on a large scale. This approach to learning is also in keeping with the constructivist view of teaching, which acknowledges that children have views and attitudes which are formed because of experiences inside and outside of the classroom. These experiences are meaningful to learning and demonstrate transferable skill sets, which must be considered if learning in both subjects is to be fully achieved (Littledyke and Huxford, 1988). The garden in this school subsequently provided the children with plenty of projects throughout the year, which encouraged a cross-curricular approach to learning, and involving the children in a very creative way.

Practical activity

A sketching trip

Experience the visual wonders of the outdoors for yourself by making a sketching trip to a local park or beauty spot. Collect drawing materials (such as those described in Chapter 4, Section 4.1: Drawing) and make a simple sketchbook out of a sheet of paper: **www.youtube.com/ watch?v=PkaeRcK2cqM**

Make a viewfinder by cutting a rectangular hole into a small piece of card, which you can use to look through to isolate areas for focused sketching.

Try the following activities.

(Continued)

(Continued)

- Where is the horizon? How can you show where the sky meets the land? Use your viewfinder and draw what you see.
- Try to view the scene in terms of shape. Draw some large shapes and block the darker areas in with charcoal. Can you see shadows? Draw those in, too.
- Look up at the sky: what colours and tones can you see? Try to draw the clouds as you can see them: what sort of marks will you have to make?
- Stand under a tree. Draw the branches as you see them; remember, there are no straight lines in nature.
- Tear coloured paper and use glue to create a collage that shows texture and patterns that you notice.

Figures 7.6.1 and 7.6.2 A sketching trip with friends or colleagues is an enjoyable way to practise your own skills, before taking your class to participate in similar activities.

A place for imagination

An abundance of opportunities exist for collaboration between art and science in primary schools, providing scope for observation, recording, creativity, imagination, experimentation and so forth. Albert Einstein gives a scientist's perspective when reflecting on his life, stating: *When I examine myself and my methods of thought, I conclude that the gift of fantasy has meant more to me than my talent for absorbing positive knowledge* (Gardner, 1993, p105). He acknowledged that facts have limited value without imagination. It is for us, as teachers, to recognise imagination as a prized attribute, and a suitable learning outcome in science as well as in art.

━━━ Practical activity ━━━

Have a go

Art and science go together well when it comes to using natural materials. These can be used for all sorts of craftwork, and have been so for centuries (see Chapter 4, Section 4.5: Craftwork and making for more on this).

Try experimenting yourself following the instructions below to colour plain fabric with red cabbage dye, or try this out with your upper Key Stage 1 or Key Stage 2 class.

Figure 7.6.3 Children learn the science of creating dyes from natural materials.

Resources: large bowl; wooden spoon; red cabbage; hot water; cotton squares; kitchen paper; dropper; vinegar; lemon; soap; bicarbonate of soda.

Preparation: Make the soda into a solution: one teaspoon to one cup of water.

1. Cut up some red cabbage and put it in a bowl.

2. Add some very hot water and stir for about five minutes.

3. Remove the cabbage leaves from the bowl.

4. Place the cotton material into the purple liquid and stir for about five minutes.

5. Remove the material and dry between two pieces of kitchen paper.

6. Place the material on fresh kitchen paper.

7. Use a dropper to make coloured patterns on the material with vinegar, lemon juice, bicarbonate of soda solution, or draw lines using a bar of soap.

(Continued)

(Continued)

8. Leave the material for a few minutes for the chemicals to react.

9. Rinse the material quickly in cold (preferably running) water, before drying.

Background information: Red cabbage is an 'indicator': i.e. it is one colour in an acid and another in an alkali. Acid means *sour* in Latin. Alkali is the chemical opposite of acid. (Toothpaste is an alkali that neutralises the acids which build up in our teeth. Indigestion tablets are alkalis that neutralise excess acid in the stomach.) The purple colour of the dyed material turns pink when it meets an acid (vinegar) and turns blue or blue/green when it meets an alkali (soda and soap).

Skills: Investigating and experimenting.

Safety: Care is needed with very hot water. An adult should cut up the cabbage.

Follow-up activities: Use leftover cabbage water to test substances such as orange juice, cola, toothpaste. What does the colour change tell you about these things?

Summary

This section has aimed to develop your understanding of the value of making links between art and science. It has demonstrated how art and science can provide many opportunities to observe and analyse, and at the same time encourage creativity in the understanding and representation of the world. Creating art from nature in many ways is a powerful way for children to interpret the world and enable them to create personal representations and responses. For the artist, as for the scientist, every act of looking has the potential to become an act of analysis. The ability to observe requires children to use all their senses in a truly meaningful way.

━━━ Further reading ━━━

Davies, D and Howe, A (2003) *Teaching Science and Design and Technology in the Early Years.* London: David Fulton.

Jeffries, S (2011) 'When two tribes meet: collaborations between artists and scientists'. *The Guardian.* Available at: **www.theguardian.com/artanddesign/2011/aug/21/collaborations-between-artists-and-scientists**

Osborne, A (2005) *Seesaw.* Norwich: SAW Press.

Be inspired by the projects listed on these websites.

Art and Science Collaborations: **www.asci.org/homepage.html**

Art & Science: **www.artandscience.org.uk**

7·7
Art and ... English
Kerenza Ghosh

Introduction

Art and literacy both engage the imagination and invite personal response from viewer and reader, putting them at the heart of the aesthetic experience. The two subjects complement one another as the integration of reading and writing within the arts can strengthen literacy skills, as well as foster creative thinking in the primary curriculum. In his research into children's literacy development, Gunther Kress observes the many ways in which children are influenced by the visual modes that surround them, including film, television, apps, picturebooks, posters, etc. In light of this, Kress states that: *As texts draw more and more on overt visual design and communication, the skills and knowledges of visual design and display will need to be fostered as a central part of any literacy curriculum* (1997, p58). It is therefore necessary for teachers to consider how to forge links between art and literacy in the classroom: fortunately, there are several creative ways in which this can be achieved.

Theory focus

Book illustration as an art form

Visiting the children's section of a bookstore can be an experience of wonder and delight. Examining the many picturebooks, we find ourselves in the presence of beautiful art of every imaginable medium and style, and an endless variety of stories. Contemporary picturebooks are now recognized as more than useful pedagogical tools or nursery entertainments: they are seen as unique combinations of literature and visual art, worthy of serious attention.

(Sipe, 2001, p24)

The above comment by Lawrence Sipe celebrates the picturebook as a work of art, as well as a stimulus for developing children's visual literacy. He states that picturebooks require time and

(Continued)

(Continued)

consideration if they are to be fully appreciated. This is not only because of the detail within the illustrations, but also the special relationship between word and image and the gaps between the two, which are left open to interpretation. In *The Act of Reading* (1978) Iser argues that every text has these gaps, which must be filled by the reader: in a picturebook, gaps arise between the visual and verbal text so, *author and reader are to share the game of the imagination* (1978, p108). The following case study describes how one such picturebook, *Leon and the Place Between* by Angela McAllister (author) and Grahame Baker-Smith (illustrator), was read with children aged nine and ten and used to make creative links between art and literacy.

Case study

In the classroom: picturebooks

Leon and the Place Between tells the story of Leon, who takes his younger siblings to a circus. At first, Leon's brother and sisters don't believe in magic, but they are soon won over by acrobats, clockwork animals and the mysterious magician, Abdul Kazam. The illustrations have been created using a variety of mixed media (drawing, photography, collage, painting) with rich use of colour and light, inviting the reader to look closely at each image. Other significant visual features include assorted typography and interactive elements (fold-outs and windows) incorporated in the layout. Given the diverse modes used to tell the story, *Leon and the Place Between* may be described as a 'multimodal' text. Multimodality refers to the range of ways in which a text communicates meaning through speech, image, gesture, music, sound and movement

Figure 7.7.1 Leon and the Place Between by Angela McAllister and Grahame Baker-Smith.
By kind permission of Templar Publishing.

(Bearne and Wolstencroft, 2007). Such texts allow children to be visual learners, contributing towards their understanding and experience of the work.

Multimodality

In modern society and in school, children encounter multimodality every day (Kress, 1997): they are expected to read images as well as print, and increasingly use computers to compose their own texts. This project sought to build upon these experiences, and the outcome was to be a poem written in response to the picturebook, making use of drawing and computing for visual emphasis. For Bearne and Wolstencroft, *Poetry is the perfect multimodal text as it sings and dances off the page* (2007, p141). They also suggest that effective visual approaches to poetry can involve children writing poems based on illustrations in printed books: throughout the project, the children were encouraged to look closely at the illustrations in *Leon and the Place Between* to appreciate the text as an art form and as a basis for their poetry writing.

Reading images

The children began the project by looking at the endpapers (these being the pages just inside the front and back covers), which give clues about the story and invite the reader to make predictions. Sipe suggests that endpapers have *'meaning-making potential' and examining them with children before the story is read will enhance their literary and visual aesthetic experience* (2006, p302). In *Leon and the Place Between* these pages are decorative and gilded, and for children this evoked ceremony, celebration and magic. Whilst the story was read aloud, the children discussed the illustrations, characters and events, commenting on objects, colours, patterns, style and atmosphere, and explored relationships between picture and text. Sharing copies of the book in pairs meant there was plenty of opportunity to look closely at the illustrations and revisit parts of the text. A spotlight tool on the interactive whiteboard was used to view a fold-out page showing clockwork animals, to focus upon detail in the illustration and to show models of descriptive phrases. These enabled children to consider the illustrations more thoroughly and make considered choices about vocabulary as they came up with their own descriptive phrases, such as 'mystical clockwork carousel'; 'dusty blue elephant'; 'snapping crocodile with glowing, red, beady eyes'.

—— Theory focus ——————————————

The Reader in the Writer

In *The Reader in the Writer* (2001) Barrs and Cork explain that exposure to quality literature is key to the development of children's writing, since *young writers, who are learning to make their own texts sound for a reader, are likely to echo the tunes and patterns of stories they have encountered* (p38). The children were encouraged to tune into the descriptive language in *Leon and the Place Between* as they collected words and phrases from the story to use in their poetry writing. A display board in the classroom offered a space to share descriptive phrases, vocabulary and ideas, and was added to continually as the project unfolded. Examples included: 'Bang! Three jugglers tumbled onto the stage to the pounding beat of a drum', and 'Trust nothing ...' said Abdul Kazam, 'but believe everything!' Extracts such as these can be adapted for poetry writing, and three techniques, as suggested by Vernon (2002), were demonstrated to the children to show them how this could be achieved.

(Continued)

(Continued)

1. Changing past tense to present tense, to make the action immediate and exciting.

2. Adding more detail for elaboration.

3. Omitting unnecessary words for effect.

Following this, the children combined their own descriptive phrases with those they had collected and adapted, to write short, free-verse poems.

> *Back and forth, up and over, the three jugglers are spinning around.*
>
> *Tumbling onto the stage to the pounding beat of a drum,*
>
> *Bang! Bang! Bang! The three jugglers stop and dive down,*
>
> *Skittles spin high and higher like a twinkle of light.*
>
> *The jugglers bow and bounce away like a shining star.*

(Adam, aged 9)

This poem clearly resembles the page from which it was inspired: it is animated and, along with Adam's illustration, effectively captures a moment in the story. The children then typed their poems onto the computer, experimenting with different fonts for visual effect as inspired by the typography within the book.

Figures 7.7.2 and 7.7.3 Children's work is clearly influenced by the multimodality of the original text.

Drawing and collage were the artistic mediums used by the children in the final stages to illustrate their poems: a variety of brightly coloured wrapping paper and sequins were provided to reflect the techniques used in the picturebook. Time was given to discussing choices made by the author and illustrator with regards to page layout, and the children made decisions informed by the length of their poem, the original illustration from the book and the materials available. Cox claims that by discussing illustrations, children can learn to *work as experts rather than learners* in justifying and making decisions with regards to how a text should be represented (1991, p211). Overall, the children had created a multimodal page that communicated meaning through word and image. Their finished products were of high quality and reflected the influence of the picturebook, as well as the children's own creative ideas and responses, as can be seen in Figures 7.7.4 and 7.7.5.

 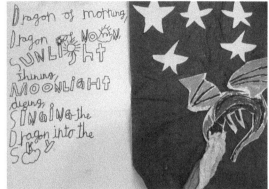

Figures 7.7.4 and 7.7.5 Using mixed media ensures that diversity of outcome is achieved.

Links with art and design

Quality picturebooks are invaluable for providing teachers with an effective stimulus for engaging children in learning opportunities that link the graphic arts and literacy. In *Children Reading Pictures: Interpreting Visual Texts* (2016), Arizpe et al. pay attention to the rich encounters that children have when they interact with picturebooks through discussion and by creating their own drawings. As Dawn and Fred Sedgewick declare, *However it works, drawing is thinking aloud: a powerful route into knowledge* (1993, p29).

Practical activity

Have a go

Choose a poem: this could be any poem you wish. It may come from a poetry book that you own, or you can search for one on the websites listed below. Once you have chosen your poem, you will need a range of artworks to look at. Ideally, visit an art gallery: there is no substitute for seeing art in real life. Alternatively, you could look online: the National Gallery website, for example, has a good tool for zooming into images of artworks. Find an artwork that links with your poem in some way: the link can be as concrete or as abstract as you like. It might be something that you are reminded of, a personal experience or a literal interpretation of the poem. Identify the lines, words or phrases within the poem that prompted the link. Perhaps the whole poem conjures up an image in your mind's eye, and you have found just the artwork to match it.

Poetry Archive: **www.poetryarchive.org/**

Children's Poetry Archive: **www.childrenspoetryarchive.org/**

Poetryline: **www.clpe.org.uk/poetryline**

Cregan Library DCU

━━━ Reflection point ━━━━

- In this Practical activity, what do you learn about interpretation and response in relation to both poetry and art?
- How could you adapt this activity to accommodate different ages, phases, or needs of individual children?

Analysis

This is a very open-ended activity, as there are no right or wrong answers: the purpose is to engage children in observation: talking, making connections and giving justifications. If it is not possible to visit a gallery, provide the children with a variety of printed images of the artworks, spread out around the classroom. Give them time to browse all of these images after they have selected a poem. Whilst having a range of poems works well for paired and class discussion, with younger children it may be preferable to read one poem together before they choose an associated artwork. To develop the approach, children could create their own artwork based upon a poem, or write a poem inspired by a piece of art.

Summary

This section has aimed to develop your understanding of the value of making links between art and English in one small example: there are endless ways in which the two subjects can be taught together. It has shown how picturebooks and poetry can provide opportunities for children to develop visual literacy and communicate through visual means. Especially, it has highlighted *drawing* and *collage* as artistic mediums that correspond well with illustration, and the use of computer skills to create texts in imaginative ways. It has also emphasised the importance of giving children opportunities to respond to literature in this way. I would like to encourage you to consider drawing as a means for teaching and learning that, together with other motivating classroom practices such as access to quality texts, choice, collaboration and opportunity to discuss, can enable all children to participate fully in a literate community.

━━━ Further reading ━━━━━━━━━━━━━━━━━━━

Evans, J (2009) Chapter 6 Reading the visual: Creative and aesthetic responses to picturebooks and fine art, in Evans, J (ed) *Talking Beyond the Page: Reading and Responding to Picturebooks*. London: Routledge.

Sipe, L R (2008) Chapter 7 Learning from illustrations in picturebooks, in Frey, N and Fisher, D (eds) *Teaching Visual Literacy Using Comic Books, Graphic Novels, Anime, Cartoons and More to Develop Comprehension and Thinking Skills*. Thousand Oaks, CA: Corwin Press.

Chapter summary and conclusion

This chapter has brought together all your learning throughout the book and contextualised subject knowledge in art and design in relation to a selection of primary subjects. Children's engagement with art, craft and design can enhance their life experiences by allowing them to explore their individuality and their identity within society: this, some may argue, is what primary education is for. One of the last century's most important theorists on art education was Sir Herbert Read. The fundamental message in his key text of 1943, *Education Through Art*, states that: *art should be the basis of education. The aim of education should be the creation of artists – of people who are efficient in the various modes of expression* (p1), which is rather a neat way to finish this book, as this theory echoes the philosophy of the Reggio schools that is exemplified in Chapter 1. We have therefore come full circle in your learning in art and design for now. I hope that you are inspired, and feeling enabled to continue your own learning journey in creativity and artistic expression; whatever form that takes in your own life. Keep in mind that your enthusiasm, encouragement and deeply rooted conviction in an arts-rich curriculum will have far reaching implications for the attitudes and the creative lives of the children you teach. If you believe in the power of art, you will always be able to find the space and time to teach this subject to the best of your ability and foster a love of learning through art and design in the next generation.

Further reading

Efland, A (2002) *Art and Cognition, Integrating the Arts into the Curriculum.* New York: Teachers College Press.

Claxton, G (2002) *Building Learning Power: Helping Young People Become Better Learners.* Bristol: TLO.

Fisher, R (2005) *Teaching Children to Think.* Cheltenham: Stanley Thornes.

Gardner, H (1993) *Multiple Intelligences: The Theory in Practice.* New York: Basic Books.

Hosack Janes, K (2014) *Using the Visual Arts for Cross Curricular Learning.* Oxon: Routledge.

OFSTED (2010) 'Learning: creative approaches that raise standards'. Available at: **http://bit.ly/2p8j3cg**

References

Adichie, C (2009) 'The danger of a single story'. TED Talk. Available at: **www.ted.com/talks/ chimamanda_adichie_the_danger_of_a_single_story**

Alexander, R J (2009) 'Towards a new primary curriculum: a report from the Cambridge Primary Review. Part 2: The future'. Cambridge: University of Cambridge Faculty of Education. Available at: **www.cprtrust.org.uk/wp-content/uploads/2014/06/Curriculum-report-2.pdf**

Alexander, R (ed) (2010) *Children, Their World, Their Education*. Oxon: Routledge.

Anderson, J R (1976) *Language, Memory, and Thought*. Mahwah, NJ: Erlbaum.

Ansberry, K and Morgan, E (2007) *More Picture-Perfect Science Lessons: Using Children's Books to Guide Inquiry*. USA: National Science Teachers.

Arizpe, E and Styles, M (2016) *Children Reading Pictures: Interpreting Visual Texts* (2nd edition). London: Routledge.

Assessment Reform Group (2002) 'Assessment for Learning: 10 Principles' (online). Available at: **www. aaia.org.uk/content/uploads/2010/06/Assessment-for-Learning-10-principles.pdf**

Atkinson, T and Claxton, G (2000) *The Intuitive Practitioner: The Value of Not Always Knowing What One is Doing*. Buckingham: Open University Press.

Bandura, A (1977) *Social Learning Theory*. New York: General Learning Press.

Barnes, J (2011) *Cross-Curricular Learning 3–14*. London: Sage.

Barrs, M and Cork, V (2001) *The Reader in the Writer*. London: CLPE.

Bartel, M (2001) 'Eleven classroom creativity killers', Goshen Education (online). Available at: **www. goshen.edu/art/ed/creativitykillers.html**

Batey M (2011) 'Is creativity the number one skill in the 21st century?' *Psychology Today* (online). Available at: **www.psychologytoday.com/blog/working-creativity/201102/is-creativity-the-number-1-skill-the-21st-century**

Bauer, Y (2004) Online Dimensions. *Journal of Holocaust Studies*, Volume 8: Fall.

Bearne, E and Wolstencroft, H (2007) *Visual Approaches to Teaching Writing*. London: Paul Chapman Publishing.

Benninga, J S (2003) 'Moral and ethical issues in teacher education'. *ERIC. Teaching and Teacher Education*. Available at: **www.ericdigests.org/2004-4/moral.htm**

Berger, J (2005) *On Drawing*. Ireland: Occasional Press.

Biddle, S J H and Asare, M (2011) Physical activity and mental health in children and adolescents: a review of reviews. *British Journal of Sports Medicine*, 45: 886–895.

Black, P and Wiliam, D (1998) Assessment and classroom learning. *Assessment in Education*, 5: 1

Blakemore, S J and Frith, U (2005) *The Learning Brain*. Malden, MA: Blackwell.

Bobbitt, F (1918) *The Curriculum*. Boston, MA: Houghton Mifflin.

Bobbitt, F (1924) *How to Make a Curriculum*. Boston, MA: Houghton Mifflin.

Bogardus, E S (1925) Social distance and its origins. *Journal of Applied Science*, 9: 216–225.

Bradburne, J (2001) Looking for clues, clues for looking. *Welcome News Supplement*, 5: Science and Art (2002). London: The Wellcome Trust.

Brown, G T L and Harris, L R (2013) Student self-assessment (pp367–393), in McMillan, J H (ed) *The SAGE Handbook of Research on Classroom Assessment*. Thousand Oaks, CA: Sage.

Bruner, J (1996) *The Culture of Education*. Cambridge, MA: Harvard University Press.

Burnard, P, Cremin, T and Craft, A (2008) *Creative Learning 3–11 and How We Document It*. Stoke: Trentham.

Burt, E and Atkinson, J (2015) Arts on referral interventions: a mixed-methods study investigating factors associated with differential changes in mental well-being. *Journal of Public Health*, 37 (1): 143–150.

Caine, N, Caine, G, McClintic, C and Klimek, K (2008) *Brain/Mind: Principles in Action*. London: Corwin Press, Sage.

Callaway, G and Kear, M (1999) *Teaching Art and Design in the Primary School*. Oxon: David Fulton.

Cancer Research (2016) 'Let's tackle children's obesity' (online). Available at: **www.cancerresearchuk. org/support-us/campaign-for-us/tackling-childhood-obesity#vgGIQqpuum1iruhe.99**

Cardon, G, De Craemer, M, De Bourdeaudhuij, I and Verloigne, V (2014) More physical activity and less sitting in children: why and how? *Science and Sport*, 29: S3–S5. Available at: **www.sciencedirect. com/science/article/pii/S0765159714001403**

Carey, J (2005) *What Good Are The Arts?* London: Faber & Faber.

Catling, S (2015) 'Pre-service primary teachers' knowledge and understanding of geography and its teaching: a review'. *RIGEO* (online). Available at: **www.rigeo.org/vol4no3/Number3Winter/ RIGEO-V4-N3-3.pdf**

CBI (Press team) (2015) 'Skills emergency could starve growth' (online). Available at: **www.cbi.org. uk/news/skills-emergency-could-starve-growth-cbi-pearson-survey**

Claxton, G, Lucas, B and Spencer, E (2012) 'Making it: studio teaching and its impact on teachers and learners'. University of Winchester: Centre for Real-World Learning.

Cone, T P and Cone, S L (2005) *Teaching Children Dance* (2nd edition). Champaign, IL: Human Kinetics.

Cooper, H (2012) *History 5–11*. Oxon: David Fulton.

Cooper, H (2013) *Teaching History Creatively*. Oxon: Routledge.

Council for the Curriculum, Examinations and Assessment (2007) 'Northern Ireland Curriculum'. Available at: **www.nicurriculum.org.uk/curriculum_microsite/the_arts/art**

Cowan, P and Maitles, H (1999) Promoting Positive Values: Teaching the Holocaust in Scottish Primaries, conference paper, University of Dundee. Available at: **www.leeds.ac.uk/educol/documents/00001208.htm**

Cox, B (1991) *Cox on Cox: An English Curriculum for the 1990s*. London: Hodder and Stoughton.

Craft A (2001) Little C creativity, in Craft, A, Jeffrey, B and Leibling, M (eds) *Creativity in Education*. London: Continuum.

Craft, A (2005) *Creativity in Schools: Tensions and Dilemmas*. London: Routledge.

Craft, A (2008) *Creativity and Early Years Education*. Lifewide Foundation, London: Continuum.

Craft, A and Hall, E (2014) Changes in the landscape for creativity in education, in Wilson, A (ed) *Creativity in Primary Education*. London: Learning Matters/Sage.

Crafts Council England (2014) 'Our future is in the making: an education manifesto for craft and making'. Available at: **www.craftscouncil.org.uk/content/files/7822_Education_manifesto@14FINAL.PDF**

Cremin, T, Glauert, E, Craft, A, Compton, A and Stylianidou, F (2015) Creative little scientists: exploring pedagogical synergies between inquiry-based and creative approaches in Early Years science. *Education*, 3–13, 43 (4): 404–419.

Crossick, G and Kaszynska, P (2016) Understanding the value of arts and culture: the cultural value project, Arts and Humanities Research Council (AHRC). Available at: **www.ahrc.ac.uk/documents/publications/cultural-value-project-final-report**

Csikszentmihalyi, M (1990) *Flow: The Psychology of Optimal Experience*. New York: Harper and Row.

Csikszentmihalyi, M (1996) *Creativity: Flow and the Psychology of Discovery and Invention*. New York: Harper Perennial.

Dann, R (2002) *Promoting Assessment as Learning: Improving the Learning Process*. London: Routledge Falmer.

Davies, M (2001) *Helping Children to Learn Through a Movement Perspective*. London: Paul Chapman Publishing.

De Bono, E (1990) *Lateral Thinking: Be More Creative and Productive*. London: Penguin.

Department for Culture, Media and Sport (DCMS) and Vaizey, E (2016) Press release: 'Creative industries worth almost £10 million an hour to economy' (online). Available at: **www.gov.uk/government/news/creative-industries-worth-almost-10-million-an-hour-to-economy**

Department for Culture, Media and Sport (DCMS) (2016) 'Creative industries economic estimates, January 2016, Key Findings' (online). Available at: **www.gov.uk/government/statistics/creative-industries-economic-estimates-january-2016**

Devlin, P (2009) 'Restoring the balance, the effect of arts participation on wellbeing and health'. Voluntary Arts England. Available at: **www.artsforhealth.org/resources/VAE_Restoring_the_Balance.pdf**

DfE (2010) 'The importance of teaching: the schools white paper' (online). Available at: **www.gov.uk/government/publications/the-importance-of-teaching-the-schools-white-paper-2010**

DfE (2013) 'Art and Design programmes of study: key stages 1 and 2'. GOV.UK (online). Available at: **www.gov.uk/government/uploads/system/uploads/attachment_data/file/239018/PRIMARY_national_curriculum_-_Art_and_design.pdf**

DfE (2014) 'Statutory Framework for the Early Years Foundation Stage'. GOV.UK (online). Available at: **www.gov.uk/government/uploads/system/uploads/attachment_data/file/335504/EYFS_framework_from_1_September_2014__with_clarification_note.pdf**

DfE (2015) 'National Curriculum in England: science programmes of study'. Available at: **www.gov.uk/government/publications/national-curriculum-in-england-science-programmes-of-study**

DfE (2016) 'Strategy 2015–2020 World-class education and care'. Available at: **www.gov.uk/government/uploads/system/uploads/attachment_data/file/508421/DfE-strategy-narrative.pdf**

DfE (2016) 'Educational Excellence Everywhere'. GOV.UK (online). Available at: **www.gov.uk/government/publications/educational-excellence-everywhere**

Dodge, D (2004) *The Creative Curriculum for Pre-school*. New York: Clifton Park.

Doherty, J and Brennan, P (2014) *Physical Education 5–11: A Guide for Teachers*. Oxon: Routledge.

Doherty, J and Hughes, M (2014) *Child Development Theory and Practice 0–11* (2nd edition). Harlow, Essex: Pearson.

Eisner, E W (1997) Cognition and representation. *Phi Delta Kappan*, 78: 5

Eisner, E W (2002) *The Arts and the Creation of Mind: What the Arts Teach and How It Shows*. USA: Yale University Press.

Feldman, E Burke (1970) *Becoming Human Through Art: Aesthetic Experience in the School*. Michigan, USA: Prentice Hall.

Gardner, H (1993) *Creating Minds: An Anatomy of Creativity Seen Through the Lives of Freud, Einstein, Picasso, Stravinsky, Eliot, Graham and Ghandi*. New York: Basic Books.

Gardner, H (2006) *Five Minds for the Future*. Boston, MA: Harvard Business School Press.

Garner, R (2014) 'Education Secretary Nicky Morgan tells teenagers: Want to keep your options open? Then do science', Monday 10 November 2014. *The Independent*. Available at: **www.independent.co.uk/news/education/education-news/education-secretary-nicky-morgan-tells-teenagers-if-you-want-a-job-drop-humanities-9852316.html**

Gleave, J and Cole-Hamilton, I (2012) 'A world without play: a literature review on the effects of a lack of play on children's lives'. BTHA and Play England. Available at: **www.playengland.org.uk**

González, N, Moll, L and Amanti, C (2005) *Funds of Knowledge: Theorizing Practices in Households, Communities, and Classrooms*. Mahwah, NJ: Lawrence Erlbaum.

Grainger, T and Barnes, J (2006) Creativity in the primary curriculum, in Arthur, J, Grainger, T and Wray, D (eds) *Learning to Teach in the Primary School*. London: Routledge.

Green, L, Chedzoy, S, Harris, W, Mitchell, R, Naughton, C, Rolfe, L and Stanton, W (1998) A study of student teachers' perceptions of teaching the arts in primary schools. *British Educational Research Journal*, 24: 95–107.

Grigg, R and Hughes, S (2013) *Teaching Primary Humanities*. London: Routledge.

Hall, A (2015) 'The prevent duty: departmental advice for schools and childcare providers', Department for Education June 2015. Available at: **www.safeguardinginschools.co.uk/wp-content/uploads/2015/07/The-Prevent-Duty-Commentary-Andrew-Hall.pdf**

Halpin, D (2003) *Hope and Education: The Role of the Utopian Imagination*. London: Routledge Falmer.

Hannaford, C (1995) *Smart Moves: Why Learning is Not All in Your Head*. Virginia: Great Ocean.

Harmat, L, Ørsted Andersen, F, Ullén, F, Wright, J and Sadlo, G (2016) *Flow Experience: Empirical Research and Applications*. Switzerland: Springer.

Heise, D (2007) *Differentiation in The Art-Room*. NAEA: Advisory.

Henley, D (2012) 'The case for cultural education', DCMS. Available at: **www.gov.uk/government/uploads/system/uploads/attachment_data/file/260726/Cultural_Education_report.pdf**

Hickey, I and Robinson, D (2013) *The Leonardo Effect*. London: Routledge.

Hickman, R (2005) *Why We Make Art and Why it is Taught*. Bristol: Intellect.

Holt, D (1997) Problems in primary art education: some reflections on the need for a new approach in the early years. *International Journal of Early Years Education,* 5: 2.

Howe, A, Davies, D, McMahon, K, Towler, L and Scott, T (2005) *Science 5–11*. London: David Fulton.

Hurford, J (2012) 'A principled approach, the teaching tomtom, design and social context', RMIT University. Available at: **www.teachingtomtom.com/2012/09/27/a-principled-approach**

Irwin, M R (2016) Arts shoved aside: changing art practices in primary schools since the introduction of national standards. *International Journal of Art and Design Education*, DOI:10.1111/jade.12096

Iser, W (1978) *The Act of Reading*. London: Johns Hopkins University Press.

Jensen, E (2000) *Learning with the Body in Mind: The Scientific Basis for Energizers, Movement, Play, Games and Physical Education*. CA: The Brain Store, Inc.

Jordanova, L (2010) *History in Practice*. London: Bloomsbury.

Jordanova, L (2012) *The Look of the Past: Visual and Material Culture in Historical Practice*. Cambridge: Cambridge University Press.

Kandinsky, W (1914) *The Psychological Working of Colour, in Concerning the Spiritual in Art*. London: Constable and Co.

Kandinsky, W (1977) *Concerning the Spiritual in Art*. New York: Dover.

Kandinsky, W (1979) *Point and Line to Plane*. New York: Dover.

Katz, L (1993) Dispositions: definitions and implications for early childhood practices, ERIC Clearinghouse on Elementary and Early Childhood Education. Available at: **scholar.google.com/scholar?hl=enandbtnG=Searchandq=intitle:Dispositions:+Definitions+and+Implications+for+Early+Childhood+Practice**

Klee, P (1955) *Pedagogical Sketchbook*. London: Faber & Faber.

Knapton, S (2016) 'Robots will take over most jobs within 30 years, experts warn'. Saturday 13 February 2016. *The Telegraph* (online). Available at: **www.telegraph.co.uk/news/science/science-news/12155808/Robots-will-take-over-most-jobs-within-30-years-experts-warn.html**

Kolb, D A (1984) *Experiential Learning: Experience as a Source of Learning and Development*. Englewood Cliffs, NJ: Prentice-Hall.

Kress, G (1997) *Before Writing: Rethinking the Paths to Literacy*. London: Routledge.

Lave, J and Wenger, E (1990) *Situated Learning: Legitimate Peripheral Participation*. Cambridge: Cambridge University Press.

Lester, S and Russell, W (2008) 'Play for a change. Play, policy and practice: a review of contemporary perspectives', Summary report. London: National Children's Bureau.

Littledyke, M and Huxford, L (1988) *Teaching the Primary Curriculum for Constructive Learning*. London: Routledge.

Lyman, F T Jr (1981) The responsive classroom discussion: the inclusion of all students, in Anderson, A (ed) *Mainstreaming Digest*. College Park: University of Maryland.

Macintyre, C and McVitty, K (2004) *Movement and Learning in the Early Years*. London: Paul Chapman.

Malaguzzi, L (1994) 'Your image of the child: where teaching begins'. *Reggio Alliance* (online). Available at: **https://reggioalliance.org/downloads/malaguzzi:ccie:1994.pdf**

Martin, F (2008) Ethnogeography: towards a liberatory geography education. *Children's Geographies*, 6 (4): 437–450.

Massey, D (2006) The geographical mind, in Balderstone, D (ed) *Secondary Geography Handbook*. Sheffield: Geographical Association.

Matthews, J (2003) *Drawing and Painting: Children and Visual Representation*. London: Paul Chapman.

McAllister, A and Baker-Smith, G (2008) *Leon and the Place Between*. London: Templar.

McGill, I and Beaty, L (1995) *Action Learning*. London: Kogan Page.

Merriam-Webster Dictionary (2017) (online). Available at: **www.merriam-webster.com/dictionary/imagination**

Morpurgo, M (2011) *ImagineNation*, Cultural Learning Alliance. Available at: **www.culturallearningalliance.org.uk/images/uploads/ImagineNation_The_Case_for_Cultural_Learning.pdf**

Moss, P (2001) The otherness of Reggio, in Abbott, L and Nutbrown, C (2001) *Experiencing Reggio Emilia: Implications for Preschool Provision*. London: Open University Press.

NACCCE (1999) 'All our futures: creativity, culture and education'. London: DfEE.

Neelands, J et al. (2015) 'Enriching Britain, culture, creativity and growth: the future of cultural value', University of Warwick. Available at: **www2.warwick.ac.uk/research/warwickcommission/ futureculture/finalreport/warwick_commission_final_report.pdf**

NSEAD (2013) 'Art and design programme of study: key stage 1–3'. Available at: **www.nsead.org/ curriculum-resources/downloads/PoS_ART_AND_DESIGN_DFE_NSEAD_combined_version.pdf**

NSEAD (2014) 'National Curriculum for England' (online). Available at: **www.nsead.org/curriculum- resources/england.aspx**

NSEAD (2016) 'The National Society for Education in Art and Design Survey Report 2015–16' (online). Available at: **www.nsead.org/downloads/survey.pdf**

OFSTED (2009) 'Improving primary teachers' subject knowledge across the curriculum'. Available at: **http://dera.ioe.ac.uk/305/1/Improving%20primary%20teachers%20subject% 20knowledge%20across%20the%20curriculum.pdf**

OFSTED (2009) 'Drawing together: art, craft and design in schools'. Available at: **www.dera.ioe. ac.uk/10624/1/Drawing%20together.pdf**

OFSTED (2010) 'Learning: creative approaches that raise standards'. Available at: **www.ready unlimited.com/wp-content/uploads/2015/09/Learning-creative-approaches-that- raise-standards-Ofsted.pdf**

OFSTED (2011) 'Geography: learning to make a world of difference'. Available at: **www.gov.uk/ government/publications/geography-learning-to-make-a-world-of-difference**

OFSTED (2011) 'Safeguarding in schools: best practice', No. 100240.

OFSTED (2012) 'Making a mark: art, craft and design education'. Available at: **www.gov.uk/ government/publications/art-craft-and-design-education-making-a-mark**

Oxfam (2006) 'Global Citizenship Guides: Teaching Controversial Issues'. Available at: **www.oxfam. org.uk/education/global-citizenship/global-citizenship-guides**

Page, J S (2010) Challenges faced by 'gifted learners' in school and beyond. *Inquiries Journal/Student Pulse*, 2 (11). Available at: **www.inquiriesjournal.com/a?id=330**

Pavlou, V (2004) Profiling primary school teachers in relation to art teaching. *International Journal of Art and Design Education*, 23: 35–47.

Polanyi, M (1967) *The Tacit Dimension*. New York: Anchor Books.

Preston, L (2014) Australian primary pre-service teachers' conceptions of geography. *International Journal of Research in Geographical and Environmental Education*, 23(4).

QCA (1999) 'National Curriculum for England, 2000' (online). Available at: **http://webarchive. nationalarchives.gov.uk/20100202100434/http://curriculum.qcda.gov.uk/key-stages-1- and-2/subjects/art-and-design/keystage1/index.aspx**

Read, H (1943) *Education through Art*. London: Faber & Faber.

Richardson, P (2009) 'Using images with children from a different view'. *Geographical Association*. Available at: **www.geography.org.uk/adifferentview**

Robinson, K (2006) 'Do schools kill creativity?' TED Talk. Available at: **www.ted.com/talks/ken_robinson_says_schools_kill_creativity**

Rose, J (2009) 'The Independent Review of the Primary Curriculum'. Nottingham: DCSF Publications. Available at: **www.educationengland.org.uk/documents/pdfs/2009-IRPC-final-report.pdf**

Rosen, M (2010) in *Imagine: Art is Child's Play*. BBC. Available at: **www.bbc.co.uk/programmes/b00svrvx**

Sackes, M, Trundle, K and Flevares, L (2009) Using children's books to teach inquiry skills. *Young Children*, 64 (6): 24–26.

Sax, L (2007) *Boys Adrift: The Five Factors Driving the Growing Epidemic of Unmotivated Boys and Underachieving Young Men*. New York: Basic Books.

Schoenberg, A and Kandinsky, W (1984) *Letters, Pictures and Documents*. London: Faber & Faber.

Schon, D (1983) *The Reflective Practitioner: How Professionals Think in Action*. London: Temple Smith.

Scottish Government (2010) 'Scottish Curriculum for Excellence'. Available at: **www.gov.scot/Topics/Education/Schools/curriculum**

Sedgewick, D and Sedgwick, F (1993) *Drawing to Learn*. London: Hodder and Stoughton.

Sharp, C and Dust, K (1997) *Artists in Schools, A Handbook for Teachers and Artists*. Slough: NFER.

Shusterman, R (2006) Thinking through the body, educating for the humanities: a plea for somaesthetics. *The Journal of Aesthetic Education*, 40 (1): 1–21.

Sipe, L R (2001) Picturebooks as aesthetic objects: literacy teaching and learning. *International Journal of Early Reading and Writing*, 6 (1): 23–42.

Sipe, L R (2006) Picturebook Endpapers: Resources for Literacy and Aesthetic Interpretation. *Children's Literature in Education*, 37 (2): 291–304.

Skinner, B F (1972) *Beyond Freedom and Dignity*. New York: Vintage Books.

Smith, M K (2002) Jerome S. Bruner and the process of education. *The Encyclopaedia of Informal Education* (online). Available at: **www.infed.org/mobi/jerome-bruner-and-the-process-of-education**

Sooke, A (2013) 'Leonardo da Vinci: anatomy of an artist', 28 July 2013, *The Telegraph*. Available at: **www.telegraph.co.uk/culture/art/leonardo-da-vinci/10202124/Leonardo-da-Vinci-Anatomy-of-an-artist.html**

Standish, A (2009) *Global Perspectives in the Geography Curriculum: Reviewing the Moral Case for Geography*. Oxon: Routledge.

Stenhouse, L (1980) *Curriculum Research and Development in Action*. London: Heinemann.

Storm, M (1989) The five basic questions for primary geography. *Primary Geographer*, 2 (4).

Suh, Y (2013) Past looking: using arts as historical evidence in teaching history. *Social Studies Research and Practice*, 8 (1): 135–157.

Thomas, N J T (2004) Imagination, mental imagery, consciousness and cognition (online). Available at: **www.co-bw.com/BrainConciousness%20Update%20index.htm**

Tomlinson, C (2001) *How to Differentiate Instruction in Mixed-Ability Classrooms* (2nd edition). Alexandria, VA: Association for Supervision and Curriculum Development.

Tredgett, S (2015) *Learning through Movement in the Early Years*. Northwich: Critical Publishing.

Turner-Bisset, R (2005) *Creative Teaching: History*. Oxon: David Fulton.

Tyler, R W (1949) *Basic Principles of Curriculum and Instruction*. Chicago, IL: University of Chicago Press.

Van der Merwe, L (2007) The 'how to' of history teaching with and through music in the GET phase yesterday. *Today*, 1: 173–192.

Vernon, J (2002) As red as a turkey's wattles: the poetry of everyday language, in Barrs, M (ed) *The Best of Language Matters*. London: CLPE.

Vygotsky, L S (1978) *Mind in Society: The Development of Higher Psychological Processes*. Cambridge, MA: Harvard University Press.

Vygotsky, L S (1987) Thinking and speech (Minick, N Trans pp39–285). In Rieber, R W and Carton, A S (eds) *The Collected Works of L S Vygotsky: Vol. 1. Problems of General Psychology*. New York: Plenum Press. (Original work published 1934.)

Wahl, E (2016) 'The importance of creativity in the workplace'. *All Business* (online). Available at: **www.allbusiness.com/the-importance-of-creativity-in-the-workplace-24566-1.html**

Ward, H (no date) 'Art as a cross-curricular tool' (online). Available at: **www.henryhward.com/art-as-cross-curricular-tool**

Watts, R (2005) Attitudes to making art in the primary school. *International Journal of Art and Design Education*, 24 (3).

Welsh Assembly Government (2008) 'National Curriculum for Wales'. Available at: **www.learning.gov.wales/resources/browse-all/art-and-design-in-the-national-curriculum-for-wales/?lang=en**

Williams, R (2014) 'End of the creation story? Design and craft subjects decline in schools'. Tuesday 11 February 2014. *The Guardian* (online). Available at: **www.theguardian.com/artand design/2014/feb/11/design-craft-subjects-decline-in-schools**

Wingert, P (1991) 'The best schools in the world'. 12 February 1991. *Newsweek*. Available at: **http://europe.newsweek.com/best-schools-world-200968?rm=eu**

Wrenn, A et al. (2007) *(T.E.A.C.H.) Teaching Emotive and Controversial History 3–19*. London: The Historical Association.

Wynne, E A (1995) The moral dimension of teaching (pp190–202), in Ornstein, A C (ed) *Teaching: Theory into Practice*. Boston, MA: Alyn and Bacon.

Yair, K (2011) 'Craft and wellbeing'. Crafts Council. Available at: **www.craftscouncil.org.uk/content/files/craft_and_wellbeing.pdf**

Zorich, Z (2011) A chauvet primer. *Archaeology Archive*, 64 (2). Available at: **www.archive.archaeology.org/1103/features/werner_herzog_chauvet_cave_primer.html**

Index